FISHERS, MONKS AND CADRES

FISHERS, MONKS AND CADRES

Navigating State, Religion and the South China Sea in Central Vietnam

EDYTA ROSZKO

UNIVERSITY OF HAWAI'I PRESS
HONOLULU

Printed in the United States of America

26 25 24 23 22 21   6 5 4 3 2 1

Published for North America by
University of Hawai'i Press
2840 Kolowalu Street
Honolulu, HI 96822
www.uhpress.hawaii.edu

This paperback edition of *Fishers, Monks and Cadres*
is published by arrangement with NIAS Press.

ISBN 978-0-8248-9055-1 (paperback)

First published in 2020 by NIAS Press

Publication of this volume was assisted by generous financial support received from
the European Research Council (ERC) Starting Grant under the European Union's
Horizon 2020 research and innovation programme (Grant agreement No. 802223)
and the Danish Council for Independent Research in Culture and Humanities (Grant
agreement 0602-02917B/FKK), for which the author expresses her warm thanks.

A CIP catalog record for this book is available from the Library of Congress

University of Hawai'i Press books are printed on acid-free
paper and meet the guidelines for permanence and durability
of the Council on Library Resources.

Cover image: *Vietnamese fishers celebrating the opening of
a new fishing season, Sa Huỳnh (photo by author).*

For Oscar

Contents

List of Illustrations

Acknowledgements

This book has grown out of a dissertation submitted to the Max Planck Institute for Social Anthropology and Martin Luther University Halle-Wittenberg in 2011. My initial interest in Vietnam began in 2002 when I went there as part of a postgraduate programme arranged by the Polish Ministry of Education and Sport. Since then, many individuals and institutions have helped me throughout this project. Before I thank them and acknowledge my gratitude and indebtedness for their constant support and encouragement, I will briefly describe how it happened that I decided to carry out research in Vietnam.

Some failures turn out to be our best friends. When in 2001 I failed to win a scholarship to study in China, I thought that I would have to give up my dream of doing research in the country that had long fascinated me. I was learning Chinese and wrote my master's thesis on Buddhism in China with a view to conducting research there. During that same year, I began attending seminars on Southeast Asia organized by Małgorzata Pietrasiak at the Institute of International Relations (University of Łódź). 'Why you don't apply to go to Vietnam?' she asked me. I had never thought about going to Vietnam and I knew very little about it. Moreover, it was my last year of study at university and, according to the rules, I was no longer eligible to apply. When I had almost given up the idea, my thesis supervisor Sławoj Szynkiewicz exclaimed, 'More go-getting energy, Ms. Roszko!' Their enthusiasm, encouragement, support, and trust helped convince the dean of the University of Łódź to allow me to submit my application. Ten months later, just after my graduation, I received confirmation from the Polish Ministry of Education and Sport in Warsaw that I had won the scholarship! Without Sławoj Szynkiewicz and Małgorzata Pietrasiak's help, I would not be where I am now.

My three-year stay in Vietnam (2002–2005) would have been impossible without financial support from the Polish Ministry of Education and Sport, which not only provided a grant but also, in an exceptional gesture, extended its scholarship to me twice. I particularly want to thank Jacek Wojtaśkiewicz (Department of International Cooperation), whose assistance and efficiency helped to overcome many formal constraints and make my stay in Vietnam possible. I would like to extend my thanks to the Polish Embassy in Hanoi, where I was warmly received and which assisted me whenever I needed during my early stay in Vietnam.

Upon my arrival in Hanoi in 2002, I would never have been integrated so quickly into Vietnamese society had it not been for the lively environment at the Vietnamese Academy of Social Science in Hanoi, in particular the Institute for Religious Studies, with which I was affiliated from 2002 to 2005. I am particularly grateful to its director, Professor Đỗ Quang Hưng, who helped me innumerable times with bureaucratic challenges. I am also grateful to the late Prof. Cao Xuan Phố and the late Dr. Nguyễn Quốc, as well as Dr. Ngô Văn Doanh and Dr. Đào Thế Đức. Special thanks also to the younger researchers: Dr. Nguyễn Ngọc Quỳnh, Dr. Nguyễn Thị Minh Ngọc, Dr. Nguyễn Văn Dũng, Dr. Lê Tâm Đắc, Mrs. Phan Tường Vân, and many other colleagues with whom I not only had lively discussions, but also took field trips outside of Hanoi. They were my first guides through the culture and everyday life of Vietnam.

My adventure in Vietnam could not have taken on such serious and professional proportions without Andrew Hardy, the head of the École Française d'Extrême-Orient (EFEO) in Hanoi, who provided advice and support at critical moments during the first years of my stay in Vietnam. The EFEO also generously offered me two years of funding to study Vietnamese. In 2007 Andrew invited me to join his multidisciplinary project, 'The Long Wall of Quảng Ngãi', which he was organizing in cooperation with the Vietnam Institute of Archaeology. Andrew's and Nguyễn Tiến Đông's assistance and expertise in the field and their excellent relations with the Quảng Ngãi provincial authorities were invaluable for my PhD project. Much appreciated support in transcribing interviews and in collecting various documents was provided by Nguyễn Hồng Nhung. For teaching me Vietnamese, I am indebted to two professional teachers from Hanoi National University, Lê Thị Thu Hoài and Nguyễn Thị Phương Thùy, who tirelessly corrected my pronunciation and guided me through linguistic nuances. They were not only my tutors; they also became my good friends.

My doctoral studies formally began in the winter of 2006 when I became enrolled in the joint PhD programme of the Max Planck Institute for Social Anthropology and Martin Luther University in Halle. My doctoral fieldwork in Vietnam in 2006–2007 was made possible by financial support from the Max Planck Institute for Social Anthropology. Chris Hann, my principal advisor, was most important in welcoming me to the Max Planck Society and helping me orient myself to the research project 'Religion and Morality', which he initiated. What Chris Hann offered to my dissertation in terms of a postsocialist studies approach and a solid ethnographic focus, Burkhard Schnepel of Martin Luther University – my second advisor – provided in guiding me through maritime history and polytheistic religions and by sharing his enthusiasm for 'small islands'. In the course of my PhD trajectory I benefitted greatly from comments and suggestions from colleagues not only in informal discussions, but also when I presented earlier drafts of several chapters at conferences, workshops, and seminars or sent my papers directly to them. I want to specifically thank Fridrich Binder, Irene Becci, Pascal Bourdeaux, Andrew Hardy, Lâle Yalçın-Heckmann, Kirsten Endres, Tobias Kölner, Nathan Light, Agata Ładykowska, Agnieszka Pasieka, Małgorzata Rajtar, Detelina Tocheva, Philip Taylor, Markus Schlecker and Gábor Vargyas.

At this point, I would like to thank the Institute of Culture Studies and, particularly, Prof. Lê Hồng Lý, who arranged my visa during my stay in Vietnam from September 2006 to September 2007, and Prof. Nguyễn Thị Phương Châm, who continued to arrange my research visas between 2011 and 2018. I am aware that my 'hyper-mobility' in Vietnam caused many troubles for the institute that hosted me and was responsible for my research and my whereabouts. I highly appreciate their patience, help, openness, and goodwill, all of which made this project possible. I would like to acknowledge that the Quảng Ngãi authorities helped me carry out my project in central Vietnam. I am particularly grateful to Nguyễn Hoàng Sơn, Dr. Nguyễn Đăng Vũ, Phan Đình Độ, Nguyễn Kim Sơn, Hoàng Nam Chu, and Lê Hồng Khánh. I also owe my thanks to the authorities of Phổ Thạnh commune (Đức Phổ District) and of Lý Sơn District, who warmly welcomed me as a foreigner and organized my stay in their communities.

I owe numerous other debts of gratitude to those who helped me through my entire stay in Vietnam. It is impossible to mention them all, so here I must limit myself to only a few names. My deepest thanks go to the people of Sa Huỳnh and Lý Sơn, whose hospitality, help, and candor touched me more than I can say. Specifically, I would like to mention Lê Tấn Lại, Hồ Kiếm, Trần Nên, Trần Phẩm, Mai Phầu, Nguyễn Bảy, Nguyễn Dư, Nguyễn Tuấn Hải, Nguyễn Song, Đăng Năng, Nguyễn Bé, Hoàng Thị Hảo, Huỳnh Thị Thu Thảo, Nguyễn Mới, Phạm Hiến, Trường Hoài Dư, Sâm Nhung, Võ Tấn Công, and Võ Nghìn. Chị Bình and her family hosted me for almost a year in the Thế Vĩnh roadhouse. Their generosity, help, and patience were invaluable throughout my entire stay in Sa Huỳnh. Lê Ở, Điển Lễ, Nguyễn Công Tiến, Nguyễn Hấp, Pham Đình Thọ, Ngô Xương, Nguyễn Quảng Nghị, Nguyễn Thanh Tùng, Võ Hiến Đạt, Nguyễn Đình Trang, Phạm Thoai Tuyển, Trần Đỗ, and Mỹ Linh gave me unwavering support during my research on Lý Sơn Island. Võ Văn Út and Phan Quyên and their relatives not only endlessly supported my fieldwork in Lý Sơn, but also took me into their homes and considered me a family member. There are so many more whom I simply do not have space to mention. I am grateful to you all.

The project was also supported by a generous writing fellowship from the Research Center for Humanities and Social Science, Academia Sinica. I am deeply grateful to the Center of Asia and Pacific Area Studies (CAPAS) for providing me with an office, the impressive collections of books in their library, and assistance throughout my two-year stay in Taipei. I would like to thank Cheng-Yi Lin, Hsin-Huang Michael Hsiao, Chang Wen-Chin, Ota Atsushi, and my advisor Shiu Wen-Tang. Chang Wen-Chin and Shiu Wen-Tang in particular not only welcomed me at CAPAS, but made my stay in Taipei more cheerful. I also extend my thanks to Lin Shu Hui, Chiang Ginger, Chen Erin Yi-Fang, and Chien Hsinyi, who guided me through the intricacies of administrative requirements. Postdoctoral fellowships from the European Commission at Durham University and from the Danish Council for Independent Research in Culture and Humanities at the Department of Cross-Cultural and Regional Studies at the University of Copenhagen gave me time and resources to revisit my field sites in Vietnam in 2014 and to turn the thesis into this book. Much of the rethinking and rewriting that went into this book happened during my visiting fellowship at the Institute for Religion, Politics and Society of the Australian Catholic University in Melbourne in 2015. I am particularly grateful to Bryan S. Turner for inviting me to Melbourne to work on this project. Ingolf Thuesen, the head of the Department of Cross-Cultural and Regional Studies at the University of Copenhagen, provided me with the office space and library resources at a time when I most needed it. The Christian Michelsen Institute in Bergen created time for me to complete the book.

Earlier versions of some parts of this book have been published elsewhere. Parts of the Introduction, Chapter 4, and a fragment of the Conclusion appear in the article 'A Triad of Confrontation: State Discipline, Buddhist Purification, and Indiscipline as a Local Strategy in Central Vietnam', published by the *Journal of Contemporary Ethnography* (Roszko 2019). Parts of Chapter 1 and fragments of Chapter 3 appear in a book chapter, 'Geographies of Connection and Disconnection: Narratives of Seafaring in Ly Son' (Roszko 2016), in *Connected and Disconnected in Vietnam: Remaking Social Relationships in a Post-socialist Nation*, edited by Philip Taylor and published by ANU Press. Parts of Chapter 2 appear in the article 'From Spiritual Houses to National Shrines: Religious Traditions and Nation-Building in Vietnam', published in the journal *East Asia: An International Quarterly* (Roszko 2012). Parts of Chapter 5 appeared in the essay titled 'Commemoration and the State: Memory and Legitimacy in Vietnam', published in *Sojourn: Journal of Social Issues in Southeast Asia* (Roszko 2010). And some fragments of Chapter 5 appear in the article 'Maritime Territorialisation as Performance of Sovereignty and Nationhood in the South China Sea', published in the journal *Nations and Nationalism* (Roszko 2015).

Profound intellectual and personal debts of gratitude are due to Erik Harms and Hue-Tam Ho Tai. Hue-Tam Ho Tai was the first to give helpful suggestions regarding how to turn my thesis into a book. Erik Harms read the entire manuscript and provided invaluable suggestions about how to refine the argument of the book. His influence on my work has been profound. Bill Hayton lent his critical eye for historical details and helped to put them into place. I would especially like to thank Brian Donahoe, editor and fellow anthropologist, whose sharp comments went far beyond editorial suggestions, as well as Gerald Jackson at NIAS Press for his genuine trust in me and in this project. To Jutta Turner go my grateful thanks for the preparation of the maps.

I would like to finish these words on a personal note. My stay in Vietnam in the earlier years would not have been possible without the support of my parents Henryk and Danuta Roszko, and my brother Daniel and his wife Ewa, who have been enormously patient and understanding through my long physical and intellectual journey. My nephew Igor Roszko – who sweetly asked me to take a ride with him on the roller coaster at Tivoli and, when I did, asked 'What's wrong with you, aunt'? – challenged me as nobody before. My deepest thanks go to my husband and harshest critic, Oscar Salemink, who brought out the best in me. The curiosity, intellectual rigour, fun, and joy he has brought through all these years of our journey together have enriched my life immensely. I dedicate this book to him.

Note on Transliteration
and Translation

Vietnamese is a tonal language. Formerly, the Vietnamese language was written using original Chinese characters – called *chữ Hán* – and a system of newly created and modified characters called *Hán-Nôm*, which rendered Vietnamese pronunciation. In the sixteenth and seventeenth centuries a romanized system called *Quốc Ngữ* was invented by Portuguese Christian missionaries and then developed by a French Jesuit, Alexandre de Rhodes. Under French colonial rule, the script became official and was required for all public documents, but it only became universally used when nationalists saw it as a tool in the fight against French colonial power. Present-day *Quốc Ngữ* consists of the standard English alphabet plus extra letters such as â, ă, ê, ô, ơ, ư, đ. Diacritical marks indicate tones and particular vowel sounds. This means that there can be as many as six words that are written identically (except for the diacritical marks), but differ in tone and, therefore, in meaning. For example, *tinh* means 'sharp-witted', *tính* means 'temper', *tình* means 'affection', *tỉnh* means 'province', *tĩnh* means 'quiet', and *tịnh* means 'absolutely'. To avoid any semantic confusion, I have chosen to transcribe Vietnamese terms with diacritical marks. The only exceptions are Vietnamese words which will be familiar in English to the reader. Thus, I write Hanoi instead of Hà Nội, Ho Chi Minh City instead of Hồ Chí Minh, and Vietnam instead of Việt Nam.

In the text, terms in languages other than English are rendered in *italics*. The only exceptions are personal names and place names. Each term is followed by an indication of its language (if it is not clear from the context) and then by an English gloss of its meaning (in some cases the order is reversed, with the English gloss being given first and the Vietnamese following in parentheses). In addition, foreign terms in titles or subtitles are rendered in italics. Except for the names of lineages and recognized historical and public figures, all personal names are pseudonyms. Unless otherwise stated, all translations herein are mine.

Glossary

ADMINISTRATIVE TERMS

chủ tịch	chairman
Công an Biên phòng	Border Guard Command
huyện	district
Sở Văn hóa, Thể thao và Du Lịch	Provincial Office of Culture, Sport and Tourism
thôn	village or community
tỉnh	province
xã	often translated as "commune"; refers to an administrative unit denoting municipality consisting of various villages or *làng* – residential units or "villages" or "communities."
Ủy Ban Nhân Dân (UBND)	state institution of the People's Committee

TERRITORIAL DENOMINATIONS

ấp	hamlet (typical for southern Vietnam)
Hoàng Sa	Paracel Archipelago
làng	village
lân	sub-hamlet
Trường Sa	Spratly Archipelago
vạn	self-ruling fishing organization, fishing community
vạn chày	floating fishing community (see also religious denominations)
xóm	hamlet (typical for northern Vietnam)

TERMS FOR ORGANIZATIONS

Giáo Hội Phật Giáo Việt	Buddhist Association of Vietnam, created by the Party-State in 1981
Phật Giáo Thống-nhất Việt Nam	Unified Buddhist Church of Vietnam (UBCV), unrecognized by the Party-State

RELIGIOUS DENOMINATIONS

âm hồn	soul of the dead person
chùa	Buddhist pagoda
chủ làng	village senior, master of the ceremony
chủ vạn	head of the fishing community
dinh	literally: "palace" – here "temple"
đình	communal house, political and religious centre of the village
lăng	literally: "mausoleum" or "tomb" – here communal temple of the fishing community
mê tín dị đoan	superstitious/superstition
miếu	shrine, temple
Quan Âm	Quan Yin in Chinese
tín ngưỡng	religious beliefs
vạn	fishing religious organization

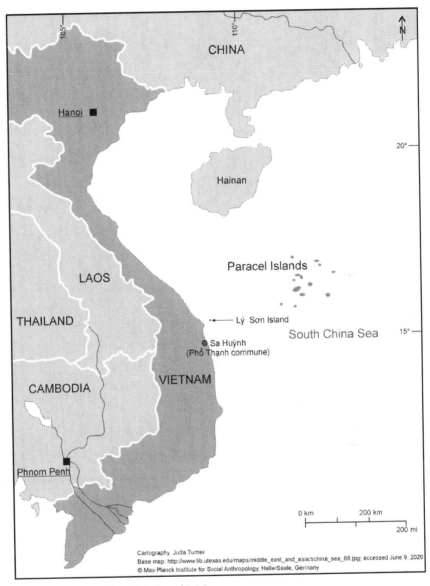

Map 1: Field sites of Sa Huỳnh and Lý Sơn.

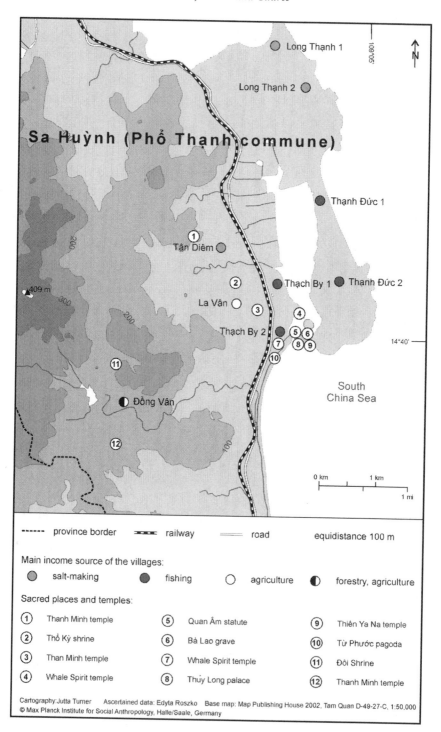

Long Thạnh 1

Long Thạnh 2

Sa Huỳnh (Phổ Thạnh commune)

Thạnh Đức 1

① Tân Diêm

② Thạch By 1 ● Thạnh Đức 2

La Vân ③

④

Thạch By 2 ⑤⑥
⑦⑧⑨
⑩

⑪

Đồng Vân

⑫

South China Sea

409 m

0 km   1 km

1 mi

109°05'

14°40'

- - - - - province border   ▬▬▬ railway   .... road   equidistance 100 m

Main income source of the villages:

⬤ salt-making   ⬤ fishing   ◯ agriculture   ◑ forestry, agriculture

Sacred places and temples:

① Thanh Minh temple   ⑤ Quan Âm statute   ⑨ Thiên Ya Na temple

② Thổ Kỳ shrine   ⑥ Bà Lao grave   ⑩ Từ Phước pagoda

③ Than Minh temple   ⑦ Whale Spirit temple   ⑪ Đồi Shrine

④ Whale Spirit temple   ⑧ Thủy Long palace   ⑫ Thanh Minh temple

Cartography: Jutta Turner   Ascertained data: Edyta Roszko   Base map: Map Publishing House 2002, Tam Quan D-49-27-C, 1:50,000
© Max Planck Institute for Social Anthropology, Halle/Saale, Germany

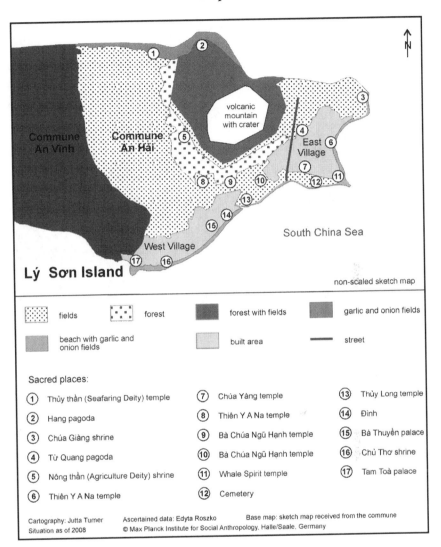

Map 3: Religious sites in An Hải Commune, Lý Sơn Island.

Map 2 (opposite): Religious sites in Sa Huỳnh, Quảng Ngãi Province, Central Vietnam.

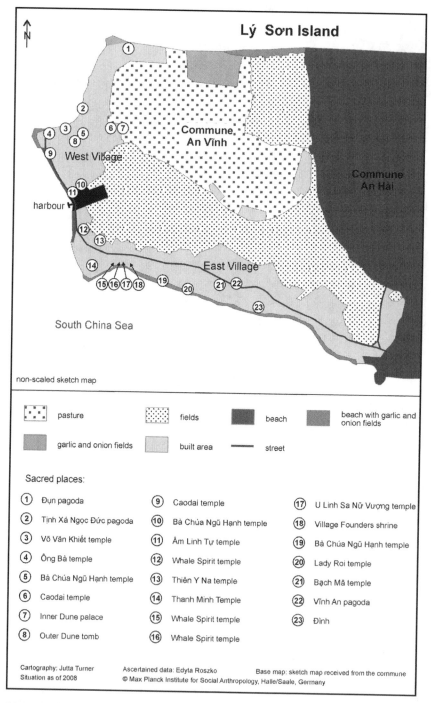

Map 4: Religious sites in An Vĩnh Commune, Lý Sơn Island.

Figure 1: A wooden statue recovered by fishermen from the South China Sea.

A Triad of Confrontation

In February 2007, fishermen from Sa Huỳnh pulled a one-metre-high wooden statue out of their net while fishing in the South China Sea – or 'East Sea' (*Biển Đông*) in Vietnamese – in the vicinity of Lý Sơn Island, about 30 kilometres off the shore of Quảng Ngãi Province in central Vietnam. The wooden carving depicted a Chinese dignitary seated on a throne with armrests in the shape of a dragon's mouth. The statue had survived quite well, although the places where the paint had come off were covered with shellfish. The fishing crew that made this unexpected discovery placed the statue in the yard of the boat owner's house, next to an open-air altar dedicated to the Earth Spirit (*Thổ Địa*). A fence was carefully erected around the statue, and an umbrella was set up to protect it against rain. The fishers believed that the statue was an image of a king of the Vietnamese Lê dynasty (1428–1788) and considered the finding a sign of luck, security, and good health for their families.[1] This narrative was soon enriched with reports of the statue's supernatural power (*linh thiêng*) to provide miraculous protection to fishers against various misfortunes. Until very recently, fishers were most fearful of storms, but this fear has been superseded by China's and Vietnam's competing claims to the South China Sea and the associated risk of capture, detention, and confiscation of their vessels by the Chinese coastguard. As a consequence, the fishers felt that the statue needed a more appropriate abode and wanted to build a proper shrine to better protect and honour it. They reported their finding as 'historical heritage' to the People's Committee of Sa Huỳnh Commune and asked for permission to erect the shrine. However, the petition was dismissed

---

1. To avoid the highly gendered language that privileges men and excludes women, I use the term *fishers* as the 'best gender-neutral plural for people working in the fishing industry' (Subramanian 2009: xiii). When I am referring specifically to males or females, I use the terms *fishermen* and *fisherwomen*.

1

by the cultural office on the grounds that building a shrine for the statue would constitute 'superstition' (*mê tín dị đoan*). A local policeman drew up a protocol of the occurrence and instructed the fishers not to display the statue publicly. Consequently, the group of fishers kept the statue out of the communal space and held private rituals for themselves.

The sea has always been synonymous with insecurity for the humble fishers who ventured onto it. The wooden carving that the fishermen pulled out of the South China Sea likely traces its origins to one of the many merchant ships that went down in a storm or in pirate attack while navigating the coast of what today is Vietnam. The wooden statute thus provides a silent testimony to the hazards of seafaring, an activity which – if successful – could prove profitable, but which could also fail and cause major losses for the ship owner. As the vignette above suggests, the art of navigation may require not only steering a ship in the most literal sense against winds and currents, but also in a more symbolical sense between the strong hand of state authoritarian power and the geopolitical perils of the South China Sea dispute. Taking our cue from Greek mythology, the fishers had – and have – to find a way to navigate between the sea monsters Scylla, taking the form of a rocky cliff that may stand for Vietnam's authorities, and Charybdis, a roiling whirlpool that in this case can symbolize the South China Sea dispute. In that sense, the fate of the wooden statue is a silent witness to the fishers' efforts to call on their religious practices to navigate the various dangers in the seascape of everyday life and global politics.

This book is about fishing communities living on the fringes of the South China Sea and the various ways they interact with state and religious authorities while at the same time responding to new geopolitical challenges. The focus is mainly on coastal people and the ways they have navigated religion and politics over the decades of massive change since their incorporation into the Socialist Republic of Vietnam in 1975. The sea plays a major role in this study, as does the location: a once-peripheral area now at the centre of a globally important struggle for sovereignty, legitimacy, and control in the South China Sea. The South China Sea is one of the busiest sea-lanes in the world, and the unimpeded flow of maritime traffic is vital to the economies of East and Southeast Asia. A number of countries make competing and overlapping claims of sovereignty over the many small, uninhabited islands, islets, and reefs in order to justify access to the resources in the territorial waters surrounding them (Hayton 2014). The Paracel (Hoàng Sa) and Spratly (Trường Sa) Islands in particular have become a bone of contention between China and Vietnam. The Philippines, Malaysia, Taiwan, and Brunei all claim partial sovereignty there as well, but China is the dominant military force and Vietnam its main challenger. The maritime boundaries between China, Vietnam, and other countries have been only partially fixed. However, by law, all official Vietnamese maps must portray the Paracel and Spratly Islands within the national borders of Vietnam; all Chinese maps, conversely, must show the islands as being part of China.

One of the principal research sites in this book is Lý Sơn Island, which was thrust into the national limelight as a symbol of Vietnam's historical and present-day sovereign rights in the South China Sea. Lý Sơn is a small atoll lying about 16 nautical miles (ca. 30 km) off the shore of Sa Kỳ port in central Quảng Ngãi province, connected to the mainland by a private hydrofoil service. One hundred twenty-three nautical miles (approximately 228 km) separate Lý Sơn from the Paracel archipelago, to which both Vietnam and China lay territorial claims. Because of its proximity to and discursive association with the Paracels, Vietnamese authorities consider Lý Sơn Island a sensitive border zone and a strategic defensive position. The second principal research site, Sa Huỳnh, is associated with the disputed parts of the South China Sea not in terms of geographical proximity, but rather in terms of its fishing legacy. In recent times, the fishing communities in both sites have come to be viewed as custodians of a maritime culture and hence as key actors in Vietnam's resistance to Chinese claims over the South China Sea. While Lý Sơn is now depicted as a 'heroic vanguard' (*tiên phong anh hùng*) of Vietnam's sovereignty, Sa Huỳnh – picturesquely located on a sand dune facing the sea – has become symbolic of idyllic, long-standing fishing communities that are now in need of cultural protection. These two fishing communities – Sa Huỳnh and Lý Sơn – are at the heart of this study. They are considered peripheral not so much because of their geographical remoteness, but for the alleged social 'backwardness' (*lạc hậu*) associated with coastal settlements and the mobile livelihoods of their residents. As a result, fishers only partially fit into the dominant imaginary of Vietnam's territory and nation, propagated over the course of the various Indochina wars, as predominantly agrarian (Gourou

1936, 1940; Mus 1948, 1952; McAlister and Mus 1970; FitzGerald 1972; Scott 1976).

Sa Huỳnh comprises a string of rural, coastal settlements trapped between the Trường Sơn mountain range (also known as Annamese Cordillera) to the west and the South China Sea to the east. While there are rice paddies along with the fish and shrimp farms and salt marshes, the broad sandy dunes and marshy plains create more favourable conditions for fishing and salt production than for wet rice cultivation. For that reason the majority of Sa Huỳnh's 20,000 people make their living from fishing, production of salt and fish sauce, fish breeding ponds, boat construction, animal husbandry, and seafood restaurants and shops. People in the poorest quarter of Sa Huỳnh live in sheds built right on the beach; those who are better off live in solidly built houses by the beach and further inland.

National Route 1A and the parallel North–South Railway line cut directly through the various settlements making up Sa Huỳnh, connecting the capital Hanoi in the north with Ho Chi Minh City in the south. National Route 1A is crowded with trucks, speeding buses, and mopeds and motorcycles pulling small trailers that carry most of Sa Huỳnh's fish and other aquatic resources to the nearest markets in Đức Phổ and to more distant centres inland. The shops that have mushroomed along the highway offer to passing travellers a range of local products, including dried fish and a famous local elixir made of sea horses preserved in bottles of rice liquor. Next to these stalls, simple restaurants offer cheap bowls of noodles. For the more discriminating traveller, there are motels scattered along the main road where one can refresh oneself after the journey, renting a room for the night and dining on fish, rice, and vegetables washed down with alcohol. For some of its length, running between tightly packed houses then continuing parallel to the coast, the tracks of the North–South Railway mark a border between the sandy beaches of the coast and the rice paddies to the west. Passing with a terrible roar day and night, the trains trouble Sa Huỳnh residents and fuel stories about the ghosts of those who failed to heed the approaching train and were run over. Most of the time, however, people take advantage of the railway line to sell their goods and refreshments to passengers, thereby supplementing their meagre incomes. Whenever the express train stops in Sa Huỳnh, local women rush out to sell dried cuttlefish, sweets, and dry pancakes (*bánh tráng*) to the passengers peering out of the windows.

Beyond the tracks lie the flooded rice fields, dotted with small clusters of houses and groves of coconut palms stretching to the foot of the mountains. Shining emerald green in the bright sunlight, these rice paddies are irrigated by a stream that comes down out of the mountains, flows under the railway and highway bridges, and then turns to the south and flows for one kilometre parallel to the beach and finally out to the sea. Except in the driest months of the summer, the green section of the canalized stream right above the beach, covered with water ferns and grass, creates a perfect grazing area for cows. The canal itself functions as a fish trap. In the early morning, fishers paddle upstream and check their nets in search of small fish pushed into the canal at high tide.

The long beach constantly changes throughout the year. In autumn and winter the sea is very rough and every wave – crashing against the shore – brings a huge mass of sand that forms dunes. At this time, the sea is full of unexpected holes, steep drops, seething whirlpools, and rapid currents that can pull a person under. With the arrival of spring, the sea softens. When summer comes, the kilometre-long beach resembles a golden caterpillar basking in the sun on the leaf of the turquoise sea. This is a happy time for village children, who splash in the sea and play football on the beach, taking advantage of the fading afternoon heat.

Lý Sơn's population is nearly the same size as Sa Huỳnh's, but with steep volcanic hills covering two-thirds of the island, Lý Sơn residents have to take advantage of whatever space is available for housing and agriculture. The mineral-rich basalt soil of the plains, which descend right down to the sea, is unsuitable for rice cultivation but perfect for growing garlic, onions, and maize. Forming a green patchwork of fields stretching to the craggy cliffs of the three large volcanoes on the island, the long, round shoots of garlic and the flatter stalks of onions shimmer green-gold in the sunlight, much like the rice stalks in Sa Huỳnh.

Rising from the sea, the bowl-shaped craters of three extinct volcanoes dominate the landscape of Lý Sơn. The deepest point of the largest crater Thới Lới, with its ragged cliffs walling off the island on its north side, was long ago turned into an artificial lake that functions as a source of water for the island's residents. The sea cliff itself is famous for the Hang (Cave) pagoda and for its impressive formations of volcanic rock and coral sandstone. On the other side of the island, the Giếng Tiền volcanic depression – covered with grass, shrubs, and coniferous and pineapple trees – provides both pastures for cows and a recreational space for Lý Sơn residents and tourists. Rising to the sky and then dramatically falling into the sea, the crater's steep side offers a splendid panoramic view of the island and the sea. At its foot stands a twenty-seven-metre-tall image of the bodhisattva Quan Âm (Guanyin in Chinese), erected by former Lý Sơn residents now living overseas to watch over and guard the South China Sea. Because it obstructs the view of the dramatic Giếng Tiền cliff side, the Buddhist statue has become a subject of heated discussion among residents and some guests from the mainland, with some arguing that it adds to the beauty of the landscape and others viewing it as an eyesore that defiles the natural beauty. A similar debate is sparked by the mushrooming hotels, restaurants, and pubs, often built illegally right in the middle of the island's most scenic spots. Newspapers in Vietnam lament that the massive – and often unplanned – buildings and tourist hotspots that taint the island's landscape and have damaged its fragile marine ecosystem beyond repair.[2]

On the fringes of the South China Sea, Sa Huỳnh and Lý Sơn have become the nodal points of Vietnam's newly rediscovered maritime culture. This book thus charts the contours of Vietnam not from its firm terrestrial base of urban and agrarian centres, but by attending to its 'loose ends' – its sandy shorelines and territorial waters – to show how the places seen as remote or marginal are central to understanding Vietnam and the Vietnamese state (Harms 2011a: 12). What becomes visible on the ethnographic chart is not just the design formed by weaving different coloured threads into a tapestry of the nation-state, but also where its loose ends get tied together into a knot anchoring the fabric of the national narrative.

Beyond the coastal fringe of central Vietnam

In the eighteenth and nineteenth centuries, the Paracels historically constituted fishing grounds for Lý Sơn fishermen, but the group of islets was also frequently visited by local fishermen from Hainan and by Malay

---

2. See 'Ly Son Island harmed by unplanned building', available at https://en.vietnamplus. vn/ly-son-island-harmed-by-unplanned-building/100317.vnp, accessed 27 April 2020.

and Buginese sailors who responded to the growing Chinese demand for luxury marine commodities (Lê Quý Đôn [1776] 1972; Warren 1981; Tagliacozzo 2011). Around the same time, Sa Huỳnh – located at the sea's edge with access to sandy bays, estuaries, and rocky headlands, as well as to the mountainous forests of the Trường Sơn range – exchanged salt and fish with highlanders – Cham, Khor, and Hrê – who in return provided forest goods, buffaloes, and rice (see Hardy 2009). Rather than being a border zone between discrete societies, the resource-rich highlands and waters surrounding the Paracels were zones of interaction and exchange of locally developed knowledge, technologies, and networks that generated livelihoods for coastal people (see Hardy 2005, 2008, 2009; Salemink 2013, 2018a).

In that sense neither Sa Huỳnh nor Lý Sơn really corresponds to the stereotype of isolated and remote settlements: the coast was always reachable from both land and sea, and the island has 'all-round "connectivity" … accessible to the seaborne' (Pearson 2006: 358). What qualifies Sa Huỳnh and Lý Sơn as remote or peripheral is not so much geographical distance, but rather the presumed social 'backwardness' of fishing communities, which supposedly do not live up to the generally accepted conception of a monolithic 'Vietnameseness' that ignores regional, cultural, and historical differences. Colonial sources shaped influential territorial imaginaries of Vietnam centred on the terrestrial rice-growing Red River Delta as 'the cradle of Vietnamese civilization'. The colonial era is also the source of the cliché of the Vietnamese village as a politically autonomous, socially homogeneous corporate community surrounded by a hedge and rice paddies – thus an isolated and remote entity (see, for example, Gourou 1936, 1940; McAlister and Mus 1970; Scott 1976; Kleinen 1999a). Moreover, the classic tripartite division of Vietnam into North, Centre, and South – metaphorically characterized as '"two rice baskets on a pole" to describe the supposedly rich agrarian North and South held together by the poor but hardworking Centre' – is still alive in many popular discourses and accounts (Wheeler 2006: 129–130). Keith Taylor (1998: 971) has convincingly argued against the 'pan-Vietnamese village morphology' that produced the Vietnamese hierarchy, which puts rice farmers at the top of the social ladder and fishers at the bottom, pointing out the many different ways of being and acting Vietnamese that have existed through space and time.

Taylor's critique of stereotyped representations of Vietnamese history, culture, and territory that affirm unity and continuity is echoed in the work of Charles Wheeler (2006), Li Tana (2006), John Whitmore (2006), and Nhung Tuyet Tran and Anthony Reid (2006), all of whom pay particular attention to Vietnam's maritime frontier. By conceptualizing the littoral in terms of networks of transregional (dis)connectivity and flows, they offer a new perspective on Vietnamese society as seen from the sea. Like the littoral, which is in a constant state of flux, this society must be seen as fluid and flexible as well (Pearson 1985, 2003).

The ethnographic material that is at the heart of this book shows that potent intersections of religion, economy, politics, and ecology are particularly visible in such a contact zone, where the state struggles to establish and increase its presence. The problematic conceptualization of a monolithic Vietnamese nation and culture (Evans 2002) tends to underplay the regional, historical, and cultural diversity, and to marginalize places such as coastal fishing villages because they are seen as representing an extreme, unusual, and unsettled situation that does not stand for the imagined Vietnamese territory and nation. Occasionally, such coastal societies might also be exoticized and viewed as guardians of an ancient fishing culture and a symbol of heroic sacrifice in the name of Vietnamese citizens, who started to identify themselves with the 'Vietnamese waters' vis-à-vis China's competing claims over the South China Sea. Probing the social life of such marginalized places requires bringing to light many pasts that were driven by ecology, politics, and local actors themselves (Taylor and Whitmore 1995). The spatial marginality and ambivalence of such communities remains a major concern of the state, which tries to incorporate them through various cultural agendas and development programmes. These often contradictory and dispersed processes in the coastal communities reveal the uneven status of places and their different relationships with the state.

There is nothing new in the idea that people in every society perceive themselves as being at the centre of the universe that they live in, see, and experience. At the same time, they recognize that other universes exist, and are sometimes more powerful than theirs is (Anderson 1991: 13). Anna Tsing (1993), in the case of the Meratus Dayak communities living in the mountainous forest areas of South Kalimantan, Indonesia, convincingly shows that marginality is not just a direct construct of a centre–periphery dichotomy, but is, rather, a process or a way of being. What constitutes in Vietnam the 'centre' (*trung ương*), the 'local' (*địa phương*), the 'periphery' (*ngoại vi*), or a 'remote area' (*vùng sâu vùng xa*) very much depends on the relative vantage point of a person in relation to other geographic and political locations. For Lý Sơn Island, the centre is the Vietnamese mainland; for Sa Huỳnh it is the provincial city of Quảng Ngãi. But for Quảng Ngãi, the point of reference is the capital, Hanoi. What, then, constitutes the centre for Hanoi? Perhaps this could be the imagined *trung ương* or central state with its various agencies spread across the city. Neither the centre nor the periphery is a stable entity; they are, rather, relational categories that are always localized by people from their specific perspectives at various levels and in different locations. Likewise, it refers to their relationship with the state.

It is for this reason that I take a closer look at two fishing communities in Quảng Ngãi Province, which before 1975 had been part of the Republic of Vietnam, also known as South Vietnam. Both Sa Huỳnh and Lý Sơn expose the social, cultural, and historical unevenness of the place and remind us that locality does not simply exist, but has to be produced and achieved against the backdrop of perennial change, conflict, and threat (Appadurai 1996). Although Sa Huỳnh did not escape the modern nation-state's vision of national culture and development – focusing on both fisheries and tourism – these processes take on very different shapes on the coast. As the opening vignette shows, the desire of Sa Huỳnh people to turn their local worship of the statue recovered from the South China Sea into national 'historical heritage' was labelled 'superstitious' and was consequently dismissed by local authorities. This is because Sa Huỳnh, firmly located on Vietnam's shoreline, is not granted much latitude to diverge from the Vietnamese ideal. Lý Sơn, on the other hand, because of its perceived territorial and geopolitical vulnerability and 'otherness', needs to be absorbed and properly linked to the 'centre' (see Ardener 2012).

No matter how alien Lý Sơn people's livelihoods seems to be in the eyes of mainlanders, their 'island indigenousness' – whether in the form of seafaring tradition, fishing occupation, or beliefs – is necessary for Vietnam's project of constructing a new 'maritime' nation. Lý Sơn's connectedness with the state and the mainland has to be constantly enacted not only through more prosaic means such as the improvement of boats, fishing operations, and a submarine cable that transmits electricity from the mainland's national power grid, but also through positive reinforcement of the island's historical and cultural legacy. What might be considered 'superstitious' and 'backwards' in Sa Huỳnh could, on Lý Sơn Island, provide evidence of maritime heritage and hence Vietnam's long-standing sovereignty in the South China Sea, which is then invoked to counter China's claims to the same territory. The ability of Lý Sơn to appropriate its alleged remoteness as a resource to claim various benefits from the state not only depends on its connectedness to surrounding zones, but also to the 'dominant zone', to use the term employed in this context by Ardener (2012: 532). Within this framework, both Sa Huỳnh and Lý Sơn stand out as 'singularities', an image that is reinforced by 'perceptions' from the dominant zone about what constitutes Vietnamese culture. In contrast, this book features Sa Huỳnh and Lý Sơn in terms of spatial and temporal connections, without obscuring the complexity of geography, local histories, and ways of acting 'Vietnamese' (Li 2006; Tran and Reid 2006; Wheeler 2006). I conceptualize Sa Huỳnh and Lý Sơn as part of coastal society whose livelihoods are connected to both the foreland and the hinterland. Occupying the shore and exhibiting mix of land and sea in their occupations, this society could be considered truly 'littoral' – a concept used by Michael Pearson to specify people living in coastal zones, on the beach, and along the intermediate frontier on land (Pearson 2006).

By focusing my analysis on Sa Huỳnh and Lý Sơn, I do not aim to compare or homogenize the two settings, but rather to show how different localities stand out as 'pluralities' representing different levels of (dis)connectedness to state power. Sa Huỳnh's and Lý Sơn's histories and their entanglements with modernity at the national and global scales underscore the inadequacy of undifferentiated notions of state and society, religious and secular, and mainland and island. Contemporary religious practices are inscribed in the nuanced texture of everyday concerns, national debates, and international agendas, showing the actors' rich arsenal of tactics and strategies in navigating binaries across and within the state–religion–village triad of contested domains. To fully recognize these everyday concerns and their connections with religious practices, one needs to pay attention to various groups of people who seek to transform, organize, and control their environment not only through such ritual activities as conducting ceremonies, evoking and consulting spirits, and making offerings, but also through more profane technical and social practices such as building, renovating, and maintaining sacred spaces. The ritually transformed environs are purified when the state institutionalizes and nationalizes gods and spirits by selecting spirits, designating sacred spaces, and granting certificates in order to keep them under control and effectively 'pin' them down. In this process, villagers carry out their own counter-purification, as they sometimes choose to foreground the aesthetic or 'national' value of objects and spaces while temporarily backgrounding their religious value. By moving between opposing ideas of secular and religious rationalities and positioning themselves discursively and ritually against the backdrop of constant change, the villagers create and reinvent their religious practices in recognizable religious forms. In this sense, each of the settings – Sa Huỳnh and Lý Sơn – represents a different dimension in terms of local histories, practices, territory, and relations with the state and the wider world. For that reason, I argue, interactions across and within the triad of contested domains of state–religion–village assume sharper contours, and hence become more visible.

Charting the contours of religion in Vietnam

The opening vignette speaks of contestations between state agents and villagers over what constitutes legitimate religious practice in understudied central Vietnam.[3] My particular focus in this book is on the proliferating and shifting encounters between state and religious authorities; between religious authorities and fishers; between fishers and farmers; and between men and women. These categories and individuals – divided by age, gender, class, and profession – often adopt conflicting understandings and strategies to achieve their goals vis-à-vis the state, represented by central, provincial, and local officials, scholars, and journalists. These different confrontations involve relationships experienced and expressed in terms of mutually exclusive binaries, the poles of which are in fact neither mutually exclusive nor stable, as the examples below well illustrate.

While protests in Vietnam's major cities against China's installation of an oil rig in what Vietnam considers its territorial waters were seen by the

---

3. Kwon (2006, 2009) and Avieli (2012) are among the rare studies focusing on central Vietnam.

Vietnamese authorities as politically harmful for the country's relations with China (Ciorciari and Weiss 2016), the delegation of Buddhist monks that went to the Spratly archipelago to re-establish abandoned temples was seen as helping to assert Vietnam's sovereignty over the disputed islands.[4] This is because, in contrast to the bold anti-China protests that challenged the Vietnamese state's authority and legitimacy, the political 'transcript' (Scott 1990) of the Buddhist mission to the South China Sea was veiled by a religious agenda that heeds a different source of authority and indexes different moral tensions. Accordingly, the high-profile 2014 celebration for the peace of the Paracel and Spratly sailors (*lễ cầu siêu lính Hoàng Sa và Trường Sa*) – held on Lý Sơn Island by a delegation of Buddhist monks from Huế – was considered to be purely religious. The people of Lý Sơn nevertheless added a personal (and political) touch to the celebration by making sure that the Buddhist altar prepared for the ceremony accommodated ancestral tablets (*bài vị*) with the names of local fishermen who had gone missing in the vicinity of the disputed archipelagos while bravely 'clinging to the fishing grounds to defend national sovereignty' (*bám ngư trường để bảo vệ quyền tổ quốc*), as well as that of the 67-year-old woman from Ho Chi Minh City who self-immolated to show solidarity with fishermen affected by China's deployment of the oil rig in waters claimed by Vietnam.[5] Both the 2014 anti-China protests in the streets of Vietnam's main cities and the woman's self-immolation in the same year added fuel to the debate about the disputed areas of the South China Sea and to the allegation that Vietnam's Party-state is weak in its dealings with China. However, when folded into the context of the celebration of Paracel and Spratly sailors, the potentially sensitive case of the woman's self-immolation became subsumed under the rubric of religious rather than political expression, demonstrating that the opposing poles of religion and politics are not absolute and can be skilfully navigated by both religious authorities and Lý Sơn people. Yet to treat this ritual performance as apolitical would be to deny 'the creative agency of its myriad participants' (Bowie 2017: 268).

---

4. See 'Vietnam to send Buddhist monks to Spratly Islands', available at https://www.bbc.com/news/world-asia-17343596, accessed 29 April 2020.

5. See 'Vietnamese woman dies in self-immolation protest against China', available at https://www.theguardian.com/world/2014/may/23/vietnamese-woman-dies-self-immolation-protest-china, accessed 29 April 2020.

This book approaches binary oppositions such as institutionalized religion versus beliefs, religion versus politics, modern versus traditional, science versus superstition, cultural versus political, mainland versus island, Việt versus Cham, farmers versus fishers, masculine versus feminine, and ancestor versus ghost not as absolute, everlasting, or antagonistic, but as constantly changing and shifting in pragmatic tactics employed within and across the triadic relationship between the state, villagers, and more institutionalized versions of religion. Binary ways of thinking about social phenomena have long been present in Western social theory. It comes as no surprise, then, that many of the debates about the state, religion, and society have been structured through the sacred–profane dichotomy posited by French sociologist Emile Durkheim (1995 [1915]) and through the legacy of Weberian thinking that places traditional/non-Western and modern/Western categories, or politics and religion, or individual beliefs and secularism on opposite ends of a spectrum (Weber 1951, 1966; Day 2002: 6). At the same time, there has been a growing awareness among scholars that binary oppositions that separate religion from politics or the sacred from the profane are generally not universally applicable categories, but a product of European thought transmitted to other parts of the world through colonialism (Goody 1961; Stanner 1967; Granet 1975; Coleman and White 2006; Turner 2006; Ashiwa and Wank 2009). Scholars have shown that these concepts are virtually irrelevant in practice in Asia, but they often nevertheless inform and transform the relations between state, religion, and society by creating a more universal category of 'religion' – one that is either relegated to the private realm or institutionalized and exploited in order to create and uphold a 'national culture' (DuBois 2009; Turner and Salemink 2015). As a result, the reductionist binaries of religion and secularism or religion and individual belief in Asia are constantly constructed and reconstructed across all levels of society and state. But to debunk or simply dismiss these binaries as irrelevant would mean to turn a blind eye to people who themselves are making and unmaking these categories on a day-to-day basis in their tactical engagement with authoritative state and religious discourses.

Right after the end of the Second Indochina War (1975) and Vietnam's formal reunification (1976), the Party-state sought to control all facets of life and relegated everything religious to the suspect category of 'superstition'. With the Đổi Mới reforms, which began in 1986, Vietnam's Party-state ceased to play the strong ideological role in people's lives, as it adopted neoliberal reforms in partnership with the World Bank, the International Monetary Fund, the United Nations Development Programme, and foreign donors that affected the state and the market more than Marxist–Leninist ideology did (Salemink 2008b: 282; see also Taylor 2001). This led to a situation in which the state to some extent retreated from various domains such as health care, education, and welfare, and people themselves had to pay for the services they needed – a process known as *xã hội hóa* (socialization) that mostly affected the poorest sector of Vietnamese society (Salemink 2008b: 282). However, the Party-state did not refrain from regulating the place of religion in society; rather, it standardized and instrumentalized religious practices so as to provide moral and cultural reinforcement for the state's various policies and projects. As sociologist Bryan Turner (2006: 210) argues, 'national, secular politics is typically parasitic upon deeper, more embedded, religious traditions' because political power lacks the persuasive authority of religious rituals. Meanwhile, religion itself is considered a competing source of power and morality that needs to be controlled, purified, and hybridized in order to exercise legitimate power over the population (Turner 2006: 211).

The relationship between state, religion, and society is not a new topic of debate in anthropology, especially in the context of an authoritarian country like Vietnam. Two distinct anthropological approaches can be identified when we talk about religion in Asia, which is home to all 'world religions' (Judaism, Christianity, Islam, Buddhism, and Confucianism) and a breeding ground for less institutionalized religious practices such as ancestor and spirit worship, Mother Goddess worship, and whale worship, to mention just a few among many (Turner and Salemink 2015). Religion in Asia is either approached through a dichotomous and often antagonistic framework of state–religion interactions (Anagnost 1994; Duara 1995; Van der Veer and Lehmann 1999; DuBois 2009; Salemink 2015) or through the framework of embodied and experienced religious practices that leaves the state out (Tsing 1999; Morris 2000; Keane 2003, 2007, 2008; Pedersen 2011). One of the aims of this book is to refocus those debates by asking how people engage, selectively accept, and eventually subvert state discourses when it comes to religious practices. Whereas Yoshiko Ashiwa and David Wank (2009: 7) define the confrontation between state and religion as 'the process of institutionalizing the modern concept of religion in the state and in religion', this book tackles the ways in which state and non-state actors seek to navigate the ideology of the state by continuously rupturing and rearranging secular and religious binaries. While the state cannot be ignored in Asia, state–religion binaries that reduce the state to a Foucauldian disciplinary apparatus and people's actions to resistance or co-optation obscure the full spectrum of interactions between the two realms.

Navigating a triad of contested categories: state–religion–village

Deriving from the Latin words *navis* ('ship') and *agere* ('to drive'), navigation describes the process of 'accurately determining and controlling the movement of a [water]craft ... along the desired course. This can only be accomplished by finding the navigator's position compared to known locations' or landmarks.[6] To ensure the vessel's safe movements on the sea, successful navigation relies on accurate mapping not only of natural and man-made features, but also those more elusive features that at certain times rise above the water's surface and on other occasions remain submerged.

In a more symbolic sense, navigating could be interpreted as the way in which we 'act and react in relation to our current position within social terrain, in response to current constraints, possibilities and configurations of power, as well as in relation to our perception of the future terrain and its unfolding' (Vigh 2010: 159). Henrik Vigh (2010: 159) wrote that 'in order to move towards where we wish to go, we sometimes take detours, sometimes refrain from acting and sometimes engage in apparently illogical acts, shaped in anticipation of what is to come'. Vigh's anthropological account of 'social navigation' (2008, 2010) indicates that it is directed towards the condition of constrictions and confinements, changes and possibilities, that arise in situations of chronic crisis created by a war, protracted violence, or persistent poverty. Within such a framework, crisis and chronicity form a 'condition' in which instability

---

6. See 'Navigation', https://www.marinelink.com/articles/maritime/navigation-100154, accessed 30 April 2020.

and 'disorder [become] the expected order of things' (Vigh 2008: 15). Yet the normalization of crisis is not tantamount to indifference or apathy; rather, it is a kind of agentive experience that forces people to attune their 'movement and action to an opaque and fluctuating social environment' (Vigh 2008: 18). When crisis is endemic rather than episodic, it becomes the 'context' for provisional action, navigation, and meaning in everyday life (Vigh 2008). While I fully agree that 'navigation' is a sort of 'motion within motion' that can only be anchored in praxis (Vigh 2010: 140), I wish to show in this book how navigation can also be enacted in situations of relative stability and order. Here, navigation is directed towards the unpredictability and constriction created not by chronic crises, but by authoritative visions of state and religion. Such social navigation takes place when social actors find themselves caught between competing sources of authority – powerful state and religious figures – and between seemingly impossible alternatives and desires that confront them with perils no matter what direction they face.

Here the binary oppositions arise: the mythical monsters Scylla and Charybdis who, on opposite sides of a narrow sea strait, work in tandem to block passage. To steer away from Charybdis means veering too close to Scylla and being dashed to pieces against the rocky outcrop of the six-headed giant. To avoid Scylla means steering the vessel too close to Charybdis and being sucked into the vortex of the sea monster's whirlpool. The art of navigation thus demands from social actors a vision that not only takes these binary oppositions into account but that also – when choosing to deal with one pole – allows them to keep one eye on the other pole in order to safely traverse the gap between the two. Analogically speaking, navigating the binaries of everyday life and everyday politics requires that Sa Huỳnh and Lý Sơn fishers establish their position by braving one or the other monster – that is, either powerful state figures or religious authorities. The other option is to adjust their course and pass through the violent currents of new geopolitical challenges and national preoccupations, avoiding direct encounters with the monsters while passing within sight of them, much as Jason and his Argonauts did when they took a detour through the Wandering Rocks on their way to retrieve the Golden Fleece, thereby avoiding Scylla and Charybdis. This analogy quite neatly encapsulates the triadic relationship of state-religion-village that I develop throughout this book. It represents a model of social relations that is never fixed, that is always changing and changeable.

The state–religion–village relationship is understood here as a triad of contested categories which do not necessarily 'collapse into dichotomies of domination versus resistance' (Harms 2012: 737), but emerge in a proliferation of shifting binaries, such as one type of discipline versus another; discipline versus indiscipline; secular versus religious; island versus mainland; fishers versus farmers; local ritual versus Buddhist doctrine; and female versus male religious practices. While confrontations do occur between different sides, they do not involve monolithic entities with a singular agency, like state and society, but occur between heterogeneous actors representing different and often conflicting ideas and disciplines (Salemink 2013:173; see also Malarney 2001, 2002, 2003; Day 2002; Luong 2003; Taylor 2007; Ashiwa and Wank 2009; Harms 2011a, 2012; Herzfeld 2016; Subramanian 2009). In this book I argue that binary oppositions do exist in Vietnam between the state, villagers' vernacular expressions of religion, and the more institutionalized versions of religion such as Buddhism, but they often shift and realign in unexpected and pragmatic ways. They are flexible, temporary, and spatially limited, as different social actors might subtly deny or selectively use, accommodate, and modify authoritative religious and cultural languages to legitimize their various, often contradictory, interests and goals.

Three analytical concepts – *semiotic ideology, purification,* and *indiscipline* – help me explain the kind of shifts in binaries required by state officials, different categories of villagers, and doctrinally minded religious authorities to navigate secular and religious rationalities as well as diverging practical interests. I draw on the concept of *semiotic ideology* to analyse the words, signs, and meanings that various social actors use to achieve their goals. Webb Keane (2003, 2007, 2008) employs semiotic ideology to denote the dynamic interconnections across authoritative religious languages in the context of the cultural encounter between Protestantism and local ancestor worship practices in Indonesia. However, my use of semiotic ideology captures the words, signs, and meanings that build on both religious and state ideologies. In Vietnam, the appropriation of religion as a representation of culture and nation transcends political, linguistic, and religious boundaries and has generated a vast repertoire of religious traditions and practices that compete with the state's semiotic ideology (Salemink 2015; see Chapter 2 for a detailed discussion). As Michael Herzfeld shows, such binarism itself is not static, but 'creates a kaleidoscopic range of possibilities', some of which may be institutionalized by one group of people and completely rejected by another (Herzfeld 2016: 24). The vignette at the beginning of this introduction gives a snapshot of how different actors move between the opposing poles of shifting secular–religious binaries. Aware of the state policy of protection and promotion of cultural heritage, fishers used the secular argument to get permission to build a shrine for the statue they recovered from the sea. This was, however, not enough to convince the local state representatives, who considered such a project 'superstitious' and potential grounds for opportunism and selfish motives in the name of 'religious beliefs'. On the other hand, as this book shows, there are occasions when villagers successfully negotiate their religious practices, proving themselves to be remarkably skilled at re-adapting the national discourse on heritagization for their own purposes (see Herzfeld 2016). Institutionalized religions, vernacular expressions of religion, and the ideologies of the post-socialist state are mediated, interpreted, and rationalized across different social fields by political and religious semiotic ideologies. The ability of state and non-state actors to navigate these semiotic ideologies and to 'recognize [their] forms as "the same" depends on certain ways of framing them, since their very materiality means they are always open to other unrealized possibilities' (Keane 2007: 21). This book tackles the multiplicity of ways in which semiotic ideologies are mobilized in response to the materiality of religious practices and objects, thereby allowing the reader to see how the binaries across and within the triad of contested domains of state–religion–village are continuously drawn, interrupted, and rearranged in everyday life experience (see Harms 2012).

One of the ways in which state and religious semiotic ideologies respond to the materiality of religion is through *purification*. According to Mary Douglas's analysis of purity and pollution situated within a Durkheimian dichotomy of sacred and profane, purification means 'separating, purifying, demarcating and punishing transgressions ... to impose system on an inherently untidy experience' (2001: 4). In Chapter 4 I will show that if, in the late 1970s, a religious object such as the statue of the Buddhist bodhisattva Quan Âm in Sa Huỳnh appeared as 'polluting' to the policemen who carried out the task of vacating a local pagoda, this was because their state semiotic ideology rejected the Buddhist statue as 'matter out of place', to use Douglas's (2001: 41) words. Almost thirty years later the new head monk of the local Buddhist pagoda saw the villagers' placement of the same Buddhist statue in a non-Buddhist space as matter out of place because, in his religious semiotic ideology, 'Buddhist' was to be kept strictly separate from 'non-Buddhist', just as religious practices and spaces had to remain separate from secular and superstitious ones. Thus, purification works through demarcation and the sharpening of distinctions among different categories and domains of social life, as Keane argues (2007: 83).[7] Building further on Keane's notion of purification, in this book I understand purification as cleansing religious discourses and practices by rejecting those elements that do not conform to orthodoxy and orthopraxy in modernist political or religious semiotic ideologies. Such purification includes the institutionalization and heritagization of religion – an exclusionary process in which religion assumes a highly organized form – as exemplified by UNESCO's recent recognition of the Mother Goddess worship as an Intangible Cultural Heritage of Humanity (Salemink 2015, 2016a, 2016b). Working through separation, demarcation, and cleansing of various categories, purification therefore sharpens binary oppositions within the triadic relationship of state–religion–village.

While state and religious semiotic ideologies draw boundaries between binary categories, they are undermined by an *indiscipline* that blurs such binaries (Mbembe 1992). Rather than centre my analysis on Foucault's (1975, 1991) approach, which privileges the apparatus of state power and the strategies through which state discipline is produced and internalized by the population, I track the exact procedures and means

---

7. In his critique of modernity, Bruno Latour (1993) uses the term *purification* to describe the process of ontologically separating the categories of human (culture) and non-human (nature), as is done in 'modern' science, in contradistinction to religion. In contrast, Keane argues that purification does not necessarily exclude the category of religion from the 'modern' (2007: 23–25), which is congruent with my own ethnographic material, as shown in my discussion of religious purification. Moreover, whereas Keane draws on Latour's concept of purification as sharpening the boundaries between things and persons, he criticizes Latour for not explaining how purification really works.

used to obscure those binaries by focusing on the ways in which various actors in the triad of contested categories – state, religion, and village – rework semiotic ideologies. Assuming that agency is located within rather than outside structures of power (Giddens 1979; Keane 2003, 2007; Ortner 2006), I show how state and non-state actors in Vietnam use indiscipline as a common tactic in response to forms of religious and state discipline (Certeau 1984; Mbembe 1992; Mahmood 2005; Harms 2012). By 'indiscipline' I mean the use of strategic, improvised tactics by different actors, not necessarily to resist or reject selected political and religious repertoires, but to draw on them in order to pursue their own agendas. This has the effect, however, of subverting the dominant semiotic ideologies and rupturing, rearranging, and blurring binary oppositions. Denoting *in*subordination through continuous bargaining and re-invention, indiscipline stands in contrast to Foucault's (1975) concept of discipline, and thus better captures the temporality and unpredictability of everyday interactions and practices through which subjectivities are formed and enacted (Mbembe 1992). However, the idea of indiscipline cannot be considered without the idea of discipline, as both are part of the same dialectical relationship.

By bringing together these three analytical concepts – semiotic ideology, purification, and indiscipline – in my ethnographic material, I examine how different actors locate and redefine their positions in binaries that change and shift across and within the triadic relationship between state officials, villagers, and religious modernizers. Focusing on how state agents, fishers, and religious figures impose and subvert rules not by rejecting them but by invoking the dominant semiotic ideologies, I argue that binaries between state and villagers, between state and religious authorities, and between religious authorities and villagers are realigning all three categories. Yet, diverse religious practices, including their material articulations, exist simultaneously in the local community and indicate shifting allegiances in which state and non-state actors in central Vietnam sometimes align with the selected categories of the state or religious semiotic ideologies, and sometimes do not.

Multi-sited research and methodology

The material for this book was collected during a year-long period of documentary and field research from September 2006 to September

2007 in Quảng Ngãi Province, central Vietnam, and complemented with follow-up visits totalling four months in 2011 and 2014. In Vietnam, access to the field requires not only approval both of national research institutions and government officials, but also cooperation with local authorities. My Polish background and the lingering effects in the present of the sense of fraternity among former Communist bloc countries, together with my ability to speak and understand Vietnamese, were crucial to my gaining permission to conduct extended fieldwork in Sa Huỳnh and particularly on Lý Sơn Island, which, due to its border status, was a politically sensitive zone closed to most foreigners at that time. The Quảng Ngãi authorities had their own understanding of my role in the province and also of the research I was carrying out. In my PhD project the Provincial Office of Culture, Sport, and Tourism saw a chance to raise the profile and visibility of the province not only within the country, but also outside its borders. Promoting Sa Huỳnh, which was associated with the colonial period's discoveries of a Bronze Age civilization of the same name (part of the so-called Đông Sơn culture), and Lý Sơn Island as a not yet 'discovered' place was part of that agenda.[8]

My focus on religion determined the character of the ethnographic research that I carried out. People and their religious practices and worldviews turned out to be much more dynamic, mobile, and unpredictable than I had assumed when I carefully designed my plan to stay in a small community. The idea of a 'small fishing community' itself turned out to be a fiction, as mobility and commercial networks across the South China Sea have been the hallmarks of this coastal society for centuries (Li Tana 1998). The invitation of provincial authorities to include Lý Sơn Island encouraged me to change my initial plan and design a new project after I had already arrived in the field, one which took into account the fact that the two sites might provide me with the exciting possibility of exploring the relationship between the state and religion, and how religion might play out in a 'peripheral' border security zone. I did not conceive of it as a comparative research project, as fieldwork

---

8. Đông Sơn culture is the name given to societies that lived in northern Vietnam from c. 600 BC to c. 200 AD. It is usually associated with bronze and early iron age civilizations and the discoveries of Đông Sơn bronze drums across the Southeast Asia, with the greatest concentration in northern Vietnam (Solheim 1988-1989).

in different geographical places is often envisioned. To the contrary, following the paths and movements of people, objects, and narratives, I collected data that gave me a more complex and complete picture of the state, religion, and society in central Vietnam and forced me to rethink differences and connections found in the two settings (Malinowski 1961[1922]; Gupta and Ferguson 1992; Marcus 1995, 1998).

Because 'religion' in Vietnam plays out quite differently from the institutional monotheistic religions in the Western context, I had to figure out how to collect data regarding less formalized and institutionalized Vietnamese religious traditions. Villagers in Sa Huỳnh and Lý Sơn do not form religious organizations in which members meet and pray regularly to a particular spirit. Village temples were only open during communal ceremonies. Although people felt obliged to contribute money, they were free to decide whether they wanted to attend these events or not. Their presence was not obligatory since there were elders in charge of the rituals. Often, villagers' religiosity was transactional and ritualistic rather than exclusively devotional. During my ethnographic immersion, I gradually began to comprehend the 'native' point of view about what 'religion' is and what it means 'to be religious' in Vietnam. I realized that although I was able to classify a particular spirit and determine general patterns, in everyday practice all gods and places merged with one another in a very flexible way that depended on the historical and political circumstances or individual preferences. This book sheds light on how such flexibility leads to a never-completed project and creates endless 'hybrids' across different social fields, geographical locations, and temporalities, mixing objects and categories (Latour 1993; Douglas 2001; Keane 2008).

An ethnographic approach that traces the recent past through the accounts of people and records the present – shared between the ethnographer and the subject in real-time interaction in the field (Kumar 2016: 54) – proves useful for conceptualizing the way in which binary forms of contestations emerge, dissolve, and re-emerge at different points in time among various groups of actors. Connecting the dots between temporally disparate events, practices, and people allows me to reveal a triad of confrontation that is unstable over time. The value of this ethnographic method lies in the possibility of analysing and theorizing these connections at different temporal and spatial scales, thereby developing an analytical model that goes beyond a simplistic demonstration of the top-down exercise of naked state power on villagers or a study of straightforward bottom-up resistance of individuals and groups in the village seeking to challenge the hegemony of the state. By ethnographically mapping different structural positions and goals in the triad of confrontation at various moments and locations in time, the structure of this book demonstrates the complexity and temporality of these interactions in which the lines of dispute, of cross-cutting allegiances, and of tactical positions are constantly shifting.

Structure of the book

The structure of the book traces the multifarious and boundary-crossing religious and ritual practices from the perspective of fishers and farmers, men and women, and religious leaders and state officials. The ethnographic insights in the chapters highlight the role of the sea in people's lives – not just in their livelihoods but in their cosmology as well. A view that takes the sea into account as part of the ecology and cosmology of coastal people is more common in the ethnography of Oceania and the island nations of Southeast Asia, but is still rather new for continental Asia and especially for Vietnam, which until recently was defined, and defined itself, primarily as a land-based, rice-growing, agricultural civilization. Thus, the distinctive focus on the sea as part of ritual practices highlights the fact that navigating state and religious authorities in Vietnam's maritime periphery is a dynamic, flexible, changeable, and interconnected process. Making and doing religion is affected not only by larger socio-cultural forces, but also by the embodied actions of the relevant actors. The ethnographic examples in the chapters show that there are real confrontations between these groups, but also temporary and pragmatic coalitions and manipulations of state and religious discourses allowing various categories of actors to achieve often contradictory goals within the same semiotic ideology. By describing how these confrontations and contestations become visible in Vietnam's maritime periphery, both in terms of *discipline* – as a state project – and of *indiscipline* – as a common tactic people use to navigate state and religious ideologies – I offer an in-depth analysis of the triadic relationship of state–religion–village in a relatively little-known part of Vietnam.

Chapter 1 starts by addressing the spatial dimensions of the sea with reference to religious practices. I briefly discuss the historical and vernacular geographies of the field settings and religious sites. I emphasize the overlapping histories of the Kinh (*Việt*) and the Cham and the gradual absorption of the Cham seafaring legacy by the Kinh. Moving away from the tendency to segregate Cham and Vietnamese histories (Wheeler 2006), I also question the idea of 'Vietnameseness', which glosses over regional, historical, and cultural differences. Chapter 2 opens with a discussion of the category of religion in the context of Vietnam against the broader backdrop of Asia. Like other parts of Southeast Asia, in Vietnam a separate term that could refer to 'religion' only emerged in the context of European colonialism and in connection with Western narratives of modernity. During the period of High Socialism in Vietnam, 'religion' was often conflated with the Sino-Vietnamese term *mê tín dị đoan* ('superstition'), according to which religion appeared as archaic, unscientific, and politically heterodox. In the early years of the Đổi Mới era (1986–1990s), the Vietnamese state gradually abandoned the interpretation of religion as 'unscientific' and 'irrational', but continued trying to draw a line between those informal, vernacular religious practices that were designated as having a 'national character' (known as *tín ngưỡng*) and therefore were worthy of recognition, and those considered 'superstition', which were to be suppressed and eradicated.[9] This led the state to reformulate meanings connected with diverse religious traditions in line with the new, 'purified' category of religion as 'cultural heritage' and to design new measures for controlling such practices. By zooming in on binary opposites such as *institutionalized religion* versus *beliefs*, *religion* versus *politics*, and *science* versus *religious superstition*, I prepare the ground for the discussion not only of how these binaries inform people's action, but also how they are subverted in everyday practice by people acting to promote their own personal or collective interests.

Chapter 3 moves into the main empirical arguments of the book, providing an outline of the history of the two main forms of socio-economic organization in the coastal society over the centuries, those of rice cultiva-

---

9. While the Đổi Mới reforms have never 'ended' and so are, theoretically, still in place, I refer to the Đổi Mới era as the initial period of active reforms, starting in 1986 and going through the 1990s.

tion and fishing. In pre-colonial and colonial times, the latter was always the more marginal; the activities of fishers were seen as less valuable and prestigious and they were physically excluded from the village settlements and ritual practices of the former and from the hierarchical apparatus of the state. They formed instead their own, more egalitarian forms of social organization. Nevertheless, the two organizational structures most representative of this binary opposition – the agriculture-based village (làng) and the guild-oriented fishing organization (vạn) – were always interdependent and symbiotic, and their linkages are especially evident in their shared cosmology. In postcolonial times, the historically subordinate fishers availed themselves of the Party-state's efforts to break down the hierarchical structure of the old society. In post-Đổi Mới times, the fishers became richer and enhanced their social position vis-à-vis the farmers through ritual investment in agriculture-based temples. Throughout the chapter, I argue that by resisting exclusive ritual control of the village temples by farmers, fishers have managed, in part, to turn the tables and subvert the old hierarchy that had excluded them from the ritual and political domain of the village.

Chapter 4 describes the confrontation between a Buddhist monk, fishers, and state agents for control over sacred places. I start by sketching the antireligious measures taken by the state shortly after Vietnam's reunification in 1975. In Sa Huỳnh, the policemen who carried out the task of vacating the village pagoda had to quickly decide what to do with a two-metre-tall image of the Buddhist bodhisattva Quan Âm that was too heavy and unwieldy to take to the district office. Reluctant to destroy the Buddhist statue themselves, the policemen latched onto the fishers' offer to take the statue away, which allowed the policemen to report that they had fulfilled their task. Both sides saw Quan Âm's translocation to a nearby hill as an opportunity to act in accordance with state policies and their own personal preferences. However, twenty-eight years later, the presence of Quan Âm on the hill created a problem for the new head monk of the village pagoda, who found it inappropriate that a sacred image of the Buddha was placed in a non-Buddhist space and demanded that fishers return the statue to its original location. The chapter illustrates that this encounter was an ideological struggle between competing purifying disciplines of, on the one hand, state agents who transformed local religious practices to align with present-day realities of postsocialist

Vietnam, and, on the other hand, monks who held that neither cultural interests nor local customs had a place in 'pure' Buddhism.

Chapter 5 analyses one of the state's commemorative projects devoted to glorifying the Paracel and Spratly seafarers on Lý Sơn Island and preserving all temples and relicts related to their activities. The state project can be seen as part of a strategy to claim sovereignty over the Paracel and Spratly archipelagos in the face of competition among several states, including China. However, the Vietnamese state is also challenged by alternative accounts from Lý Sơn islanders, particularly the efforts of one of the families to have their female ancestor officially inducted into the pantheon of Paracel heroes. Focusing on the dual process of appropriation and reworking of national narratives by the island community, I show that provincial authorities were more willing to accept male ancestors of Lý Sơn as potential heroes of the eighteenth-century Paracel and Spratly flotilla than their female kin because they aligned not only with the interests of village lineages, but also with the broader interests of the nation-state. On the more theoretical level, the intersection of commemorative process with lineage competition and with the state authorities' interests and preferences illuminates how the binary of state and society collapses in upon itself and how the maritime periphery becomes the centre in the performance of sovereignty played out along the lines of the state-religion-village triadic relationship.

Chapter 6 provides an analysis of how women deal with men's exclusionary claims to religious authority and ritual practice. Women, like fishers, constitute a subaltern group that suffered from discrimination in the village religious space, but also found a way to take advantage of the state's cultural policy. In one case a woman in Sa Huỳnh enhanced her status as a religious specialist by cultivating her reputation as a spirit medium, which had the unintended but welcome consequence of helping her cope with financial insecurities brought about by the volatile market. This woman's ultimate success in her quest for religious authority, which had previously been the exclusive preserve of men in that part of Vietnam, was made possible through transgression of symbolic gender boundaries in ritual practices. Thus, by focusing on women and their religious activities I provide an account of the ongoing process of redefining gender roles in ritual contexts in coastal communities and of various regional dynamics of ritual life in postsocialist Vietnam

In the concluding chapter, I address the implications of fishers' imbuing their religious practices with a political dimension as they navigate their way through multiple-level contestations and confrontations. I propose that Michel de Certeau's (1988) understanding of dialectical relations beyond servility or resistance is crucial for scholarly work on state, religion, and society. It provides important insights into the dynamic creativity of everyday interactions and the dominant semiotic ideologies that are always related to and function in particular social situations and power relationships. Within a framework that foregrounds the centrality of the maritime periphery, state, community, and religious authorities are mutually drawn into doing and making religion through their improvised tactics – not simply to resist, reject, or acquiesce, but to pursue their own agendas by drawing on selected political and religious repertoires. While state and religious ideologies insist on drawing sharp boundaries between binary categories such as *religion* and *politics* or institutionalized *religion* and popular *beliefs*, the categories are undermined in everyday practice by an *indiscipline* that blurs and shifts the boundaries of such binaries. This approach allows me to show that doing and making religion is neither exclusively a state nor a community practice, but rather the always temporary and incomplete product of tactical manoeuvres and interactions of various actors who invoke, enact, and embody binary positions, often appropriating the same or similar semiotic ideologies in order to subvert them.

Figure 2: Sa Huỳnh, Central Vietnam.

CHAPTER 1

The Coastal Society: Historical and Vernacular Geographies

Sa Huỳnh, a coastal region of central Vietnam, and the island of Lý Sơn have long been socially and economically oriented around the South China Sea. Both places are associated with a distinct Bronze Age culture of Austronesian seafarers referred to as the Sa Huỳnh culture, which flourished in central and southern Vietnam between 1000 BC and 200 AD.[1] The Sa Huỳnh archaeological sites, named after the village where the discovery took place and where I conducted my fieldwork, provided evidence of intercultural links to maritime Malay cultures and extensive trade networks across the South China Sea as early as 600 BC (Wheeler 2006; Vickery 2009), predating the Cham period by a millennium or more. For centuries, then, the sea was a space that integrated and facilitated the circulation of wealth, power, and knowledge, while the seacoast was a point of cross-cultural contact rather than a borderline (Wheeler 2006).

Charles Wheeler (2001: 6) notes that most of the seaports in the central and southern parts of Vietnam were established during the Nguyễn period (1802–1945) on the foundations of former Cham seaports that had had extensive trade relations with seafaring merchants of predominantly Chinese origin (see also Đồng Khánh Địa Dư Chí 2003 [1885]; Ngô Đức Thọ and Nguyễn Văn Nguyên 2006).[2] Historically,

---

1. In 1909, the French scholar M. Vinet identified jar burials, pottery, and other objects with characteristic ornaments in the coastal village of Sa Huỳnh. The first discovery of artefacts in Sa Huỳnh was followed by excavations by Vietnamese archaeologists in other settings, including the most recent one on Lý Sơn Island.

2. In Quảng Ngãi Province alone there were six ports – Sa Huỳnh, Thới Cân, Sa Kỳ, Lý Sơn, Đại Cổ Lũy, and Mỹ Ý – that are of Cham origin.

the Cham port network included Sa Huỳnh and Lý Sơn and stretched as far as Hainan Island and Guangzhou, where Cham merchant communities existed for over a thousand years, interacting, and engaging in commerce with Chinese as well as Arab, Persian, Jewish, and Indian merchants. The coast served as a 'nexus for sea, coastal, riverine, and land traffic that integrated Vietnamese regions and linked Vietnam with maritime Asia' (Wheeler 2001: 6).

The Cham were known throughout Southeast Asia not only as skilful seafarers and successful merchants, but also as 'pirates', due to their naval raids on coastal areas that employed ethnically diverse maritime peoples (Hall 2011: 80). Between the seventh and fifteenth centuries, the Cham established their rule over coastal plains and mountainous zones in what is now south-central Vietnam (*Nam Trung Bộ*), a region that stretches from Quảng Nam to Bình Thuận provinces. Although the Cham sovereign polities never formed a unified kingdom (Vickery 2009: 45), the Cham and Cambodian inscriptions as well as Chinese sources from the seventh century refer to them as 'Champa'. In the fifteenth century, Champa was invaded by Đại Việt – the name of the Việt polity at the time – which gradually took control of the entire Cham territory. It was not until the sixteenth and seventeenth centuries, however, that Nguyễn lords were able to establish their power in the south. The civil wars between the Nguyễn and the Trịnh lords (1627–1672 and 1774–1775), which divided Vietnam into northern and southern realms, created conditions that allowed Việt migrants living in the south to form their own distinct way of life. Central Vietnam was part of the southern realm and provided an option for northern Vietnamese migrants who, driven by a shortage of land, famine, internal conflict, and struggles for power, were seeking a better life elsewhere.

Historian of Southeast Asia Li Tana (1998) points out that the Việt, who arrived in the seventeenth century, had to settle into a new and different environment and engage with Cham communities. Their gradual extension into new areas in the south allowed migrants to escape domination by the northern court of Trịnh in the Red River Delta, and to adopt such local elements as Cham deities and spirit cults, which were free of Confucian restrictions (Li 1998: 101–116). Vietnamese migrants colonizing the old Cham territory worshipped tutelary spirits that they had never worshipped in their places of origin. The new experience of the sea, the encounter with the unfamiliar Cham civilization, and interethnic marriages produced patterns that were quite different from those that existed in northern Vietnam (Li 1998). Therefore, to gain an adequate appreciation of contemporary religious practices and the sites of spirit worship in Sa Huỳnh and Lý Sơn, one must take a closer look at the historical legacy of the Cham, at different ways of being Vietnamese, and at the complex history of this coastal society.

Cham and Việt legacies

In Sa Huỳnh and Lý Sơn there are numerous temples and shrines located where anthropomorphized deities and terrestrial and maritime spirits are venerated by the local community. Many of these temples bear traces of assimilation of Cham elements into Việt culture, while others show a strong Chinese influence. As we will see in Chapter 3, they cast an interesting light on the history of the two locations, but also reveal an interrelated series of binary oppositions involving mainland and island, inland and coast, and land and sea, and thus different relationships between people and space. While Sa Huỳnh villagers almost never expressed anxiety about the previous Cham inhabitants of the land, the Việt residents of Lý Sơn Island were acutely aware that they were only the latest residents in a long history of settlement. This was a source of anxiety, as was the fact that the archeological record indicates that the Cham civilization was present prior to the Việt arrival on Lý Sơn in the seventeenth century. Islanders assuaged such unsettled feelings by seeking to convey a sense of genealogical continuity with larger entities such as the mainland and the nation. During my conversations with islanders, many of them betrayed a sense of unease regarding the previous Cham presence. One of the Lý Sơn villagers told me:

> In the past Bình Thuận was the place of origin for the Cham people, but from there they spread to central parts, entering Đà Nẵng and Quảng Nam. In Lý Sơn there were not so many of them, so [the land] out here was intact. There was no one to have an exchange with at all. For that reason in the sixteenth and seventeenth centuries the Việt people occupied Champa and stayed there. Well, back then, people from all provinces were moving in and out ... to other provinces. There were also people here [on the island] and the Cham also came here, but then [Việt] occupied the islands. After that [Cham] did not come here

31

anymore, they were not able to (laughing). ... The Việt caught crabs, fish, and snails, which they ate through the day to survive. When more Việt occupied the island and stayed here, civil harmony with Champa people began.

When I asked the villager what he meant by 'civil harmony with Champa', he replied:

> There were still a few Cham people here – they lived on this land. After those regarded as Cham died, they did not enter the island anymore; they were gone so the Việt people flocked together here.

The passage quoted above is not an isolated example of the sense of discomfort associated with the prior Cham presence on the island. It reveals an immediate defensive reaction of the islanders, who felt the need to convince me of the absence of Cham people at the time when their ancestors arrived on the island. Despite the historical evidence that Champa consisted of several states that occupied the south-central coast of Vietnam from the end of the first millennium BC (Southworth 2004; Vickery 2009; Hardy 2009), many islanders maintained that the Cham were originally concentrated only in the southern part of Vietnam, in present-day Bình Thuận Province. Many villagers claimed that those Cham who stayed on the island gradually vanished and, generally, the Việt people outnumbered them. In this way Lý Sơn people wanted to clear up any doubts about their identity and their rights to the land, and to forestall any accusations of violence during the process of settling on the island. Nevertheless, surnames such as Mai, Đinh, Tiêu, and so forth suggest that the Vietnamese migrants on Lý Sơn Island intermixed with the Cham natives (very few of whom still lived in the area). In the process, the descendants of these interethnic marriages masked their Cham origins by absorbing and retaining most of the beliefs of the agrarian villages from which their Việt forefathers had come.

While Việt people took possession of various islands in the South China Sea as Việt territory by means of a Việt-centric settlement history, they did not establish themselves on empty soil. Lý Sơn villagers had to assimilate and interact with the Cham who were already there, even though they might claim that those Cham who stayed gradually vanished and that the Việt people simply came to outnumber them. However, control over territory is not only about the occupation and use of the land, but also about cultural attempts to produce *locality* and create the type of localized sociality that Appadurai calls 'neighbourhood' (Appadurai 1996). Such production of locality might require newcomers to perform ritual procedures that would pacify local spirits of the defeated and dispossessed indigenous inhabitants and incorporate them into the pantheon of the newly dominant community (Kammerer and Tannenbaum 2003). For example, Việt villagers ritually inscribed themselves in Lý Sơn and Sa Huỳnh history by cultivating relations with the Cham spirits that are to this day worshipped in many temples on the island and mainland. The ritual relationship with these spirits was predicated on the existence of a more powerful spiritual domain and was maintained through the ritual of 'buying or renting land' (*lễ tá thổ*) (Li 1998: 131; Tạ Chí Đài Trường 2005: 264). Right into the twentieth century the inhabitants of both Lý Sơn and Sa Huỳnh would engage a local 'sorcerer' to perform a 'ritualized bargain' with a Cham ancestral couple, Chúa Ngu Ma Nương, and make lavish sacrifices in order to keep the land fertile (see Li 1998: 131; Tạ Chí Đài Trường 2005). One of the oldest inhabitants of Lý Sơn Island described the ceremony concerning land ownership:

> In the past, the northern part of Lý Sơn belonged to the *Chiêm Thành* (Cham Kingdom). Our Kinh forefathers fought with the Chiêm Thành, who were defeated and had to leave their land. The land remained and it was sacred (*linh thiêng*); if our ancestors who wanted to inhabit it refused to worship them [the Cham deities], they would bring serious illnesses upon the village. That is why the forefathers installed an altar [on the old Cham territory] for a wife and a husband, Chúa Ngu Man Nương. The couple managed the land and every five years the village organized the 'request for land' ritual, during which many oxen and buffaloes had to be offered to keep peace. The ceremony was great and lasted several days and nights. The *phù thuỷ* (sorcerer) was invited too. He called the couple and asked them if they were satisfied with the offerings. If they said 'yes', the villagers could stop, but if the couple said 'no', they had to continue to make sacrifices of animals. The land belonged to the couple, and without the offerings the village would be punished. If the husband required five pigs, they would give him exactly five pigs. If asked, they complied; the husband was easygoing, but it was very difficult to satisfy his wife!

By performing the large ceremony for such Cham spirits as the goddess Uma and Chúa Ngu Ma Nương, the newcomers not only established themselves as the rightful patrons of the new land, but also tacitly apologized for taking the land away from the Cham natives.[3] As the new owners of the territory, they ritually paid tribute to the fact that other inhabitants once ruled over the land and its fertility. But this is just one dimension of the ritualized bargain and the newcomers' way of inscribing themselves into the new territory. Another symbolic dimension appears when we look at the ritual of 'buying or renting land' as a reconciliation of binary Cham and Việt ethnicities. By adopting cosmologies and spirits and engaging ritually with land and sea, the Việt newcomers downplayed and even masked their foreignness. In that sense, the ritualized propitiation by the Việt became the symbolic surrender by the previous owners of the land and thus provided the newcomers with protection against sanctions from the Cham spirits (see Arno 1976).

The close interaction with the sea and the encounter with Cham prompted the Việt in Sa Huỳnh and Lý Sơn Island not only to adopt foreign spirits and beliefs into their own religious practices, but also to willingly experiment with the material culture of their predecessors. Việt migrants learned seafaring techniques from the Cham, and even the construction of their ships followed Cham principles (Li 1998: 112; Pham, Blue, and Palmer 2010; Pham 2013). Lý Sơn's family annals (*gia phả*) indicate that from the seventeenth to the nineteenth centuries, many of the islanders, due to their excellent seafaring abilities, were recruited by the feudal state to collect precious sea products and goods from wrecked ships in the Paracel and Spratly archipelagos. The eighteenth-century Vietnamese historian Lê Quý Đôn (1972 [1776]: 210) reported on Vietnamese from mainland villages near Sa Kỳ who were allowed to move to Lý Sơn and were granted a royal concession to explore the sea. Such practices were not unique to Vietnam, but also took place in other regions of Southeast Asia. In his interesting account of the eighteenth- and the early nineteenth-century migration and trade practices of 'sea people' in south-west Kalimantan, Atsushi Ota (2010: 69) observes that during this period many migrants, referred to as 'pirates' by Europeans, set up their communities in the coastal areas and 'were engaged in

---

3. Uma is the name for the great Hindu goddess Paravati, usually associated with mountains. Chúa Ngu Ma Nương is the Cham spirit of the ancestral couple.

various profitable activities such as trade, fishing, and cultivation, supplemented by occasional raids on traders, fishermen, and the villagers'. By calling these maritime migrant communities 'sea people', Ota (2010: 69) makes the interesting point that those communities were 'within the political reach of states and settled under state rulers' approval, but they were not completely politically integrated, maintaining privileges in certain activities, such as settlement in certain places and plundering'. This is analogous to Lý Sơn's loose connection to the mainland's political apparatus, which came to be formalized as the Paracel and Spratly navy, consisting of villagers recruited from Lý Sơn who operated in the vicinity of the Paracels and Spratlys, which until recently constituted the fishing grounds of Lý Sơn fishers (Lê Quý Đôn 1972 [1776]: 203, 210).

Local mobilities vis-à-vis highlands–lowlands–islands

Sa Huỳnh and Lý Sơn villagers proudly talked about their ancestors' engagement with other societies and their extraordinary mobility over land and sea. Lý Sơn people in particular underlined their past explorations in an effort to contest and change their present status as a remote, 'sea-locked', and 'outlandish' fishing community. Indeed, mobility and commercial networks between Cham, Chinese and Việt across the Central Highlands and the South China Sea were of long standing.[4] Up until the nineteenth century, mountain and forest areas of Quảng Ngãi Province were famous for the production and trade of cassia and eaglewood (Hardy 2009). At that time, cinnamon trees were farmed by highlanders, and the bark was purchased by Vietnamese and Chinese traders for resale to merchants based in Hội An. The mountain areas were home to important markets for trade in highland products – especially cassia, buffaloes, and rice – that attracted people from lowland population centres such as Sa Huỳnh.

Out in the middle of the South China Sea, the Paracel and Spratly archipelagos sustained mobility and cultural and economic exchanges among small island communities around the South China Sea. Throughout the seventeenth, eighteenth and nineteenth centuries, Lý Sơn sailors capitalized on various cosmopolitan and commercial links in the South China Sea by gathering gold, silver, swords, ivory, porcelain, cloth, wax, and other goods from the wrecked ships in the Paracels and Spratlys

---

4. For the region of the Mekong Delta, see Taylor (2007).

and supplementing them with large quantities of mother of pearl, snails, tortoises, and sea cucumbers, all of which were handed over to the royal court in Huế. The sailors were allowed to keep a significant portion of the harvested marine produce for their own profit (Lê Quý Đôn 2006 [1776]: 155). The beautiful and well-preserved ancestor house built during the reign of Emperor Minh Mạng (1820–1841) by the family of Mr Tứ (born in 1930)[5] – the uncle of my host on Lý Sơn – bears testimony to the extraordinary profits coming from that trade and the extensive maritime networks that connected Lý Sơn villagers and Chinese merchants. During their voyages to the Paracels, the Paracel and Spratly sailors occasionally met Chinese fishermen on the high seas and exchanged information (see, for example, Lê Quý Đôn 1776: 82b-85a, in Nguyễn Q. Thắng 2008). In the nineteenth and twentieth centuries, some Fujianese and Hainanese who ventured into the Nanyang region (present-day Singapore, Malaysia, and Indonesia) to procure their catches of sea cucumber (*hải sâm, bêche-de-mer*) would stop off in Lý Sơn to get fresh water and peanut oil for cooking. Mr Tứ told me that the generations of his family built their wealth on the lucrative trade that involved the sea cucumber – a highly appreciated delicacy among Chinese. Unlike the Chinese, however, for a long time Lý Sơn villagers did not develop a taste for sea cucumbers, but they knew how to process the animal in order to sell the product in Hội An – a former Cham port that from the seventeenth century onwards attracted many Chinese as well as Japanese, Muslim, and European merchants.

Under French colonial rule, the Paracel and Spratly flotillas ceased to exist, but the seafaring and trading skills of the islanders enabled their voyages to the south, where they continued to explore new markets and expand their networks through translocal and transregional trade. Islanders traded with the mainland and sold whatever they caught and farmed, which included beans and peanuts, although they were most famous for their production of fish sauce, peanut oil, and fishing nets made of a special fibre from a tree (*cây gay*) that grows on Lý Sơn. At this time fish preservation in Sa Huỳnh was inextricably linked with the production of salt, which entailed directing sea water into the fields and allowing the sun to evaporate the water, leaving just the salt. The salt-making technique remains the same to this day in Sa Huỳnh. It was

---

5. All personal names are pseudonyms.

learned from Cham, who specialized in a mixed economy based on irrigated agriculture, salt production, and fishing. In the colonial period
the French controlled salt production, and the finished product from
Sa Huỳnh was sold to Tonkin in northern Vietnam and Cochinchina in
southern Vietnam. Although the French salt monopoly aimed to control
the highlands and ethnic groups for whom the salt was essential to their
livelihood, an illicit and clandestine trade in salt and fish sauce with Hrê
and Cơr ethnic groups living in the highlands flourished. Elderly fishers from Sa Huỳnh reported that in the past they used to travel into the
mountains to Ba Tơ, a trip that lasted about five days, to trade the salt,
usually for rice.

While Sa Huỳnh fishers exploited overland connections to the
mountain and forest regions, Lý Sơn people relied on their seafaring
skills and maritime trade connections. One of my Lý Sơn informants
said that in the 1930s his late father worked as a 'trader assistant' (*lái
phụ*) for one of the boat owners (*chủ tuyền*) on the island and used to
travel south on the winter monsoon and return north with the summer
monsoon. In November the northerly winds would begin blowing and
over the next few months, Lý Sơn people would sail in their vessels
(*ghe buồm*) down to Saigon, where they would spend the lunar new
year. Because rice could not be cultivated on the island due to the poor
soil and the shortage of water, the trip to the south was undertaken in
order to buy rice, which was an essential component of the diet of the
people of Lý Sơn. The father of my informant did not take these trips
alone; he would be accompanied by a group of other sailing boats. On
the way down to the south he would usually buy sugar (*đường phên*) in
Quảng Ngãi and salt in Sa Huỳnh but his trade networks also allowed
him to go to Quy Nhơn, Nha Trang, and Hà Tiên in search of bargains.
Disembarking in Saigon or Cà Mau, he and the rest of his crew would
hire themselves out as labour to the French or Chinese, which gave them
additional income for the purchase of rice. At some point in March the
wind would shift northwards, and the trip back could be commenced. In
early summer with a full load of rice, he would sail along the coast and up
to the north, passing different ports on the way. Sometimes he took on
board Cham traders of medicinal plants (*thuốc nam*), which were highly
sought after and needed by islanders. The Cham traders would board at
the port of Bình Thuận and sail with him all the way to the island. The

father of my informant would stop again in Sa Huỳnh to buy salt, which then would be sold back in Lý Sơn. However, reaching home did not mean that his voyage was completed. Taking advantage of the southerly wind he would resume his journey up north through the ports of Hội An and Huế, where he would typically buy blocks of ironwood (*gỗ lim*), used for building ancestral houses, as well as Chinese porcelain, which was in high demand on Lý Sơn Island.

While Sa Huỳnh and Lý Sơn villagers cognitively differentiated the *mainland* from the *island* and the *highlands* from the *lowlands*, their mobility stretched far beyond these binaries. These territorial categories were not self-contained; they were, rather, subverted by people's movements, continuously transgressed and interlinked (see Salemink 2018a). Brought into contact through trade and mobility, the qualitatively different worlds of highlands, lowlands, and islands became a translocal, even domestic, space that Sa Huỳnh and Lý Sơn villagers traversed as they temporarily settled in distant places. Their diasporic networks and engagements with distant markets and ports promised a good profit (see Ho 2006). Venturing out into the Central Highlands or navigating through the South China Sea was not just a matter of contacting new people but, as Eric Tagliacozzo (2009: 114) points out, more often a matter of renewing already existing ties and networks. These connections and relations were sufficiently intimate and prolonged to allow people to go back and forth between various modes of life as they navigated through different geographical spaces.

Post-revolutionary realities and economic liberalization

The outbreak of the First and the Second Indochina Wars brought new political and economic pressures to the people of Sa Huỳnh and Lý Sơn, who found themselves trapped between two forces – the National Liberation Front and the U.S. troops. In 1954, after the First Indochina War, the United States supported the establishment of an anti-communist government south of the demilitarized zone between Quảng Trị and Quảng Bình provinces. Consequently, Sa Huỳnh and Lý Sơn – like the whole Quảng Ngãi Province – were assigned to the Republic of Vietnam, commonly known as South Vietnam, and disconnected from the liberation movement that they strongly supported. Due to a solid communist tradition (Fall, 2005 [1961]), much of the population continued to support the Hồ Chí Minh regime even when the first regular American troops entered Quảng Ngãi. While Sa Huỳnh served as a base for the U.S. Army, the strategic location of Lý Sơn Island was used both by the Naval Forces of the Republic of Vietnam to control passing ships and trawlers in the South China Sea and by the communist guerrillas to, for example, hide stolen weapons. Lý Sơn fishermen were occasionally used by the Vietnam Naval Forces as guides in military missions to the Paracels.

However, in contrast to Sa Huỳnh, Lý Sơn's geographical position enabled it to some extent to avoid the turmoil of war. In 1975, after the Second Indochina War had ended and the country was unified again, the revolutionary state tried to impose a socialist vision of society on the South and unsuccessfully attempted to pursue a policy of collectivization (see Taylor 2001; Kerkvliet 2005). As a provincial official in Quảng Ngãi stated in an interview with me in 2007, relations between more and less prosperous peasants were never as harsh in the South as they were in northern villages. According to the official, many of the farmers in Central Vietnam were knowledgeable persons who treated their labourers well and provided help if necessary. While this commonly held view of the situation is most likely highly idealized, it nevertheless demonstrates my interlocutors' desire to point out that the state's policy ended in a complete fiasco. They claimed that when the poor farmers joined cooperatives, their situation often became worse than it had been when they worked for hire. In Sa Huỳnh and Lý Sơn, fishing cooperatives established in 1979 and 1980 only survived a few years, as they met with resentment from the people. In the 1980s the fishing cooperatives stopped operating, although they have never been officially dissolved.[6]

Calling this period the 'catastrophe' (*hầm họa*), Sa Huỳnh and Lý Sơn villagers reported that when cooperatives were introduced, the village temples were stripped of their property and, in some cases, were severely damaged. Sacred statues were removed from temples and placed in the local offices of the People's Committee, and the temples

---

6. There was also a fundamental disparity between fisheries in the northern and southern regions. By the 1980s, only 10–15 per cent of the boat owners in Central Vietnam had joined cooperatives, and most of them were in the provinces known today as Quảng Bình, Quảng Trị, Thừa Thiên, Ninh Thuận, and Bình Thuận (Nguyễn Duy Thiệu 2002).

were closed. In Lý Sơn, people who had ancestral wooden panels embellished with Chinese characters or lacquered boards at home were forced to bring them to the communal house, which had been turned into a warehouse. However, some of the local cadres were aware of the great religious value of these objects and allowed people to take them back home piece by piece.

Consequently, continuous bargaining, *bricolage* and navigation of state discipline were part of people's daily survival repertoire. In the period of the subsidized collectivist economy (1977–1986), the mobility and trading networks of Sa Huỳnh's and Lý Sơn's residents were also severely restricted. Lý Sơn villagers reported that there were shortages of the most basic products, such as rice, sugar, and salt, which had to be brought from the mainland. To sail to Quảng Ngãi they needed to obtain special permission from the local authorities. Such permission specified clearly how many days they were allowed to stay away. On the day of the trip their names would be shouted out by the authorities, and only after presenting a valid document would they be allowed to embark on a small motorboat. The islanders recall that the boats were filled with more people than they could actually accommodate, and many of them had to stand or squat in uncomfortable position for eight or more hours before they reached Sa Kỳ. Villagers would still manage to smuggle out some of their local products, such as garlic and onions, to sell in Saigon on the black market in order to be able to buy rice. Hidden in baskets full of vegetables, the rice was then illicitly transported on the boat back to the island. Villagers recalled that they had so little rice that they had to cook it with sweet potatoes in order to fill their stomachs. For the people of Lý Sơn, the time had come to capitalize on their seafaring skills.

In 1982 Mr Nha (born in 1948) was the first fisherman on the island who, using a simple administration map stolen from the local People's Committee Office, made the daring journey to the Paracels to fish there. Later that same year he guided another seven fishing boats. Navigation technologies or nautical charts were not available at that time because the local government feared that fishers might try to escape the country by sea. Initially, in the Paracels, the fishers caught mainly flying fish (*cá chuồn*), which were suitable for preservation in salt. A year later, when ice-making technology became more accessible, they expanded their fishing territories, catches, and methods. Fresh fish from the Paracels and Spratlys was transported to Đà Nẵng, from where they obtained the ice. Again, this changed along with the new market opportunities that appeared in the late 1980s. Most of the Lý Sơn fishers chose to sell their catches to local women traders in Đông Ba market in Huế and later in Sa Kỳ port – the closest mainland harbour to Lý Sơn. In 1989, Sa Kỳ port began to operate under the Border Guard Command (*Công an Biên phòng*), which provided the logistical facilities for the development of the local fish market.

In Sa Huỳnh, fishing has been an intensive activity in the coastal waters for a long time. Fishers employed mainly traditional fishing techniques such as trawling, hooks and lines (*lưới giả cào*), lift nets (*lưới rút vay*), and seine nets (*nghề câu*) to catch fish far off shore. All these methods required hard manual labour. Fishing close to the shore and in the lagoon demanded profound practical knowledge. The most popular methods of using nets were *lưới bén* and *chài lưới* for catching fish and shrimp. The fishers also relied on their ability to locate various species and to gather and drive them together into the net (*đuổi cá*).

After 1989, due to increasing demand for marine products in domestic and international markets, Sa Huỳnh, like Lý Sơn, was incorporated into a regional market economy. As a result, Sa Huỳnh entered into a modernization phase in which fishers increased their harvesting capacities. Larger boats enabled them to reach new fishing grounds, the expansion of the lagoon and intensification of shrimp cultivation increased harvests, the development of ice-making techniques enabled the preservation of fish from a few hours to a few days, and better transport and roads allowed the local fish trade to reach distant markets. Around this time, the Sa Huỳnh fishers got involved in intensive fishing in Bà Rịa, Vũng Tàu, Hải Phòng, Đà Nẵng, and Bình Ty, where they sold their catches. Women tried to do their best to take care of their families in their husbands' absence. At the beginning of the 2000s, women who did not have small children and could afford to do so would go once a month to mediate the transfer of money from Sa Huỳnh fishers working in distant ports to their wives staying at home. One of them, a 35-year-old woman named Phương, was appointed by the women as 'a note keeper' (*chủ ghi*). Three days a month the fishing fleet of Phương's husband went ashore in Vũng Tàu to repair nets and fishing gear and sell the catch. Thus, every month she undertook the trip by bus to Vũng Tàu Port, rented a small room in a cheap hotel, and spent a few days working in the fish trade alongside her husband. She collected her husband's earnings and those of the other men and took them back to Sa Huỳnh.

Around the same time, with regular fishing expeditions to the Paracels and Spratlys and using a hazardous diving technology that relies on compressed air, Lý Sơn fishers were able to collect sea cucumbers in deeper waters and thus revive the old trade in the Chinese delicacy.[7] With the booming fishing market, some of the Lý Sơn people who in the late 1960s and 1970s had emigrated to Quảng Ngãi, Nha Trang, or Saigon anticipated the upcoming opportunities for profitable business. They connected with exporters, often of Sino-Vietnamese origin, who provided them with credit to buy the marine products directly from Lý Sơn fishers. Initially, the cargo of sea cucumbers, shark fins and, occasionally, turtles and sea urchins was sent to urban markets in central and southern Vietnam for export to China and Cambodia, but more recent destinations also included ports in northern Vietnam. In the north, out of sight of customs patrols, fish and various marine products from Lý Sơn are traded across the border at fishing villages in Móng Cái and transferred to Chinese fishing vessels at sea or transported directly by Sino-Vietnamese traders to Guangxi, Guangdong Province, and Hainan Island.

However, this thriving trade in marine goods has been caught between two opposing forces – the liberalization of cross-border trade between China and Vietnam and the simultaneous enforcement of borders at sea. The Qing dynasty (1636-1912) of China first began to show interest in the uninhabited islands of the Paracels in 1909. The Republic of China and the French colonial authorities in Indochina made rival claims to them in the 1920s and 1930s. France made a separate claim to the Spratlys in 1933 and China followed suit in 1946 (Hayton 2019). But it was not until decades later that China denied Lý Sơn fishers rights to use fishing grounds that for generations they had considered their own. In 1982 – the year in which Lý Sơn people recommenced their trips to the Paracels and deep-sea fishing began – a new United Nations Convention on the Law of the Sea (UNCLOS) was formally adopted, which came into force in 1994 when Guyana became the sixtieth coun-

---

7. Fishermen usually dive down to 50 m or more and breathe through a thin plastic tube that is connected to an air compressor on the boat above them.

try to ratify the agreement. This created a new international legal regime governing maritime resources, in particular the idea of an 'exclusive economic zone' (EEZ). However, most of the boundaries of the rival EEZs in the South China Sea have never been agreed upon, leaving plenty of room for confrontation at sea. Fishers from Lý Sơn and Sa Huỳnh have found themselves accused by Chinese authorities of illegally entering restricted zones, while the new unilaterally enacted Chinese laws have turned them into 'poachers'. With its far greater economic, political, and military power, China has been able to enforce a seasonal fishing ban in parts of the South China Sea, seize and detain Vietnamese fishers, and even destroy their vessels (MacLean 2014). China's increasingly assertive actions in the South China Sea during the 2000s have further exacerbated tensions and incidents in the region. The region's common history of commerce, exchange, and interest in protecting marine life has been superseded by tensions over rival territorial and maritime claims. On occasion, anger has erupted into anti-Chinese protests across Vietnam (MacLean 2016). The crisis became a turning point for Lý Sơn, which found itself at the centre of attention because of the fishers' presence in the disputed waters, interpreted by many in the country as a brave defence of Vietnam's maritime borders and national sovereignty (see Chapter 5). As a result, Lý Sơn villagers have had to maintain a low profile regarding their trading activities with China.

Shifting administrative boundaries

Both borders and names of places have changed frequently in Vietnam throughout the course of history. Two identical temples located next to each other, known as *miếu Đôi* (the Twin Shrines), recall the story of the former border between the provinces of Quảng Ngãi and Bình Định, which in colonial times was located much further east than it is today. It also tells the story of the former border between the two villages of Đồng Vân and Tân An. According to legend, in this place local people found the head of a white horse that had belonged to a Chinese general. They decided to erect a temple in order to worship the spirit of the White Horse (*Bạch Mã*). However, the discussion about which side of the border would be the right place to worship turned into a heated argument between the two villages over who had the right to claim the spirit and to erect the temple. Consequently, the authorities of Phủ, a province in colonial times, gave both villages the right to build separate temples and worship the spirit, but on the condition that the temples be identical in all features, including height and external ornamentation. At the time of my fieldwork, the Đôi temples still stood on either side of the former border, serving as a reminder of the old argument between locals about who owned the right to worship the local spirit. The dynamic that emerged between the two communities also reminds us that any present-day 'village' unit is a product of historical contingency.

Sa Huỳnh – the coast

Initially, 'Sa Huỳnh' – both a historical and common name used by local people – did not refer to the cluster of villages but was in fact the name of one of the six seaports located in Quảng Ngãi Province.[8] Today, Sa Huỳnh is officially known as Phổ Thạnh Commune (*xã*), situated in the vicinity of the present-day border between Quảng Ngãi and Bình Định provinces. The term *xã*, often translated as 'commune', refers to an administrative unit denoting a municipality consisting of various *làng* – residential units or 'villages' or 'communities'. Depending on the region in Vietnam, sometimes the term *thôn* is used instead of *làng* to refer to 'community'; in other places the two terms are used interchangeably. In some cases, *làng* can refer to a unit of the *thôn*. The *làng* or *thôn* might be broken up into smaller units such as *xóm* or *ấp* ('hamlets') and *lân* ('sub-hamlets'). In Sa Huỳnh the term *thôn* is used by local authorities to denote the smallest type of settlement; however, people referring to their 'community' might also talk about *làng* or *vạn chày* ('fishing community'). Since the terms are used in a flexible way and the rules vary from region to region, it would be incorrect to consider the case of one particular setting as representative for all of Vietnam (Kleinen 1999a, 1999b).

8. The name 'Sa Huỳnh' dates back to the reign of the Nguyễn lords in the southern realm (Đàng Trong or 'Inner Region', 1558–1777). Lê Quý Đôn explains: 'This is the land of Hoàng Sa [Sa Huỳnh], a drainage basin that lies east of the Trường Sơn mountains with seawater continuously washing over the shore' (quoted also in Đảng Bộ Phổ Thạnh 1985: 3). The name 'Sa Huỳnh' is derived from the Sino-Vietnamese term *Sa Hoàng* (literally 'sand [and] golden') meaning 'golden sand' (*cát vàng* in modern Vietnamese). Interestingly, the term is also the name of the Paracel Islands (Hoàng Sa), but with the noun placed after the adjective and sometimes translated as 'Strip of Yellow Sand' (ĐNTN-LTNV 1973 [1882]).

Today, Phổ Thạnh Commune, with an area of more than 24 square kilometres and a population in excess of 20,000, comprises six *thôns*: Thạch By, Thạnh Đức, La Vân, Đồng Vân, Tân Diêm and Long Thạnh. Figures published in 2006 indicated that Thạch By comprised 1,852 households with a total population of 10,000 people. At the time of my fieldwork, more than half of them were still of working age, which in Vietnam is from 15 to 60 years of age for men and 15 to 55 for women. La Vân, relatively small in comparison to Thạch By, consisted of 466 households with a population of 2,307. Tân Diêm had 310 households and 1,514 inhabitants. The majority of the population in those villages made a living from fishing, fish breeding and selling, salt and fish sauce production, boat construction, animal husbandry, and small restaurants and shops.

According to data obtained from a local government office of the People's Committee, 80 per cent of Thạch By – the most densely populated community – lived off fishing. However, the official authorities emphasized the increase in unemployment among fishers in the last few years. The official statistics to which I was referred to presumably did not take the informal sector into account,[9] but instead concentrated on the fact that most of the fishers in Thạch By were landless and during the off-season could not switch to farming. Another possible explanation for the high unemployment statistic is that the fishermen's wives, who usually stayed at home and took full responsibility for the household during their husbands' absence, were most likely regarded as unemployed.

In recent times, Sa Huỳnh has also experienced fluctuations of incoming and outgoing migration. Many young people moved to Đà Nẵng, Quy Nhơn, and Ho Chi Minh City in search of better-paying jobs. The temporary stay of young persons in the city often became permanent when they found work and started a family. Hy Van Luong (2009: 92–93) reports that an overwhelming number of migrants from Quảng Ngãi were young people between the ages of 15 and 35. In Sa Huỳnh, those who could afford to do so would make their way to Ho Chi Minh or Quảng Ngãi City and pay for a basic Japanese or Korean language course that would allow them to apply for a work permit abroad. They

---

9. Most of the villagers were still involved in small-scale artisanal production, including activities such as cultivating ornamental plants, weaving bamboo baskets and fishing nets, processing dried sea products for sale, and tailoring.

hired themselves out as labourers in Japan or South Korea, where they would stay for several years. Young women who did not see chances for marriage in their native villages would go to Ho Chi Minh City or Hanoi in the hope of finding a job and a husband (see Luong 2009: 91). Those who were already married but wanted to escape poverty or were just looking for adventure also moved to the big city. In turn, girls under the legal working age from neighbouring Bình Định Province waited tables at roadside restaurants and bars for 'a bowl of rice' or a small salary in Sa Huỳnh. Some of them voluntarily dropped out of school, but the vast majority were forced to do so because their parents were unable to pay for their education. These girls grew up in poverty, and by moving to Sa Huỳnh they hoped for changes that would enable them to help their parents and start a better life.

My fieldwork focused mainly on Phổ Thạnh Commune and the twin fishing villages of Thạch By (divided into Thạch By 1 and Thạch By 2), the agricultural village of La Vân, and the salt-producing village of Tân Diêm. In the past Tân Diêm had been a sub-hamlet (*ấp*) of La Vân, but today it constitutes a separate village (*thôn*). Although I tried to confine the area of my research, it was impossible to focus exclusively within the boundaries of these communities because their ritual landscapes are continuously expanding. People organize and participate in religious ceremonies and festivals not only in their own communities, but also in neighbouring villages, including Phổ Châu Commune, which was part of their ritual landscape. Therefore, regardless of administrative divisions, the whole township, including Phổ Thạnh and Phổ Châu Communes, was known among locals by the name Sa Huỳnh. Following the local perception of space, I therefore use Sa Huỳnh to refer in general to this coastal settlement area, and the names of individual villages when I wish to single out a particular process or phenomenon.

As I began to explore religious life in Sa Huỳnh, I realized that I had missed part of the story by focusing exclusively on Sa Huỳnh and assuming that it was self-contained. In particular, I saw ritual and religious links with Lý Sơn Island, located only about 30 km off the Quảng Ngãi coast. According to local narratives, at the beginning of the twentieth century Sa Huỳnh fishers found the body of a woman that had been thrown by the sea onto rocks below the temple of the goddess Thiên Y A Na at the foot of *Cấm Núi* (the Forbidden Hill), which forms a part of the Sa Huỳnh peninsula. They took her body away and buried it in the vicinity of the temple. Many fishers believe that she was a trader from Lý Sơn Island. In Sa Huỳnh she is known as Bà Lao, although some people argue that her name was Ngô Thị Khinh, while others say that her real surname was Tô, which indicates a Chinese origin. In the 1980s, villagers inducted Bà Lao into their pantheon of three goddesses – Thiên Y A Na, Thủy Long, and Quan Âm – worshipped on the Forbidden Hill. Consequently, this place became known among villagers as 'the place of four ladies' (*chỗ bốn bà*). Nowadays, people perceive Bà Lao as a particularly sacred spirit because she was young, unmarried, and died prematurely. For example, Tự, a middle-age fisherman whom I met making offerings at her grave, said that a few years ago his ship got bogged down in shallow waters close to the place where Bà Lao's grave lies. He was convinced that she raised the water level so his ship could safely enter the port.

Phận, the old caretaker of Thiên Y A Na's temple, stated in an interview that a few years earlier relatives of Bà Lao from Lý Sơn Island came to him and enquired about her grave. They said that they heard about the location of her grave through a spirit medium. The family, wanting to fulfil their ritual and ceremonial obligations towards their newly revealed divine ancestor, asked Phận to take care of the grave and gave him some money to renovate it. I was not able to find Bà Lao's family during my visit to Lý Sơn, but islanders told me another story which led me back again to Sa Huỳnh. I learned from fishers that in one of the temples devoted to the worship of the Whale Spirit in Lý Sơn, they keep the head of the most powerful whale. When I asked islanders what happened to the rest of the whale's body, they replied that it had drifted in to Sa Huỳnh and is now kept in a similar temple near Thạch By village in Sa Huỳnh. Although neither side could confirm the other's story, their narratives continue to reveal symbolic connections between the two places.

I took these stories as metaphors of the interconnections of coastal society. Just as the head must be joined with its other remains to form a complete body, Sa Huỳnh and Lý Sơn are joined by the sea and constitute an interconnected space in which beliefs and narratives constitute elements of cohesion. Therefore, when in February 2007 I got the chance to expand my research, I started to work at a second site,

Lý Sơn Island, parallel to my mainland fieldwork in Sa Huỳnh. Each setting shed light on the other and significantly enriched my knowledge about important changes that happened along the maritime periphery of Central Vietnam. By looking at the two I was able to form a more complex picture of how people navigate state and religious authorities in the border zones.

Lý Sơn – the island

Lý Sơn Island is a small atoll, formerly named Cù Lao Ré. While 'cu lao' is a Vietnamese pronunciation of the Cham word *pulao*, denoting island, the meaning of the term 're' is unclear. Local people us the word *re* to refer to the special fibre made from a tree that grew on the island and was used to make fishing nets. However, according to historian Andrew Hardy, the toponym *ré* and the current term *lý* bear an etymological relationship to the names given by highland people for Quảng Ngãi's main rivers.[10] While one cannot be sure about true meaning of these terms, the Cham-Việt name and the Sino-Vietnamese record of the name Lý Sơn index different territorial and ethnic affinities, which Việt settlers attempted to blur and reconcile through ritual propitiation of the previous owner of the land. The Sino-Vietnamese name Lý Sơn (*sơn* literally means mountain) draws our attention to the three long-extinct volcanoes on the island that played an important economic and defence role during the Nguyễn dynasty. Still today, the Lý Sơn mountains, like those in Sa Huỳnh, are used by the Border Guard Command (*Công an Biên phòng*) as military observation posts and play an important role in exercising sovereignty and in monitoring Vietnam's territorial waters, especially now, with both China and Vietnam claiming the Paracel and Spratly archipelagos as their own.

As in the case of Sa Huỳnh, what today constitutes the district (*huyện*) of Lý Sơn is a product of historical contingency. Lý Sơn Island changed its name and administrative status several times. In 1808 the king Gia Long changed the name Cù Lao Ré into Lý Sơn and made the island a *canton* (or sub-district – *tổng*) of Bình Sơn District (Quảng Ngãi Province). After the August Revolution of 1945, the island, consisting of two communes, maintained the status of *canton* but changed its name

10. Hardy and Nguyễn Tiến Đông (2019) argue that the population of Champa's port cities and coastal plains included both Austronesian- and Austroasiatic-speaking people.

to Trần Thành. In 1946 the *canton* was renamed and became the commune of Lý Sơn. In 1951, the French colonial authorities placed Lý Sơn Commune under the administrative supervision of Đà Nẵng Township (*thị xã*) in Quảng Nam Province. In 1954, the South Vietnamese authorities again made Lý Sơn a commune of Bình Sơn District. In 1993, Lý Sơn was separated from Bình Sơn and became an independent district. Today, Lý Sơn is one of the fourteen districts of Quảng Ngãi Province.

In Vietnam local government officials are appointed at the level of the province (*tỉnh*), district (*huyện*) and municipality (or commune, *xã*). Local state power in Lý Sơn and Sa Huỳnh was exercised by officials recruited from the region and represented in the state institution of the People's Committee (*Ủy Ban Nhân Dân – UBND*), which is tied to the district and provincial offices. The People's Committee Office, represented by the chairman (*chủ tịch*) at the apex, oversees several administrative departments responsible for economic and administrative management of the area, guiding and organizing cultural events such as religious festivals, and managing such practical affairs as police work, updating fishers about new regulations, issuing sailing licenses, and investigating complaints and grievances, just to name a few of their many duties.

At present, Lý Sơn District has an area of 10 square kilometres with 20,000 citizens living in three communes: An Hải and An Vĩnh on the island of Lý Sơn, and the third commune, An Bình, located on the neighbouring Bé Island (formerly called Cù Lao Bờ Bãi), which has only recently been inhabited and was included in Lý Sơn District. Lý Sơn Island, which remained unscathed during the First and Second Indochina Wars, was considered among provincial authorities as a storehouse of data on the settlement and development of the Việt people in Central Vietnam, and in 2014 gradually developed into a 'patriotic' tourist destination.

The two *làngs* on Lý Sơn proper today constitute *xã* of An Vĩnh and An Hải. An Vĩnh consists of two *thôn*: West (Tây) and East (Đông). An Hải comprises three *thôn*: West (Tây), East (Đông), and Central (Trung Hòa). Before the advent of tourism on the island, An Vĩnh had 2,500 households with a population of 11,422 people, while An Hải had 1,814 households with 8,214 people. An Bình Commune, located on the neighbouring Bé Island, consisted of 106 households and its population reached 476 people. Local state power in Lý Sơn was represented by the district People's Committee office and two commune-level People's Committees. The three offices on the island were governed by a single chairman who supervised the administrative work, managed local affairs, and organized protection against typhoons, among other duties.

Since rice could not be grown on the island, Lý Sơn people always had to be more strategic than Sa Huỳnh villagers for their economic survival – as their past maritime ventures showed. They also experimented on an individual basis. Due to a shortage of fresh water for agricultural and domestic use, Lý Sơn people tried alternative crops in an effort to make a living off the sandy soil. In the 1950s they tested red rice plants taken from Central Highlanders, but the cultivation turned out to be too demanding and farmers were forced to look for more suitable crops like sweet potatoes. However, a major success story in Lý Sơn's agrarian history has been the islanders' ability to grow garlic and shallots in the sand. This started in the 1940s, when a farmer covered the clay beds near the seashore with a layer of sand, allowing water to percolate through and thereby making garlic and shallot cultivation possible. In the early 1960s, the method was improved and adapted by others, who started to use sand from the seashore and even seawater for garlic crops.[11] In the period of the subsidized collectivist economy, the success of this experiment allowed them to sell garlic and shallots to Ho Chi Minh City. However, between 1988 and 1989, overexploitation of sand on the island caused the beaches to disappear almost entirely. Although islanders developed a method to recycle the sand, the shortage of sand was too severe, leading to a crisis in the garlic industry. In 2008 the situation became so serious that farmers were forced to buy sand from people who dug it from the seabed. Today, garlic and shallots are, next to fishing, one of Lý Sơn's most important tourist attractions and a symbol of the sacrifices the islanders were willing to make in order to develop a barren land in the sea. Most tourists from northern and southern Vietnam perceive Lý Sơn to be a geographical and cultural backwater and their inhabitants as undeveloped fishers overcoming the odds to

---

11. For a similar case of successful experimentation with the cultivation of shallots in south-eastern Ghana, see Akyeampong (2001).

survive and thrive between Vietnam's land mass and the Paracels and Spratlys, stoically standing at the forefront of national sovereignty.

♒

According to the universally accepted myth of origin, the Vietnamese descend from the union between the elements of water and land. Lạc Long Quân (Dragon Lord of Lạc), who came from the realm of the water, married the beautiful, fiery Âu Cơ, who came from the mountains. After the wedding, Âu Cơ gave birth to an egg sac, from which one hundred human children hatched and grew. However, the couple decided to split because Lạc Long Quân always found his heart longing for the coast, while Âu Cơ constantly yearned for the highlands. They split up their children, of whom fifty followed the dragon father Lạc Long Quân to live by the water and the other fifty followed their fiery mother Âu Cơ to dwell in the highlands. The Lạc children of Âu Cơ and Lạc Long Quân are considered the progenitors of the Vietnamese people who settled in the Red River Delta (Vo 2012: 100). While the legend of the creation of the Vietnamese nation begins with the union of the realm of water and mountains, and hence with the connection of the mountains to the rivers and the sea, the sea aspect has been neglected in most Vietnamese historical analyses. As Wheeler (2006: 125) puts it, 'Ironically, Vietnam's territory is the product of the very maritime engagements its Vietnamese nationalistic perspective ignores.'

Until recently, the region of the Red River Delta in Vietnam was seen as the undisputed cradle of civilization and the exemplar of 'authentic' Vietnam and its wet rice culture. However, the increasingly strident international contestations over the South China Sea have led to a significant change in rhetoric, recasting Vietnam from the village-based, rice-growing nation depicted during its various wars against foreign occupiers to a maritime nation (*nước biển*) oriented towards the 'East Sea'. This discursive shift from land to sea is marked by stories about the most recent 'turn towards the ancestral sea islands' (*hướng về biển đảo quê hương*) and the idea of Vietnam as a *nước biển*, which is a contemporary invention of tradition that discursively places Vietnam in Tony Reid's (1999) 'Malay World'. The most recent propaganda posters that draw the maritime margins into the centre and blur boundaries between mainland and island are part of that effort. They proclaim that 'Vietnam is a maritime country' (*Việt Nam là một quốc gia biển*), 'The island is a home and the sea is a homeland' (*Đảo là nhà biển là quê hương*) and 'Every Vietnamese is a citizen of the sea' (*Mỗi người Việt Nam là một công dân biển*). Until this shift, fishers and the fishing industry were portrayed mainly in terms of socialist production – alongside agriculture and forestry – but the most recent move in Vietnam's state rhetoric turns Vietnamese fishers into the heroic vanguard of national sovereignty in the 'East Sea'. Complementarily, novel expressions of national identity and citizenship can be seen in T-shirt slogans such as 'The Vietnamese nation is determined to preserve each plot of the Vietnamese land and sea islands' (*Dân Tộc Việt Nam Quyết Tâm Gìn Giữ Từng Tấc Đất và Biển Đảo Của Việt Nam*) and 'Vietnam turns towards the East Sea' (*Việt Nam hướng về Biển Đông*). These T-shirts became increasingly popular among many young Vietnamese tourists in Lý Sơn who wanted to publicly express their identification with fishers and the sea.

This aesthetic shift is accompanied not by militarization but by a changing geography of *affect* (Navaro-Yashin 2007), by which people who have never been on the Paracels or Spratlys claim a deep emotional bond with these 'ancestral' places and the desire to defend their 'sovereignty'. This affect is performed in a wide variety of ways: national commemoration of the Paracel and Spratly sailors; building a wall around Lý Sơn Island to protect against Chinese invasion; emotional demonstrations in the streets of Hanoi and Ho Chi Minh City against the Chinese occupation of 'ancestral' seas; and mainlanders performing solidarity with islanders – supposedly victimized by Chinese vessels – through patriotic tourism, donations, and cultural campaigns. Furthermore, the changing geography of affect creates new spaces for interaction between state and society, but which also bring religion into the mix. The 'ancestral' deep sea territory, fishing practices, new maps of the national geo-body, new development plans, and a new style of patriotic tourism in Vietnam's coastal areas illustrate the multitude of ways in which affect is provoked and people respond to local and global economic and political discourses. As stated in the Introduction, the global competition for marine resources, the geopolitical conflict over the disputed archipelagos in the South China Sea, and tourism development in Sa Huỳnh and Lý Sơn – these are not the main foci of this book. However, it was my hope in this chapter that attending to such local histories of maritime periphery will destabilize the powerful and hegemonic idea of 'Vietnameseness' that dismisses regional, historical, and cultural differences and sidelines places – such as Sa Huỳnh and Lý Sơn – that do not represent the imagined culture of northern Vietnam. Sa Huỳnh and Lý Sơn themselves should also not be homogenized, but rather pursued through their spatial and temporal connections and discontinuities. By telling the story of how the people of Sa Huỳnh and Lý Sơn navigate state, religion, and the South China Sea, my wider goal in this book is to show religious practices in their continuity with earlier legacies and with different ways of acting and being Vietnamese.

Figure 3: An altar in the yard of a house for the Earth Spirit, Sa Huỳnh.

CHAPTER 2

Doing and Making Religion in Vietnam

Hưng (born 1948), a former guerilla fighter, a member of the village team responsible for rituals, and a fisherman, often shifted between joking about the Party – warning me that the Communist Party allowed me to carry out my research and for that reason my intentions must be pure – and relating critical stories of the preceding years of severe restrictions. Before taking me to meet the local healer and exorcist (*thày đuổi tà ma*) – known for his defence of a Buddhist statue during the antisuperstition campaign – he had asked me, 'Why is the Communist Party only one, not two?' Then, pointing to the sky and laughing, he answered his own question: 'Because it does not tolerate competition and for that very reason there is no religion (*tôn giáo*).' Then he continued, 'But because of a new policy up there, the Communist Party has to spread propaganda about a return of freedom, freedom of religious beliefs (*tự do tín ngưỡng*), which was limited in the time of state collectivization. Now there has been a real change, but [the Party] watches closely. I tell you young lady … understanding Communism is not simple!' Hưng's remark about the complexity of Communism raised much laughter among the men gathered around, but his underlying desire to share the bitter events of the antisuperstition campaign in Sa Huỳnh was palpable. However, in his game of beating state discipline with his own indiscipline, he publicly warned me that my reasons for learning about local history must be 'cultural,' not 'political', and thus I needed to recognize a clear boundary between those two realms.

Binary oppositions such as institutionalized religion versus beliefs, religion versus politics, high modernism versus (backwards) religion, science versus religious superstition, and cultural versus political appeared in almost every conversation I had with Vietnamese people with regard to their religious practices. As Erik Harms (2011a: 226) persuasively argues, 'To dismiss these binaries as false would be to ignore a fundamental element of the social landscape', regardless of whether these binaries are seen as accurate or not. While such ideal oppositions help people make a sense of their world in everyday life, they are often blurred and merged to serve personal interests. In order to understand the ways in which such binaries are produced and invoked by state agents and by villagers like Hưng, it is necessary to take some time to discuss the regulatory character of the Vietnamese state regarding religious practices. By zooming in on the important transformations in state policy towards religion, this chapter thus prepares the ground for a discussion about the various categorical binaries informing people's actions, as well as how these binaries are undermined in practice by different actors.

The chapter opens with a brief discussion of the category of religion in Vietnam as it emerged through modern state formation. Drawing on Scott's (1998) argument on state simplification, I discuss in the second section how the Vietnamese state appropriates and purifies religion through administrative procedures in order to standardize the complex and diverse vernacular classifications and hence make people and their religious practices 'legible' to the state gaze. The subsequent section takes a critical look at the *Official Gazette (Công Báo)* as it articulates Vietnam's official state discourse on religion. Finally, I show that in the Đổi Mới period, the state approach to religion shifted from hostility to a more pragmatic approach.[1] Whereas the Party-state withdrew from its pursuit of socialist modernity and appropriated religion by converting some influential religious forms into 'cultural heritage' and/or 'national heritage', it continues to see religion as a competing source of power that needs to be controlled and managed.

Institutionalized religion versus beliefs

During my ethnographic immersion in Sa Huỳnh and Lý Sơn, I never heard villagers using the term *tôn giáo* (institutionalized religion) to describe their belief in spirits, but I often heard them using the term *tín ngưỡng* (religious beliefs) to describe their personal and intimate re-

---

1. Đổi Mới literally means 'renovation' and refers to a period of reforms initiated in 1986.

lationship with specific spirits. Following the state, Vietnamese people make a distinction between 'religion' and 'religious beliefs' based on the presence or absence of doctrine (see Dror 2002a). As in other parts of Southeast Asia, in Vietnam a separate term that could refer to religion (*tôn giáo*) per se only emerged in the context of European colonialism (Van der Veer and Lehmann 1999; Turner and Salemink 2015). The newer term's entry into common usage has resulted in religious practices being not only labelled and controlled, but also understood as separate from the 'secular' and counterposed to 'science' (for China, see Sutton and Kang 2009). In the imperial encounter, both colonized countries and those that had successfully resisted Western hegemony coined a new concept of religion based on terms understood within Western narratives of modernity (DuBois 2009).

Such a process involved a kind of purification that reconfigured the concept of 'religion' both for those groups of people that identify themselves with religion and those that do not (Keane 2007: 83). For example, during the period of High Socialism in Vietnam, 'religion' was often combined with the Sino-Vietnamese term *mê tín dị đoan* ('superstition'), making religion appear archaic, unscientific and heterodox (Salemink 2013; see also Sutton and Kang 2009: 193–194). In the Đổi Mới period initiated in 1986, the Vietnamese state gradually abandoned the interpretation of religion as 'unscientific' and 'irrational', while still attempting to draw a line between those informal, vernacular religious practices that were recognized as having a 'national character' (known as *tín ngưỡng*) and those considered superstition (*mê tín dị đoan*) and therefore contrary to the modern project of building a 'progressive nation' (Salemink 2013; Taylor 2007). This led the state to reformulate meanings connected with diverse religious traditions in line with the new, 'purified' category of religion and to design new measures for controlling such practices (Keane 2007: 84–88; Sutton and Kang 2009).

In his analysis of religion in China, Andrew Kipnis (2001: 33) asks, '[W]hat is this flourishing thing called religion, what is the significance of calling it religion, and why is it flourishing?' According to one of the most accomplished and well-known anthropological definitions of religion – that of Clifford Geertz (1973: 90) – religion is a 'system of symbols which acts to establish powerful, pervasive, and long-lasting moods and motivations in men by formulating conceptions of a general order of existence and clothing these conceptions with such an aura of factuality that the moods and motivations seem uniquely realistic'. However, implying that religion is a coherent system of beliefs, such a definition appears to have little relevance in the case of China or Vietnam, where religion is not only a 'constructed category ... arising through modern state formation' (Ashiwa and Wank, 2009: 5), but it also lacks fixed norms and is polytheistic in its nature (Chau 2006; Endres 2011; Soucy 2012; Turner and Salemink 2015; Hoang 2017).

In trying to answer his own question, Kipnis accepts Talal Asad's (1993: 29) argument that Geertz neglects the role of social forces such as authoritative institutions, which can impose consistent interpretations of religious symbols, authorize religious practices and knowledge, and discipline religious subjects. Bringing to the table historical conditions, Asad shows that it is not possible to formulate an essential definition of religion because its contents change over time and because religion itself is a creation of a particular historical moment and a particular place. However, Kipnis still finds inspiration in Geertz's emphasis on symbols and models, especially in reference to China, where the state defines what belongs to the domain of religion and science. Instead of reading symbols as a set of 'shared beliefs', as Geertz's (2001: 34) definition implies, he points out existing contestations over religious symbols that produce an array of different interpretations and motivations rather than a unified form of thought.

Asad's sensitivity to historical context is helpful in our understanding of religion as a process, but his analysis focuses mainly on exploring religions through authoritative institutions, and thus it is reduced to *monotheistic* modes of religiosity authorizing practices and doctrines from in principle a central vantage point. Not all religious beliefs in Vietnam involve a standardization of religious knowledge and practice as in the Abrahamic monotheistic traditions (Turner and Salemink 2015). Often lacking orthodoxy and orthopraxy, religion in Vietnam is mostly polytheistic in nature and described in terms of the 'interconnection and mutual influence between major religious traditions ..., through a wide variety of rituals and in overlapping cosmologies and pantheons associated with Buddhism, Daoism, and Confucianism ..., built on a substratum of ancestor worship ... and spirit worship' (Salemink 2008b: 272; see also Kwon 2009; Soucy 2012; Turner and Salemink 2015). Also, '[i]n Vietnamese Buddhism, there is no systematized, formally imposed, orthodox practice that is required of all devotees' and, consequently, many people who engage in Buddhist and non-Buddhist practices do not necessarily experience them as being in conflict (Soucy 2012: 3–4; see also Taylor 2004). This is no less true for Sa Huỳnh and Lý Sơn, where the existing beliefs and practices such as ancestor worship, the cult of the anonymous dead, worship of the goddess Thiên Y A Na and the Whale Spirit, as well as geomancy and fortune telling, interact on various levels and are tied, albeit rather loosely, to institutions such as fishing organizations.[2] This relative absence of orthodoxy and orthopraxy constitutes a persistent challenge to state officials and doctrine-minded clergy, who wish to purify religion by eradicating those practices that they do not deem to be in line with their doctrinal interpretations. If we read the antisuperstition campaigns of the late 1970s as an attempt to do away with religion in the local village domain, it allows us to capture various local responses that sometimes required that objects – such as temples and statues – be destroyed, smashed or moved across different symbolic and political spaces and subjected to different disciplinary practices and state and religious semiotic ideologies (Keane 2008; see also Anagnost 1985, 1994; Duara 1991; Malarney 2002; Yang 1967; Young 1997).

In the case of Vietnam, it makes more sense to think about religion as 'practice' not only located, mediated and interpreted through performances, ritualization, and the creation and use of text (Asad 2001; Chau 2006, Nye 2000), but also one that builds on authoritative state semiotic ideology. A focus on religion as an *act* that is rationalized across different social fields emphasizes an ongoing process of accommodation, appropriation, manipulation, indigenization and mutual influence between different secular and religious traditions and practices. Moreover, such an approach acknowledges the existence of *many* forms of religious ideas and interpretations, of competing beliefs and their diverse expressions, which do not have to be consistent or represent everlasting authority, but nevertheless have to be reproduced afresh (Fabian 1985: 147; see also Kirsch 2004; Hoang 2017). The interplay between state and religious semiotic ideologies becomes important when we try to understand the

---

2. In Lý Sơn, Catholic, Protestant and Cao Đài religions all have their own churches. While monotheistic Christian religions were not present in Sa Huỳnh, a Cao Đài temple served a very small number of followers.

ability of people in Vietnam's maritime frontier to navigate and subvert these ideologies beyond domination or resistance.

High modernism versus religion

James Scott, in his book *Seeing Like a State: How Certain Schemes to Improve the Human Condition Have Failed* (1998), argued that the state always attempts to make a society 'legible' and arrange the population in a way that increases the state's capacity to control its citizens. This drive for the administrative ordering of society includes organizing the natural geography, settling mobile peoples, establishing population and cadastral registers, standardizing language, designing cities, and building transportation infrastructure, to recount just the most basic efforts that states make to attach their 'subjects to [their] environment' (Scott 1998: 2). This is often interwoven with the state's blind confidence in scientific and technical progress, which Scott calls 'high modernism' – 'uncritical, unskeptical, and thus unscientifically optimistic about the possibilities for the comprehensive planning of human settlement and production' (1998: 4). Such a utopian vision of a 'progressive future' requires massive changes in people's work habits, living patterns, and moral convictions and perceptions of the world and, above all, a state that is able to use its power to put the high-modernist project into effect. Scott argues that war, revolution, economic depression, and struggle for national liberation create fertile ground for the emergence of a new power – the authoritarian state that rejects the past in favour of a new revolutionary vision for its society (Scott 1998: 5).

Indeed, 'progress' and detachment from 'primordial' forms of classification took place in Vietnam against the backdrop of French colonial rule, the national political movement for independence, and the shock and trauma of the Second Indochina War. At the same time endorsement of a socialist modernity was accompanied by a strong critique of the past (see Marr 1981; Endres 2002; Ninh 2002; Pelley 2002; Taylor 2003). According to Scott's (1998: 93) argument, the simplified and thus purified 'prescription for a new society' implies a radical break with its history and traditions because, in the view of the authoritarian state, they provide fuel for backwards institutions and customs, superstition, and religious bigotry, all of which hamper the achievement of high modernism. Certainly, in revolutionary times traditional Vietnamese culture has become a subject of constant scrutiny by politicians and intellectuals. They put the blame for colonial hegemony and economic backwardness on certain aspects of the culture, such as hierarchy, wastefulness, and irrationality, which they believed were not appropriate in a modern state and should be eradicated (Endres 2002).[3]

In line with this revolutionary semiotic ideology, one of the main goals of the new socialist modernizing agenda was to strip traditional social arrangements of their sacred power and transform the Vietnamese people into a new and advanced society, with its progress based on education and rationality rather than on a religious pantheon (Keyes, Kendall and Hardacre 1994b). According to the Marxist–Leninist theory of the Party, religion will naturally disappear when humankind enters the period of communism and high modernism. In its effort to make Vietnam a secular society, Party ideologists blamed religion for the hardship and backwardness of the life of the masses, saying that people wasted time and money that could be better spent on education or national agricultural production. The Party-state was convinced that a systematic purification by selecting 'proper' aspects of Vietnamese tradition would put an end to 'depraved customs' originating from the 'era of feudalism' (Endres 2002: 1).

It is not without significance that one of the early tasks of the state's purifying discipline concerned a total restructuring of the local village religious domain in which politics and religion were merged (Malarney 2002).[4] Village festivals, life-cycle rituals, and places of worship – the spaces that sustained old power and prestige – became targets of the state's campaign against superstitions (Endres 2002). Following a Marxist analysis, religious buildings such as village temples, pagodas, and shrines were defined in terms of class struggle and considered hotbeds of feudalism, ignorance, and exploitation, not to mention a waste of village resources. Concerned with introducing a 'new way of life', the

---

3. Scott speaks of any state, not just authoritarian or socialist ones, and his argument thus remains highly relevant to an analysis of Vietnam in the Đổi Mới era, where socialist modernity has been replaced with a new vision of alternative modernity and the state's efforts to construct a society that will fulfill global standards of 'progress' and 'civility'.

4. For a very similar case of redefining the relationship between the sacred and profane in a Chinese village, see Duara (1988, 1991).

state undertook the task of turning religious buildings into spaces of secular rather than religious utility (Endres 2002: 3).

In northern Vietnam, during the land reform (1953–1955), the period of war mobilization (1960–1975), and the time of collectivization and dependence on state subsidy (1975–1986), sacred spaces had already been converted into granaries, storehouses and schools, while priest, monks and nuns were forced to adopt secular lives (Endres 2002; Hoang 2017). After 1975 this process was imposed on the South – albeit in a milder form – and lasted until 1986, when the state relaxed its enforcement of antisuperstition laws. The integration of the North and the South posed a serious challenge to the Communist state, which was confronted with a large body of religious sects and practices that had been eradicated or seriously restricted in the North but still flourished in the South despite selective control in resistance zones (Taylor 2004). In fact many of these religious sects, such as Cao Đài, Hòa Hảo, and the Unified Buddhist Church of Vietnam, had never existed in the North. The period of High Socialism (1976–79), during which the Vietnamese Communist Party unsuccessfully attempted to pursue a policy of collectivization in the South, signalled the most severe suppression of religion.[5] For example, Sa Huỳnh villagers clearly remembered 1978, the year the Communists forbade the performance of rituals and worship. Mạnh (born in 1943), who, at the time of my fieldwork, was responsible for donations and organizing religious ceremonies in local temples, depicted the strict implementation of the antisuperstition campaign:

> We lived in peace at last but oppression (*sự áp bức*) remained. Overt worship (*thờ phượng cúng*) was not allowed. Some folks adhered to [religion] so they were politically suspect (*bị chính trị*); they were arrested, imprisoned in the province or the district, hence no one dared. … All temples were tightly boarded up, superstitions were not allowed, no permission was given to lead a religious life, to enter a monastic order (*không tu hành, Phật đạo hết*). … Only at home did we have the right

---

5. In 1979 the Vietnamese Communist Party retreated from its collectivization policy and from enforcement of its centrally planned economic system by setting out new measures that were intended to enhance production. However, this shift became the Communist Party's new policy only in 1986, when the Đổi Mới programme of socio-economic reforms was officially announced at the 6th Party Congress (Kerkvliet 2005).

to believe (*quyền tín ngưỡng*); no one dared to burn incense during the full moon or pray while outside; if they did, they risked going to prison.

Mạnh's narrative underlines the confrontational relationship between the competing ideologies of state and religion that drew a sharp binary between public and domestic and, thus, between secular and religious realms. Consequently, those who dared to display religious devotion outside of their homes – in the secular space belonging to the state – were disciplined, while those who limited their religious expression to the privacy of their families were left alone. But one has to be careful about taking Mạnh's statement to denote an absolute antagonism between state and religion or state authorities and villagers. The desire to practise their religion required of people more sophisticated improvisation and legitimation tactics that complicated these different structural positions and enabled them to move flexibly and smoothly within and across religious and state semiotic ideologies (see Chapter 4). At the time of collectivization and dependence on the state's handouts, villagers in Lý Sơn remembered that the shortened and simplified versions of rituals were carried out with the utmost haste and in secret. Local authorities were aware of these illicit practices and deliberately left the temple keys in the hands of village elders after clearing the temples of sacred effigies. When in the 1990s the state's antisuperstition campaign loosened its hold, Lý Sơn villagers, with the tacit agreement of the local authorities, resumed their religious practices. Villagers also remember that in 1991, while there was still no official permit to hold rituals, there was also no strict prohibition. Between 1993 and 1994 the local offices of the People's Committee allowed the temples to be reopened, and local authorities pretended they did not see the ceremonies that villagers organized there. In the majority of cases the temples' interiors had survived intact. Two years later the nationwide relaxation of religious oversight reached Quảng Ngãi, and villagers began openly to hold communal ceremonies and to worship their spirits in the temples. At that time in the territory of the former North this process was in full swing, while in central Vietnam it had just started.

The economic reforms of Đổi Mới had brought economic liberalization, privatization and commercialization to everyday life. Ever since the Communist-led Vietnamese state integrated the country into the global economy and abandoned collectivist policies, the threat of contagion by foreign cultures had become a greater challenge to the state's legitimacy. To fill the void created after withdrawing from socialist modernity, the Party-state attempted to create its own version of modernity in which national identity played a dominant role and, as a result, took a more favourable attitude towards not only formal religions (*tôn giáo*), but also 'folk beliefs' (*tín ngưỡng dân gian*) (Endres 2002; Luong 2003; Taylor 2001, 2007; Salemink 2013). This allowed for the reinterpretation of flourishing religious practices throughout Vietnam as an expression of Vietnamese 'culture' and, above all, 'national heritage'.

Religious versus secular

As in China, in Vietnam the ongoing process of the state taking control over religious affairs in local communities was an attempt to divest local temples of their mystical aura and to show that local gods were powerless effigies. Paradoxically, at the same time, in Vietnamese official discourse there was a tradition of preservation of communal houses, temples, and shrines going back to 1945, when Hồ Chí Minh issued a decree on the protection of cultural heritage (*di sản văn hóa*) in the context of land reform (Endres 2000). Historian Patricia Pelley (2002) demonstrates clearly that the Vietnamese postcolonial socialist state, unrelenting in its defence of the country against foreign aggressors, was extremely concerned about national history and its interpretation. As early as 1943, as the 'guiding concepts for the project of building a "new culture" and a "new life"', the Vietnamese Communist Party, in its 'Theses on Vietnamese Culture', introduced three principles: nationalization, popularization, and scientism (*dân tộc hóa, đại chúng hóa,* and *khoa học hóa*) (Endres 2002: 2; see also Ninh 2002: 26–46). 'Nationalization' in particular was understood as a defence against hostile forces – France and Japan – in terms of a 'long-standing tradition of resistance to foreign aggression' and, therefore, occupied a particular place in the ideological and academic discourse (Endres 2002: 2). In the 1950s, 1960s, and 1970s, scholars debated extensively about turning points in Vietnam's history as well as about the historical figures concerned that were often 'repackaged' and represented as national heroes (Pelley 2002). This repackaging not only referred to historic figures, but also to religious structures that, in the official view, stood for a 'national tradition'. Close reading of the *Official Gazette* (*Công Báo*) from 1955 onwards reveals a gradual change in the official policy towards the local religious domain, namely, the transformation of religious buildings into 'secular spaces' that bear 'cultural heritage' and those that bear 'national heritage'. At the same time, however, it reveals that Hồ Chí Minh's directives were largely ignored.

In the North, during the land reform (1953–1955) and the time of collectivization and dependence on state subsidies (1975–1986), religious buildings suffered extensive neglect and damage as their facilities and properties were claimed by village agricultural cooperatives or simply cleared of clergy and left empty. The monks and nuns who depended largely on these properties were disconnected from the basis of their livelihoods. During the land reform, those pagodas that temporarily retained their plots of land were taxed, and their clergy were expected to work in their rice fields, shoulder to shoulder with villagers, no longer able to rely exclusively on the labour of religious followers for their upkeep (*Công Báo* 1955; *Công Báo* 1995a).

A comparison of individual issues of *Công Báo* reveals that, while the state had its own vision of how to make use of temples, it was not always clear and consistent in its policies towards religious spaces. As a result, the state's inconsistency widened a gap between the official goals for repurposing sacred spaces and its actual implementation. Moreover, the implementation of the new ideological agenda was not always as peaceful a process as the state intended. Ten years after Hồ Chí Minh issued his directives on protecting cultural heritage, Prime Minister Phan Mỹ in the *Công Báo* of 1956 lamented the pitiful situation of demolished sites of local cults, which in the official discourse had undergone a metamorphosis from religious sites into 'historical monuments' (*di tích lịch sử*), 'heritage of feudalism' (*di sản của phong kiến*), or 'monuments of resistance to foreign aggression' (*di tích kháng chiến*) (*Công Báo* 1956: 189). Thus his lament referred to the dilapidation of these buildings because, according to state semiotic ideology, they were officially of national, not religious, significance. However, as the next issues of *Công Báo* show, in the process of appropriation of religious buildings for secular purposes, national aspects were often ignored by local cadres as well as villagers.

Religious structures were demolished not only by the communist guerrillas, who had used time-tested scorched-earth tactics to deny the enemy any space to quarter their troops, but also by villagers who tore down the buildings or simply used the materials to construct their own houses. Consequently, the state showed its concern over popular reactions and feelings about the 'dilapidated situation of temples falling into ruins with pieces lying scattered around', which might have resulted in a 'negative political impression among local visitors and foreign guests,' and recommended to provincial offices of culture and the People's Committees to remove all signs of vandalism from monuments and to beautify the local landscape by planting trees (*Công Báo* 1960: 338).

In its rhetoric, the government proclaimed that although the 'communal houses, Buddhist pagodas, shrines, temples, and imperial tombs have for centuries been exploited by feudal tyrants, who used them as sources of prestige in order to get close to all classes of people and to sow superstitions among them', they should now be utilized in accordance with a new cultural project of building a modern nation (*Công Báo* 1960: 338). The state's concern was dictated by a practical interest in developing the sites as places of historical interest, cultural value, or scenic beauty that the masses could visit as tourists rather than as places of religious activity. More importantly, this development aimed at replacing 'superstitious' beliefs with a new socialist creed. Thus, the fate of these places was not a trivial and unimportant matter: their new role was to serve the state machinery in building a new society. The Ministry of Culture, aware that it was losing control over the temples and fearful of the potentially disastrous consequences of antisuperstitious zeal, blamed its own employees for 'lack of proper view' (ibid.). In a self-critical mood, the *Công Báo* (1960: 338) describes the temples' destruction:

> As a result of the need for material for new building projects, a number of objects of our age-old architectural heritage (*di sản kiến trúc cổ truyền*) have been demolished; some of them have been used to support the art of cooperatives (*văn nghệ hợp tác xã*) or the production of oil lamps for meetings, others have been turned into retail outlets, storehouses and markets, while some of them remain in the hands of superstitious old ritual masters, but no one is taking care of the majority of them. Some people with little awareness have destroyed these places or used them as private houses. ...
>
> It is prohibited to defile architectural monuments (*công trình kiến trúc*) or to use them in illegitimate ways such as: making improper drawings on the walls, pillars, statues, or objects of worship; raising chickens

and ducks [in them]; storing hay; storing manure in communal houses, pagodas, shrines, temples, or imperial tombs (*lăng tẩm*); taking memorial plaques, tiles, wood, wooden panels with Chinese characters, or lacquered boards belonging to communal houses in order to demolish them, to make piers, plank-beds, or chairs, or to bake lime.

To rectify all 'mistakes and shortcomings', local authorities were strongly encouraged to protect and preserve 'all old architectural sites and other locales of scenic beauty and use them in an appropriate way without wastage' (ibid.). The 'appropriate way' was understood as 'turning all places of worship into schools, exhibition halls, gathering places, and cultural houses', which in the official discourse were presented as places of education and thus better alternative uses for once sacred locations (ibid.). However, before the implementation of the state policy, the same issue advised local governments to consult with villagers, owners of religious buildings and provincial cultural offices about the most suitable way to utilize the religious structures. According to the government order, all Buddhist pagodas and temples – classified as sites of historical interest or scenic beauty – were to be managed by local People's Committees (*uỷ ban nhân dân*) and cultural offices (*sở văn hóa*) (*Công Báo* 1962). In practice this meant that any renovation and construction work in places of worship and of historical and cultural value had to be officially approved by these bodies. This rule is still obeyed all over Vietnam, including in Sa Huỳnh and Lý Sơn.

The six years following this public admission of shortcomings in the management of religious structures did not, however, significantly improve the situation, and the Party had to sharpen its tone. Reacting to the continuing destruction of pagodas and temples, Prime Minister Phạm Văn Đồng excoriated administrative committees (*uỷ ban hành chính*) for failing to 'preserve all places of historical interest, teach people about their value, and transform them into museums' (*Công Báo* 1966: 270). He stressed that these places had been destroyed due to the lack of interest in preserving them and even a lack of awareness of the official duty to do so, which was a reflection of the low level of training of local cadres (ibid.).

In 1973, two years before the end of the Second Indochina War, the state, specifying its policy towards Buddhist pagodas and the clergy, had to again remind local authorities of their responsibility to protect all places of historical and cultural interest. The government directive called for 'preserving thoughtfulness (*chu đáo*) and cleanliness (*sạch sẽ*)' vis-à-vis Buddhist pagodas and forbade 'hurting the feelings and beliefs (*tín ngưỡng*) of the people' by destroying Buddhist sculptures and instruments or using them in inappropriate ways (*Công Báo* 1973: 253). Vice Prime Minister Lê Thanh Nghị reminded authorities in all communes (*xã*) and urban neighbourhoods (*khu phố*) that they had a duty to coordinate mass organizations (*tổ chức nhân dân*) responsible for protecting and 'bringing into play the notion of historical monuments' (ibid.). He pointed out that these committees must invite and help monks and nuns to take direct responsibility for the protection and preservation of 'historical spaces' but, at the same time, they should not interfere with religious activities. Therefore, the state was concerned not about religious but, above all, about *national* spaces.

Theoretically, the Buddhist clergy could count on official guarantees to continue their religious activities if they voluntarily handed their land over to the village cooperatives and joined common production. The cooperatives were expected to assign the monks and nuns to brigades based on practical abilities and their religious tasks in order to ensure their livelihoods (*Công Báo* 1973). In reality, however, the clergy had little choice: the state recommended training the most suitable local clergy as tour guides. It was presumed that monks and nuns could help local cadres with instructing visitors on the history of pagodas and scenic sites (*Công Báo* 1973: 253).

One year later, in an attempt to complement the policy of 'preservation' and 'protection', the state introduced a procedure of 'classification' (*xếp hạng*) of pagodas and temples as 'historical and cultural monuments' (*di tích lịch sử và văn hóa*) (*Công Báo* 1974: 51). This was the first time that the Ministry of Culture added the adjective 'cultural' (*văn hóa*) to the term 'historical monument' (ibid.), thereby broadening the definition of 'heritage'. The subsequent issue of *Công Báo* (1975) listed twelve pagodas and temples that qualified according to this new criterion. However, between 1975 and 1979 – the time of the most zealous antisuperstition campaigns – the *Công Báo* remained conspicuously silent regarding the protection and preservation of temples.

At the beginning of the 1980s the state returned to its policy of preserving historical sites. The next issues of the *Công Báo* resumed the practice of classifying temples according to their historic, cultural, and artistic importance (*Công Báo* 1980, 1982). In 1984, when the instructions concerning cultural preservation received the higher legal status of 'state law' (*pháp lệnh*), provincial authorities were encouraged to apply for official recognition of all cultural and historical sites (*Công Báo* 1984; see also Endres 2002: 5). Judging from the growing number of official declarations of recognition published in the *Công Báo* after 1984, the state's initiative met with an enthusiastic response from local officials and villagers.[6] All these events took place on the eve of the Đổi Mới reforms.

Starting with the introduction of the Đổi Mới reforms in 1986, Vietnam gradually withdrew from its project of socialist modernity and opened its borders to the international community. Integration with global capitalism, however, came with the enormous threat of inundation by foreign cultures. This prompted the state to attempt to devise an alternative Vietnamese vision, one in which national identification was the main indicator of modernity (Salemink 2008b; Hoang 2017). One milestone in the state's policy of preservation of those local cultural practices that would simultaneously symbolize 'traditional' and 'modern' was Resolution No. 5 of the Central Committee of the Communist Party on Building a Progressive Culture Imbued with National Identity,[7] which was adopted in 1998. Although this resolution does not refer explicitly to religion, it nevertheless allowed for the interpretation of religious revival in terms of 'culture' and, above all, 'national heritage'. Salemink (2013: 161) interprets Resolution No. 5 as, on the one hand, an 'umbrella for all sorts of local, bottom-up efforts to reinvent traditions and invest these with new forms and meanings' and, on the other hand, a useful tool for the state to 'claim a greater role in the organization of rituals and festivals ... in an attempt to channel the discourse over Vietnam's identity in new directions after the withdrawal from a Socialist modernity'.

Due to its particular emphasis on the national aspect of Vietnamese modernity, it seems that Party Resolution No. 5 is much more binding

---

6. According to the Ministry of Culture, by 1996 a total of 1,860 'historical and cultural monuments' had been officially recognized (Endres 2002: 6).

7. *Nghị quyết Hội nghị lần thứ năm Ban chấp hành Trung ương Đảng về xây dựng và phát triển nền văn hóa Việt Nam tiên tiến, đạm đà bản sắc dân tộc.*

for official authorities and even academics than the 2001 State Law on Cultural Heritage, published in the *Công Báo* (2001: 2232). While the 2001 law describes 'cultural heritage' in general terms as a 'spiritual product which has historical, cultural, and scientific values preserved in memory and writings and handed down orally, through arts and crafts, science, oral philology, folk performances, a way of life, a traditional lifestyle, festivals, handicraft techniques, knowledge of traditional medicine, food culture, traditional national costumes, and different terms of folk knowledge', Resolution No. 5 helps to reconcile tensions that inevitably arise between inherently contradictory concepts such as 'socialism' and 'market', and 'cultural chauvinism' and 'cosmopolitanism' (Salemink 2013: 174).

In 2002, specifying the 2001 Law on Cultural Heritage, the government pointed out that historical and cultural sites had to meet the criterion of significance on at least one of three levels: (1) 'provincial' (*tỉnh*), (2) 'national' (*quốc gia*), or (3) 'special national' (*quốc gia đặc biệt*). While the first referred mainly to archaeological, historical, and cultural sites important for local regions, the latter two explicitly stressed the national aspects of such places. More precisely, the law of 2001 indicates that all places designated as 'national' (*di tích quốc gia*) and 'special national monuments' (*di tích quốc gia đặc biệt*) must refer to important events in national history or to 'national heroes' (*anh hùng dân tộc*) or 'famous symbolic persons having influence on the course of national history' (*Công Báo* 2002: 4051). Later in the *Công Báo* of 2002, Prime Minister Phan Văn Khải gave a detailed list of all documents necessary to apply for the official recognition, known as 'Certificate of Designation of a Historical and Cultural Relic' (*công nhận di tích lịch sử văn hóa*). In most cases, it was required that the application, certified by local authorities, must include a 'life story' (*lý lịch*) of the famous person or hero (usually worshipped by the local community as a divine spirit or god), a written statement from the applicants, and a map with the exact location of the site (ibid.).

At the time, the *lý lịch* functioned as a *political biography* that had to be periodically submitted to local authorities. In this way, the state assessed individual class background, behaviour according to socialist standards, social relations, and contributions to society (Leshkowich 2014: 143). Before 1975, the *lý lịch* was commonly used in the North as a powerful tool of economic and political class categorization and revolutionary commitment. After 1975, it was crucial for classification of southern Vietnamese 'in political terms as supporters or opponents of the revolution and in economic terms by documenting their peasant, worker, or bourgeois capitalist origin' (Leshkowich 2014: 150). However, the use of the term *lý lịch*, which is by definition political, to assess the gods' and spirits' contributions to national history provides an interesting example of state discipline 'moving productively between ideal categories' of politics and religion (Harms 2011a: 26). By demanding from the religious constituency a political biography of the spirit, the state institutionalizes religious practice and cleanses it of any connotations that are not congruent with the official semiotic ideology. At the same time, cleansing those aspects from the spirit record provides people with room for manipulation of different categories – religious and political – and for the use of indiscipline as a local tactic when acting on behalf of their gods. As I will show through my ethnography in Chapters 4 and 5, different groups of actors often draw on state semiotic ideologies and employ a common political language, but rarely agree on its meaning.

Paradoxically, the modern practice of the socialist state to grant certificates to heroes, divinities, and temples of historical and national significance has a long tradition in Vietnam, dating back to imperial times (see Wolters 1988; Boudarel 1991; Do 2003; DiGregorio and Salemink 2007). By the sixteenth century the imperial court was already attempting to gain control of the spirit cults in the villages through the establishment of a hierarchy for the spirit world that conformed to the Confucian model. Spirits were certified with a royal charter (*sắc phong*) and, at the same time, their 'spirit record' (*thần tích*) was standardized and cleansed of elements that were not congruent with the dominant, official ideology. The central authorities required that the new spirits had to be those of deceased individuals who had been moral exemplars or good officials. The central state acted as patron of these spirits and, through their standardization, tried to integrate the country and enforce a sort of unity on the regional and local levels. A closer reading of the *Công Báo* shows that the postcolonial socialist Vietnamese state continued this precolonial practice. Like the imperial court, the modern state seeks to increase its legitimacy through the careful selection and canonization of those historic figures who demonstrated moral and patriotic values and heroic resistance against foreign invaders (see Pelley 2002: 177–189; Malarney 2007: 529; Salemink 2007; Pham Quynh Phuong 2009).

In line with the imperative to 'build a progressive culture, imbued with national identity' – a famous slogan from Resolution No. 5 – local state agents are encouraged to apply for official recognition of commemorative sites that they can prove have the potential to be included in the category of 'cultural heritage' (Endres 2001, 2002: 6). At the same time, villagers who want to reclaim the sacred spaces of certain spirits and deities and reaffirm their institutional significance try to obtain such a certificate, which not only provides state recognition for the temple but also, as in the imperial past, enables people to worship their divinities in any way they wish. As such, it is also a source of personal consolation and communal pride.

However, as Salemink (2013: 173) points out, the state recognition goes beyond the cultural and historical assessment of the site as heritage, as the state 'reifies and instrumentalizes local processes under the umbrella of the nation'. By giving local practices and sites the label of 'cultural' and 'national heritage', the state rids them of their religious content and appropriates them for its own purposes. This involves not only selecting, appropriating, and modifying meanings, but also controlling and disciplining the people who are emotionally engaged in rescuing their sacred sites (Salemink 2013).

Science, beliefs, and religious superstition

In 2005, on a hot summer afternoon in Hanoi, I met with my Vietnamese language teacher. I asked her to help me interpret an article entitled 'Is it right that religion is at variance with socialism?' (*Phải chăng tôn giáo mâu thuẫn với Chủ Nghĩa Xã Hội?*). It was authored by Đỗ Quang Hưng (2004), the director of the Institute for Religious Studies, where I was affiliated from 2002–2005. She took a look at the title and then said:

> Religion still exists and this is a fact the socialist country has to accept. Marx said that religion was the opium of the masses. But now, the Party has a new interpretation, namely, that religion could have a positive effect, similar to a drug that gives people relief when they suffer a great deal of pain. In a modern society there are many different problems people have to deal with on their own, and sometimes they feel hopeless. They go to a pagoda or temple and pray, and after that they feel relieved.

As Charles Keyes, Laurel Kendall, and Helen Hardacre (1994a) demonstrate in their seminal volume *Asian Visions of Authority*, the thesis that modernization and restructuring of Asian societies in the name of 'progress' would lead to their secularization, as predicted by Marx, Durkheim, Weber, and their followers, failed to materialize. The marginalization of the religious sphere did not lead to a break with religious traditions. In fact, quite the opposite occurred: in the face of modernization, religious traditions became even more significant (Keyes, Kendall, and Hardacre 1994b: 3). The authors aptly point out that state agendas to control and standardize religion have been informed not only by theories of modernization that sought to free people from superstitious and time-consuming practices, but also by the need of modern Asian states to legitimize their rule and organize the 'masses'. This necessity, expressed in the nation-building process, entailed a different attitude to the past and to religion from that of socialist modernizing agendas.

Indeed, in 1990, the Vietnamese Communist Party debated how 'to strengthen the task of religion in the new situation' and, as a result, approved the resolution:

> Religion is a legitimate requirement of a part of society. The pending question of religion existed in the socialist system for a long time. Religious virtues and morals are, for many reasons, suitable to the new and great undertaking of national construction.[8]

However, as Salemink (2008b: 276) argues, only when the Party Central Committee adopted Resolution No. 5 in 1998 did the religious intensification begin 'to be translated into the official imaginary of the nation'. In light of this document, ancestor worship, communal houses, and the rituals associated with them appeared to be legible to the state in the sense that they were recognized as fitting material for reshaping the representation of the past and for narratives about national and revolutionary martyrs in modern Vietnam (Taylor 2007; Salemink 2008b). As in other Asian countries where the dead were 'employed' in the service of national unity (see Evans 1998; Keyes 2002), in Vietnam the belief in life after death and especially in the 'exceptional dead' became a potent symbol of national integration linking society with its heroic history

---

8. Government Regulation 24-NQ/TW 16/10/1990, quoted from the *Vietnam's Communist Party: On Religious Issues Resolutions of the 7th Plenum [9th tenure]* (The Gioi Publishers 2004).

(Malarney 2007; see also Ho Tai 2001; Endres 2008; Kwon 2009). Van der Veer and Lehmann (1999: 11) argue that 'death and afterlife form the stuff of which both religion and nationalism are made'. Consequently, in Vietnam ancestor worship has recurred as a 'hero-centered political culture' in which the centre of gravity is the exemplary service of the ancestors rather than their peaceful afterlife (Kwon 2006: 104).

The gradual change of state attitudes towards culture and religion was accompanied by scholarly debates reacting to the revival of religious traditions. Special attention was given to the 'cultural identity' (*bản sắc văn hóa*) of Vietnam, which was seen as the 'essence' of the nation. Along these lines, scholars produced articles describing at length how 'national cultural identity' contributed to the 'skills and spirit', 'vital power', and 'experience' of the Vietnamese nation, which, in turn, made it possible for Vietnam to emerge triumphantly from the trials of history. In the state semiotic ideology, 'patriotism' (*chủ nghĩa yêu nước*) and the sense of being a 'patriot' (*yêu nước*) were acknowledged as the most important characteristics of national cultural identity.

For example, Ngô Đức Thịnh (2001), one of the most devoted scholars of folklore studies, found in the realms of the supernatural (*linh thiêng*) and spiritual (*tâm linh*) symbolic elements of patriotism that were developed into 'religious beliefs' (*tín ngưỡng*) encompassing all these meanings. Vietnamese academics saw a 'will to build and preserve the country' in traditional society, especially in the popular culture of the peasants, who appeared as the guardians of the 'pure' and 'authentic' Vietnamese tradition (Pelley 1993: 114).[9] This subordination of the sacred dimensions of religion to the state's secular objectives is found in many Asian countries, where religion is seen as the essence of national culture (Kendall 1996a, 2009; Hann 2006; Kehl-Bedrogi 2006; Mandair 2009; Van der Veer and Feuchtwang 2009). Laurel Kendall (1996b, 2009: 17–19) reports that in the 1980s a new Korean middle class of intellectuals believed that the real essence of a people was in their 'folk traditions'. It should come as no surprise, then, that in Vietnam tutelary

---

9. In the post-colonial period, Vietnamese culture was divided into 'popular' and 'official', reflecting the class divide between the peasant and ruling classes. Accordingly, folklore studies focus on the 'little people' – the idealized peasants without local and historical specificity (Pelley 1993: 199). For a critique of defining Vietnamese culture in terms of class conflict, see Trần Quốc Vượng (1992).

spirits and craft ancestors, who had been erased from local landscapes during the campaign against superstitions, have returned in their full glory as historical characters. So-called folk culture and village community have become arenas in which all these notions can be articulated according to the official slogans 'family–village–nation' and 'preservation, wealth, and development of national cultural character' (Ngô Đức Thịnh 2001).

Although during the Đổi Mới era some popular practices previously labelled as superstitions became recognized as 'folk beliefs' (*tín ngưỡng dân gian*) and 'national heritage' (Endres 2002; Taylor, 2003; Salemink 2008c), the pejorative category of superstition has not disappeared entirely. In opening up public space for religion, the socialist state has neither admitted limitations to its political power nor given up control over religious practices. Although the state no longer plays the strong ideological role in people's lives that it did before Đổi Mới, it still tries to standardize religious practices. One such effort is the validation of those popular religious practices that remain in line with the state's semiotic ideology and the stigmatization of those that bear a 'superstitious' character. While identifying the first category seems to be relatively easy, the latter is more ambiguous and therefore creates a problem for the state.

The Sino-Vietnamese term *mê tín* (in Chinese: *mixin*), commonly translated as 'superstition', is associated with certain aspects of religious expression within the boundaries of the so-called great traditions of Islam, Buddhism, and Christianity and popular religious practice (Anagnost 1987).[10] In the case of China, Sutton and Kang (2009: 193–4) show that when the term 'religion' was paired with 'superstition', 'religion' 'under the shadow of superstition' appeared archaic and unscientific. Asad (1993, 2003) points out a similar phenomenon when he draws our attention to the concept of the 'secular', which emerged historically in conjunction with the notion of the religious. Like 'superstition', the concept of 'secular' cannot do without the idea of 'religion'.

In 1999 the Ministry of Culture published a volume titled *Religious Beliefs –Superstitions* (*Tín ngưỡng – mê tín*) (Hà Văn Tăng and Trương

---

10. According to the *Dictionnaire Vietnamien-Chinois-Français* by Eugène Gouin (Missions Étrangères de Paris 2002), *mê* could be translated as 'to adore', 'to devote', 'to be mad about', 'to love', 'to be blind', or 'to be unconscious', while *tín* means 'trust', 'to believe', 'faith', and 'faithful'.

Thìn 1999), which poses the problem of depicting 'superstition' with reference to the new socio-economic situation Vietnam faces. Trương Thìn, a vice director in the Ministry of Culture and Information in Hanoi and one of the volume's editors, argued that every faith and religion has a 'superstitious' (*mê tín*) character, which does not automatically mean that its nature is heterodox (*dị đoan*). Only in cases when the *mê tín*, understood here as a feeling of confidence and unwavering belief, is 'used unfairly' does it become something deformed, strange, odd, and nonsensical and, as a result, turns out to be *mê tín dị đoan*, or heterodox superstition (1999: 112–115).

As argued above, in the Đổi Mới era the Vietnamese state gradually departed from an interpretation of all religious practices as 'unscientific' and 'irrational', while still attempting to draw a line between those religious practices that were recognized as having a 'national character' and those that went against the modern project of building a 'progressive nation' and were therefore labelled as 'superstition'. To this end, the socialist state prepared a precise list of the religious practices considered 'outdated' and 'superstitious'. Life-cycle rituals and village festivals should be in tune with a 'civilized way of life' (*nếp sống văn minh*), and were therefore a particular focus of its concern. With reference to such rituals, one government regulation states:

> The state respects religious freedom (*tự do tín ngưỡng*) or the freedom not to have any religion (*tôn giáo*). Practices of ancestor worship, ceremonies in churches, temples, and pagodas ... are beliefs (*tín ngưỡng*) that the state respects. Astrology, fortune telling, soul-calling, geomancy, prophecy, amulets and incantations, spirit exorcism, and healing by spells and magic ... are superstitions that the state strictly forbids. Burning of votive paper (mannequins, many-storied houses, vehicles, dollars, and cheques...)[11] inside cultural and historical monuments or during festive occasions is prohibited. Installing incense bowls inside public service

---

11. By burning paper money and other paper items, Vietnamese people send these offerings to dead relatives in the afterlife in the belief that such offerings will help their spirits live more comfortably in the other world, and the spirits will help the living in return. In 2018 Vietnamese Buddhist Sangha issued an official document categorizing the burning of votive paper as superstition (available at https://english.vov.vn/society/buddhist-sangha-proposes-eliminating-votive-paper-burning-at-pagodas-369342.vov, last accessed 23 July 2018).

buildings, production facilities, state enterprises, socio-political organizations, or military installations is forbidden.[12]

Note that the government regulation prefers to use the term 'religious beliefs' instead of 'religion' when referring to 'religious freedom'. According to Western usage, 'religious beliefs' here are relegated to the private realm and mainly considered a personal matter (for China, see Ashiwa and Wank 2009; Sutton and Kang 2009: 194). Nonetheless, the lack of a clear differentiation between 'religious beliefs' and 'superstitions' still posed a challenge for the state's officials, and the lack of institutionalized organizations and the fluid and charismatic character of the authorities supporting them makes the practice of 'superstitions' highly resistant to state control (Anagnost 1987: 44).

Trường Thìn (1999) argues that superstitions are related to inadequate public education, and an atheist education is one of the most important aspects of a socialist upbringing when it comes to abolishing superstition. He points out that not enough attention is paid to 'scientific atheism', which should be universally taught in schools, as well as among Party members and other organizations in society (1999: 122–23). Because of their spiritual character, 'religious beliefs' and 'religion' are conducive to developing 'social evils', 'outdated practices', and 'superstitions'. All levels of government are therefore required to plan, guide, and manage religion in order to build a cultured, civilized, clean, and safe environment.

Trường Thìn furthermore argues that the 'ideology of fatalism and predestination' and the 'psychology' of praying for luck are often connected with illicit businesses, embezzlement, bribery, and damage to public health (1999: 125). Hence, in the late 1990s, even as temples and shrines were popping up like mushrooms all over the place, many popular religious specialists and their clients still remained shrouded in an aura of suspicion of malpractice and misappropriation of funds. In its struggle against superstition, the state created stricter laws in order

---

12. Government Regulation 04/1998/TT-BVHTT, quoted in Trường Thìn (1999: 121). See also *Ordinance of the Standing Committee of the National Assembly No.21/2004/Pl-UBTVQH11 of June 2004 Regarding Religious Beliefs and Religious Organizations* (available at http://www.thuvienphapluat.vn/archive/Phap-lenh/Ordinance-No-21-2004-PL-UBTVQH11-of-June-29-2004-on-beliefs-and-religions-vb76132t14.aspx, last accessed 4 June 2018).

to more easily ban fortune tellers, physiognomists, and astrologists, and to eradicate suspect places of worship such as temples and shrines in the recesses of rocky caves or on street corners. The vignette at the beginning of the book describing the fishers' effort to get permission from the authorities to erect a shrine for the statue recovered from the sea is a case in point. Consequently, article 199 of the Vietnamese Penal Code treats the practice of superstition as a crime that is liable to punishment:

> Those who use fortune telling, spirit possession, or other superstitious forms to trigger serious consequences are liable to re-education for one year or to imprisonment for a period of three months to three years. In cases where the crime of superstition has led to death or other extremely serious consequences, the time of imprisonment will be from two to ten years. (Trương Thìn 1999: 124).

The socialist efforts to abolish superstition were not limited to popular religious specialists. Since the early years of the Communist Party, the family also came under socialist scrutiny as a source of 'backwards customs and habits' that were part of everyday life. Since the 1990s, however, family and lineage rituals have been presented as the cement of village communal spirit, as having an educational role in the lives of the people, and as teaching basic concepts of morality. Trương Thìn (1999: 125–126) claims that the most effective method for combatting superstition was to expand the campaign for building 'cultural families' (*gia đình văn hóa*), 'cultural villages' (*làng văn hóa*), 'cultural quarters' (*khu phố văn hóa*), and 'civilized housing estates' (*khu tập thể văn minh*).[13] The cul-

---

13. The 'Civilized Way of Life' campaign, of which the main focus was the 'Cultural Family', had already started by the early 1960s and experienced a number of different phases; for more information see Drummond (2004). This campaign bears a striking similarity to the Chinese discourse on civilization. However, in the case of China, the concept of *wenhua* (Vietnamese: *văn hóa*) or 'culture' was used in the Cultural Revolution and had a class character. Consequently, since the 1980s it has been replaced by *wenming* (Vietnamese: *văn minh*) or 'civilized', which refers to the idea of modernization. In Vietnam, the association of the terms 'cultural' and 'civilized' with 'class' is much weaker than in China, although it is present. For example, the term 'cultural villages' (*làng văn hóa*) refers to the 'peasant class', while the term 'civilized housing estates' (*khu tập thể văn minh*) denotes educated urban elite living in residential blocks in a city. Nevertheless, in Vietnam, the terms 'cultural' and 'civilized' are used interchangeably and are associated with both the whole development of society and with nation building. At the same time, the term 'cultural' is more 'refined' than its Chinese counterpart, as it also connotes

tural campaigns were adapted to the new conditions of a market-oriented society and constituted a crucial component of the new nation-building process; they were designed to help 'prevent and drive back negative practices, social evils, and harmful cultural products' (ibid: 125).[14] The state arrogated to itself the role of educator and patron of Vietnamese society and granted certificates to those who reached the standards of 'modern behaviour', which includes well-being, progressiveness, hygiene and good health, preservation of traditional order, good customs, and civilized ways of life during weddings, funerals, and religious festivals (Drummond 2004; for China see Anagnost 1994, 1997).

〰️

What had begun with drawing a strict boundary between religion and politics in an effort to purify religion under the project of socialist modernity gradually shifted over time to a more pragmatic approach in which certain religious forms were transformed into the more secular concepts of 'cultural' and 'national heritage', while other practices were classified as 'superstition' and were, therefore, forbidden. In that sense, the Party-state continues to see religion as a competing source of power that needs to be controlled and managed. However, the presumed binary oppositions of institutionalized religion versus beliefs, religion versus politics, and science versus superstition are not in practice so clear-cut or static, and the fuzziness of the distinctions leads to the development of novel forms of religiosity that cut across not only religious, but also political, linguistic, and ethnic boundaries. The following chapters relate the events through which Sa Huỳnh and Lý Sơn villagers, state authorities, and religious figures pragmatically reconfigured these binaries and reinvented themselves vis-à-vis larger entities such as mainland, island, and nation to best serve their specific localities and interests.

---

education and literacy. For an excellent discussion of *wenming* campaigns in the context of China, see Anagnost (1997).

14. For more detail on the governmental decision regarding promulgation regulations on granting the honorable titles of 'cultural family', 'cultural village', and 'cultural quarter', see also *Công Báo* (2002a: 4045–4066).

79

Figure 4: Procession in honour of the village's founders, An Hải Village, Lý Sơn.

CHAPTER 3

Between Land and Sea: Spatial and Social Boundaries among Fishers and Farmers

There is a legend among fishers in central Vietnam that the ship of King Gia Long was rescued from sinking by the goddess Quan Âm, who tore a scrap off of her dress and threw it into the sea, creating the whale that carried the royal ship safely to shore on his back. According to local Buddhist beliefs, Quan Âm – the Goddess of Mercy – is a Buddhist bodhisattva who resigned from his search for 'nirvana' and instead assumed a female form in order to help people. Her cult is particularly popular among fishers of the south-central coast region of Vietnam, who believe that she helps them during storms.

Moved by and grateful for the whale's deed, King Gia Long brought the whale into his family and gave him the royal title 'Great General of the Southern Sea' (*Nam Hải Đại tướng quân*). Since this time, fishers in central Vietnam have considered the whale their tutelary spirit and father' (*cha*) who protects them during their voyages at sea. Therefore, whenever they find a beached whale on the shore, they organize a funeral ceremony and erect a temple, which serves as a kind of tomb or mausoleum (*lăng*) for the marine mammal. Every year those fishers celebrate the anniversary of the whale's death and make offerings at the altar in its temple.

According to local narratives, at the beginning of the nineteenth century Lý Sơn farmers found a whale beached on the shore just opposite the temple of the Goddess of the Five Elements (*Bà Chúa Ngũ Hạnh*), which belonged to the village An Vĩnh. The five statues of this goddess represent Fire, Earth, Metal, Water, and Wood, and maintain

81

the balance between *yin* (*âm*) and *yang* (*dương*) – the principles of order and disorder, internal and external, and of male and female domains. The farmers decided that the seafaring deity representing the male domain would complement the Goddess of the Five Elements. The fishers' organization, Vĩnh Thạnh, protested and claimed the property rights to the beached whale. However, the farmers did not want to yield and remained steadfast in their decision. They strongly believed that the Whale Spirit had chosen their village to send rain in time of drought and to improve crops. Subsequently, the land-oriented village (*làng*) and the fishing organization (*vạn*) reached a compromise by building two separate temples: the *Inner* Dune Palace (*dinh Cồn Trong*), representing the farmers, and the *Outer* Dune Tomb (*lăng Cồn Ngoài*), representing fishers. The two temples were designated for the veneration of the Whale Spirit, which was revered by both farmers and fishers alike under his full name, Great and Cruel General of the Southern Sea (*Nam Hải Dạ Sa Đại tướng quân tôn thần*). The farming village decided that the fishers' anniversary celebration in the Outer Dune Tomb could precede the one organized by the farmers, but as a sign of the fishing organization's respect for the agriculturally oriented village, the celebration could not be held without the presence of the village senior – the ritual master of high sacrifice and representative of the founding lineage and, hence, a farmer.

〜〜
〜〜

In traditional, predominantly agrarian Islamic, Hindu, and Buddhist societies, fishers were considered 'out of culture' and of lower social status (Serjant 1995; Chou 2003, 2010; Hoeppe 2007; Subramanian 2009). In Ming China (1368–1644), those who lived along the coast formed a separate social category within a settled agrarian society and did not have rights to permanent settlement (Xi and Faure 2016). Historian Trần Quốc Vượng (1992: 29) noted that in precolonial and colonial Vietnam, fishing was a despised occupation and fishers constituted one of the most marginalized groups in society. Landless, without roots in the village, and living in areas close to the sea and rivers, fishers were discriminated against and deprived of the spiritual and material amenities offered by the village. Even though much has changed in postcolonial times with the introduction of refrigeration, modern navigational systems, large-capacity fishing vessels, and the recent extension of economic initiatives to fishers – especially in the context of Vietnam's and China's competing claims to the South China Sea – the hierarchical divide between the worlds of the *land* and the *sea* still structures the coastal society of central Vietnam.

In his classic monograph on Malay fishermen, Raymond Firth (1964) demonstrated that in coastal areas, fishers often live side by side with people of other occupations, including farmers, with whom they maintain economic and frequently intimate relations. Michael Pearson (1985: 3), a historian of the Indian Ocean, goes a step further, stating that 'land and the sea intertwine in complex and various ways' and arguing that we have to be careful not to see the people living on the shore as totally land- or sea-oriented. Indeed, coastal people's cosmology is infused with ambivalence as they look both to the inland/mainland and to the sea as a means of livelihood and as a cosmological and sovereign centre. Yet the examples of Sa Huỳnh and Lý Sơn show that people themselves hold to a cognitive dichotomy in which the two modes of life – farming and fishing – are thought of as completely separate, even though in everyday life the two activities might mix. In Sa Huỳnh and Lý Sơn Island, the hierarchy between fishers and farmers is reproduced in the two vernacular terms *làng* and *vạn*, which appeared in almost every conversation I had with villagers.

In precolonial and colonial Vietnam, *làng* (village) constituted the territorial unit of Vietnamese society and represented an agriculture-based lifestyle, with the political and ritual system based in the *đình* (communal house). In the *đình*, villagers spiritually ensured a good harvest for the upcoming year through the worship of those who first broke the land under the plough (*tiền hiền*) and of the founders of the village (*tiền hậu*).[1] In central Vietnam, *vạn* referred both to a self-ruling fishing organization and to a territorial unit with its own religious system that was based in the *lăng*, a temple for the cult of a seafaring guardian spirit,

---

1. In central and southern Vietnam communal houses were characteristically erected in honour of the *tiền hiền* and the *tiền hậu*: those who first broke the land under the plough and the founders of the village, respectively. If the communal house was a northern *đình*, it would be a shrine for the village guardian spirit, who could be either a historical or a mythical person.

the Whale, who was usually referred to as Mr Nam Hải.[2] In the *lăng* – literally 'tomb' or 'mausoleum' – fishers kept bones of the beached whale. The fact that whales are considered seafaring guardian spirits speaks volumes about fishermen's concerns. Exposed to cold wind, rough seas, unpredictable threats, and equipment failure, fishers frequently endure great psychological stress and constant economic pressure in their everyday lives. Through propitiating the Whale Spirit they seek to ensure their own protection rather than the fertility of the land and the bounty of the harvest and, hence, the welfare of the village.

Pearson (2006: 366) writes that '[f]olk religion on the littoral ... reflects the need of its practitioners. The concerns of coastal people were usually quite different from those of peasants and pastoralists inland. On the coast religion had to do with customs to ensure safe voyages or a large catch, or a favorable monsoon so that fishing could recommence. Particular gods were propitiated for these purposes.' The vignette above is a good illustration of Pearson's point about different concerns of agriculturalists, whose main worry in this context was rain for their crops, and of fishers, who were more concerned with guaranteeing safe passage at sea. Here we touch on the heart of the problem – different perceptions of what constitutes *valuable* work.

In many Asian societies farmers have historically looked down upon fishers because fishing was considered the easier way of life. In contrast to the hard labour of a farmer, who had to invest a great deal of labour cultivating the soil and looking after the fields in order to enjoy his yields, a fisher, it was believed, just invested in his gear, went to sea, and extracted its produce, giving nothing in return. In precolonial and colonial Vietnam, rice was considered the essential staple, in part

---

2. In northern Vietnam and the northern coast of central Vietnam, the *vạn* was known in the form of floating communities that lived on boats along the banks of rivers or in the lagoons (Nguyễn Duy Thiệu 2002; Hoang Ba Tinh 2006). Called Đản in Vietnam and *Dan-jia* in southern China (Xi and Faure 2016), these boat dwellers formed small hamlets whose populations were unstable as fishers often move in search of new fishing areas (Nguyễn Duy Thiệu 2002: 91–92). In northern Vietnam there were also so-called fishing villages (*làng đánh cá*), whose inhabitants engaged in both fishing and farming. These villages resembled the fairly common 'craft villages' (*làng nghệ*) whose inhabitants were experts in goldsmithery, the production of conical hats, the manufacture of furniture, silk, and the like, alongside agriculture (see, e.g., Toàn Ánh 2005 [1968]; DiGregorio 2007).

because it could be stored for long periods and used in times of famine. In this sense farm labour was highly valued. Unlike rice, fish had to be consumed shortly after catching and, hence, just added variety to a farmer's diet, which predominantly consisted of boiled rice, sometimes with a drop of fish sauce and some vegetables (Jamieson 1985). The old Vietnamese folk proverb – 'In the village, the scholars come first, the farmers come second; but when the rice runs out and one wanders [in search of a bowl of rice], scholars come after farmers' – gives us a sense of how highly valued farming was and how a good rice harvest was seen as a guarantee that villagers would not starve (Nguyễn Duy Thiệu 2002: 118).

The introductory vignette tells us something else as well. The two religious arenas – the *Inner* Dune Palace representing farmers and the *Outer* Dune Tomb representing fishers – epitomized competing spatial imaginaries that territorialized the coast and its inhabitants as the space *outside* the hierarchical agrarian world of the *inland*. Thus, the struggle for the right to the Whale Spirit took place not only within the existing binary relationship of farmers and fishers, but also within the spatial, cognitive, and social divide between *land* and *sea*, between *inland* and *coast*, and between *mainland* and *island*. This is where the question arises: what does it mean for people living on the coast of the South China Sea to have two main livelihoods – farming and fishing – within their communities? This chapter places the discussion on fishers and farmers in historical perspective in order to explore how the distinction between these two modes of life – which often complemented each other – became the basis not only for constructing and maintaining, but also for *deconstructing* a social and ritual dichotomy of land and sea in Sa Huỳnh and Lý Sơn. As I will show, this idealized land–sea binary was never absolute, and it shifted in postcolonial times when the state's antisuperstition measures provided the historically subordinated fishers with room to challenge the old hierarchy. The fishers took advantage of the Party-state's attack on all forms of social differentiation in terms of class, gender, seating order, and ritual function that the *đình*, the village's political and ritual centre, reproduced. Uplifted by a recent reversal in economic fortunes due to the availability of trawling, refrigeration technologies, and domestic and global demand for marine produce, fishers have attained a relatively stronger economic position than farmers and, by investing heavily in agricultural temples and rituals, have turned the tables and upended the old hierarchical divide.

The recent conflict over the South China Sea has opened up a new maritime frontier in Vietnam that overemphasizes the sea as part of the rebranded 'maritime nation' (*nước biển*; literally 'water [and] sea') and, paradoxically, sharpens the spatial and social binaries between farmers and fishers. While the centrality of water has always been present in Vietnamese cosmology and Vietnamese vocabulary – as is particularly well illustrated in the Vietnamese words for 'country' (*đất nước*; literally 'land [and] water') and 'government' (*nhà nước*; literally 'house [and] water') (Avieli 2012: 28) – the term *nước biển* places a new emphasis on the sea and the coast. The state's domestication and instrumentalization of fishers draws the entire population into performance of national sovereignty and, somewhat ironically, draws the periphery – such as Lý Sơn – into the centre. Even though fishers are often seen by the dominant urban population as ignorant, backwards, and in urgent need of national development, they could be confident, even if only for a fleeting moment, that their fishing profession is seen as a sacrifice – willing or unwilling – to the nation, as they stand bravely on the frontlines in the struggle for national sovereignty.

The land–sea dichotomy

Inland versus coast

If we look at the geography of Vietnam, we see that in central Vietnam a narrow strip of lowlands linking the Red River Delta region in the north and the Mekong River Delta region in the south is sandwiched between the South China Sea to the east and the Trường Sơn range to the west. These lowlands consist of alluvial plains and sandy strips of coastal dunes. In the sixteenth to the eighteenth centuries, newcomers to Quảng Ngãi Province deforested vast areas of the region to create arable land for rice cultivation and to establish villages grounded on the patrilineages of their places of origin. These groups assumed prominent positions on the basis of their prestige as first settlers in the frontier area even though, in their place of origin, they may have been outcasts. They invested their labour in the land, thereby making it their property. Soon after a new village received its name it was included in the province register and, like in the north, the villagers could officially erect a *đình*, which, as mentioned earlier, was the political and ritual centre of the village (Nguyễn Văn Mạnh 1999).[3] The memory of their arrival and of their right to the new land was preserved in the local *đình* through the cult of the founders. The exclusive character of the founders' cult had a disadvantageous effect on later newcomers, who were refused village membership and hence the right to own land. Making the best of the natural conditions in the new environs, they formed *vạn* on sandy strips of coastal dunes and depended on fishing and trade for their livelihoods.

Toàn Ánh (2005 [1968]) observed that new 'hamlets' in central Vietnam were established not only by those who arrived later than the founding group and were denied land rights in the existing villages, but also when there was not enough land for the original settlers, if the land was barren, or if some of the founding families decided to resettle in the vicinity of a river, the sea, or the forest to earn their living fishing, producing salt, or clearing the forest. They would request permission from the village to establish a new hamlet to be run by a separate chief, although it would remain administratively subordinate to the village. In the course of time the newly created hamlet could become an autonomous village (Toàn Ánh 2005 [1968]: 23, 31, 121). This was the case for the villages of Đồng Vân and Tân Diêm in Sa Huỳnh. Situated on the most favourable land, La Vân was regarded as the head village, while adjacent Đồng Vân and Tân Diêm formed small dependent hamlets. Inhabitants of Tân Diêm – located closer to the sea – are to this day engaged in producing salt, while Đồng Vân, situated in the hills, combines forestry and agriculture. Long Thạnh, Thạch By, and Thạnh Đức, located on the sandy dunes, represent a different process. They developed into salt-making and fishing communities (*vạn*) that constituted settlements outside of the *làng* system and hence outside of the state administration.

In Sa Huỳnh, according to local narratives, the most fertile plains were occupied by the first Việt migrants coming from the north. The village 'convention' (*hương ước*) of Sa Huỳnh indicates that the agricultural village of La Vân had already been established by 1740.[4] The fishing

---

3. In many cases, villages founded by northern migrants in central Vietnam were named after their places of origin; An Vĩnh and An Hải villages on Lý Sơn were named after villages in Bình Sơn district, Quảng Ngãi Province.

4. See *Hương ước, Đức Phổ* (Village convention of Đức Phổ District). (1937). Hanoi: École Francaise D'Extrême – Orient. Unpublished manuscript, Library of Social

settlement Thạch By was established much later than La Vân, namely in 1816. This rather later establishment of the fishing settlement suggests that, at that time, the Cham population was still present in the area. The Việt who settled in the most remote parts of the coastal area intermixed with the Cham population, gradually taking over salt fields and salt production. Outnumbered by Việt, the Cham were forced to adopt some of their customs, including dress and language (see Wong Tze Ken 2016), leading to a blurring of the distinction between Việt and Cham settlements in this area. It also helps explain the conflation of professional and ethnic categories in the minds of the farming-oriented population, as all fishers, whether of Việt, Cham, or other ethnic background, were contemptuously called *hạ*, meaning 'lower rank, inferior people' living along the coast, or *mọi*, meaning 'barbarous' or 'savage' – terms that had in the past been used exclusively to refer to Cham or other ethnic minorities in the Central Highlands (see Nguyễn Duy Thiệu 2002: 88). Due to their seafaring and foraging way of life, the coastal and island people in Central Vietnam were also known as 'lowland barbarians' (*mọi hạ*) or 'sea barbarians' (*mọi nước*) (Ner 1940: 475-7).

Island versus mainland

While Sa Huỳnh's composition of fishing and farming hamlets illustrates well the division between the *coast* and *inland* and between *land* and *sea* activities, Lý Sơn provides an interesting case of an attempt to emulate the mainland pattern even though on the island there was *no* arable land for wet rice cultivation. The lack of arable land and, hence, the inability to grow rice is an important detail that sheds new light on the formation of categories such as *làng* and *vạn*. In the face of serious physical constraints to growing rice, islanders tried to control access to limited resources by reproducing the hierarchical division between farmers and fishers that they knew from the mainland. Coming from the northern coastal provinces of Thanh Hóa, Nghệ An, and Hà Tĩnh, some of the 'founders' and 'great lineages' may well have had the lower

---

Science, Hanoi. Under the Lê and Nguyễn dynasties a clash of the dual system – official and unofficial – of village administration brought about the 'convention' (*hương ước*), which was a 'mixture of administrative rules, customary laws and religious guidelines. The purpose of the convention was to regulate the interactions and relationships of each village's society' (Tonan 2008: 748; see also Grossheim 1996; Phan Huy Lê 2006; Nguyễn Thị Kim Bình 2006).

status of fishers, but in the new setting, by taking advantage of being first, they established themselves as superior *làng*.[5] The recognized descendants of the 'founders' formed dominant lineages and an unofficial channel of grassroots administration as chiefs of hamlets (*xóm*) and sub-hamlets (*lân*) operating within the context of the 'patrilineages' of the village. Other lineages whose precursors came shortly after the founders were ranked alongside the 'founders' but were not accorded the same power; these lineages were called *tộc lớn* or 'great lineages'. This hierarchical stratification survives on the island to this day and is displayed in religious and ritual practices. All these groups recorded their genealogies (*gia phả*) in ancestral halls of the individual lineages (*nhà thờ họ*). Others, who could have been either fishers or peasants, were not admitted to the *đình* order and did not share equal rights as village members because they arrived much later than the 'founders' and 'great lineages' and therefore did not have access to free land. They had to obtain permission from the 'founders' or 'great lineages' to buy plots of land and build houses within the territory of the village, but even in such cases they were not considered legitimate village members. Having been denied village membership, they joined forces and formed a *vạn* with its own civil code, although it was still subordinate to the village.

In contrast to mainland central Vietnam, where fishing communities occupied sandy dunes and, thus, could be easily distinguished from agricultural villages with their surrounding rice fields, on Lý Sơn Island fishing and farming settlements merged with each other precisely because of the lack of arable land for rice cultivation. More specifically, the two *xã* of An Vĩnh and An Hải were established in the seventeenth century as two *làng*, but shared their territory with two *vạn*: Vĩnh Thạnh and An Phú. *Vạn* Vĩnh Thạnh was positioned within the territory of An Vĩnh village, while *vạn* An Phú overlapped with An Hải village. This arrangement survives today. But those who formed a *làng* could not claim superior status on the basis of investment in rice cultivation nor could they produce the crop that would rescue the village from starvation in times of famine. Unable to maintain strict physical boundaries between the *làng* and the *vạn*, *làng* members of the two villages nurtured these separate categories through rituals and ceremonies and through claims

---

5. See local family records (*gia phả*), Lý Sơn Island.

that their ancestors were the first settlers on the island who tamed the new 'wild' land and founded the villages.

Fisher as a relational category

Thanks to the annals and local narratives preserved in Lý Sơn, as well as to historical records by Lê Quý Đôn ([1776] 2006), we know that the Paracel and Spratly navies collected and traded goods from wrecked ships. These navies consisted of both those who were members of the founding lineages and those who belonged to the organization called *vạn*. The latter group in particular most likely consisted of assimilated Cham, as it was a common practice for the imperial court in Huế to enlist experienced Cham 'fishers', who often were skilful sailors, shipbuilders, and traders, in the navy (Bộ Ngoại Giao 2013: 10–11). Moreover, according to records from An Vĩnh's temple, the *vạn* in Lý Sơn was more than just a fishing organization; in fact it was, above all, a trading organization (*vạn giao thương*), as is confirmed by their various maritime ventures to the Paracels and Spratlys as well as to Cochinchina, as described in Chapter 1.[6]

For the small island societies with a limited resource base such as Lý Sơn, salvaging cargo from wrecked European merchant ships was one of their sea-borne occupations. The recovery of gold, silver, swords, ivory, porcelain, cloth, wax, and many other goods from the Dutch, Spanish, Portuguese, and British wrecks was so profitable that Lý Sơn sailors were granted a royal concession to salvage the cargos. The spoils – often supplemented with catches of mother-of-pearl, snails, tortoises, and sea cucumber – were handed over to the royal court in Huế (Lê Quý Đôn [1776] 2006: 155) Besides being exempted from taxes, the sailors received some monetary reward and were allowed to keep a large part of the harvested marine goods for their own profit (Lê Quý Đôn [1776] 2006: 155). In an interview, a forty-nine-year-old fisher describes these activities, using the phrase 'collecting things' to refer to salvaging cargo that could be traded for profit:

> Previously Lý Sơn people used to go on sailing boats and, I think, because of that, having only sailing boats, they were still able to go to the Paracels. They kept sailing to the Paracels not because of the royal order, which at that time was just a small part of their activities, but because the Paracels were located on the Silk Road, the trade route of, for example, Chinese, Dutch, Spanish, Portuguese. All kinds of people

---

6. See the Hán-Nôm document of Vĩnh Thạnh *vạn* in An Vĩnh commune, Lý Sơn Island.

passed through there, so they [Lý Sơn people] followed that route and its trade up to the Paracels. There the Hoàng Sa [Paracel] flotilla was responsible for collecting things such as guns, steel, and porcelain. ... I tell you, some families in Lý Sơn, if they traded, they would get very rich. Lý Sơn was very rich, so the guiding principle of Lý Sơn [people] at that time was: 'To get rich one must do trade' (*muốn làm giàu phải đi buôn*) or, as they put it, 'Without trade there will be no prosperity' (*Phi thương là bất phú*), meaning that in order to get rich, you must engage in trading. So those in Lý Sơn who did trade were economically better off.

Historians provide well-documented studies showing that seasonally organized piracy, plundering, and smuggling in the South China Sea were sometimes turned into formalized trade (Antony 2014; Wang 2014; Wheeler 2015). Historically, these activities constituted an important part of local life and economy and supplemented fishing. There was a popular saying that fishers 'soak up wealth like a sponge' (*giàu bọt nước*), hinting at the perception that their profit from trade was not morally justified, especially when compared to the hard work of preparing the soil for cultivation (Nguyễn Duy Thiệu 2002: 118). Moreover, coastal settlements and, especially, islands were seen as a frontier of pirates and smugglers who could always find a good hideaway somewhere along the South China Sea coasts (see Watson 1985; Murray 1987; Kleinen and Osseweijer 2010). Known in British logbooks as Guangdong or Pulo Canton, Lý Sơn Island was a dangerous and inaccessible place for ships to anchor due to the coral reef and rocks surrounding its coast (White 1824: 75), and it was thus a perfect location for those people the Europeans called 'pirates'. A hilly, narrow tip of Sa Huỳnh peninsula that encloses a big sandbar also used to serve as a good hiding place for various smugglers and their junks. Away from prying eyes, they could secretly haul their illicit cargo from the open sea back to the sandbar or sail it further down the coast if the need arose.

Vạn as 'guild' and 'territorial unit'

In their study of two working-class neighbourhoods in a small English town, Elias and Scotson (1994: xviii) show that exclusion and stigmatization of outsiders through social control are the most powerful weapons employed by the established group 'to maintain their identity, to assert their superiority, keeping others in their place'. In the case of Vietnam, a fisherman without landed property and unregistered in the village was not allowed to marry into a farmer's family. Moreover, fishers were forbidden to settle in farming-oriented villages. Thoại, a retired fisherman in Sa Huỳnh born in 1940, described fishers as 'stateless' people by pointing out the divide between coast and inland:

> In the past, the coastline was only for those involved in marine professions, while the inland was controlled by the government, the state. … When you do fishing you do not have any land, not even a plot of ground to bury yourself; when you die your family has to ask the village (*làng*) to bury you. This is the custom of the forefathers of the poverty-stricken northern people who came here to work.

In Sa Huỳnh and Lý Sơn, the *làng* maintains its superior status through memories about the common origin of its members, collective feasts, and rituals organized in the *đình*. The *làng* despised the fishing hamlet and excluded its residents from local affairs taking place in the *đình*. In Sa Huỳnh the position of fishers was particularly inferior because they were permitted to occupy only the narrow strip of sandy dunes. Being spatially separated from the agrarian village, fishers did not have agricultural land and, thus, could not produce rice.

Nguyễn Duy Thiệu (2002: 334) points out that in precolonial and colonial times, the *vạn* in the southern part of central Vietnam did not have a formal administrative apparatus and was, above all, a *religious* organization. However, Thoại's statement suggests that the *vạn* in Sa Huỳnh was also a settlement. Indeed, Sa Huỳnh *vạn* has its genesis in a *professional* and *religious* organization, but it was also a 'territorial unit' which functioned according to its own rules, similar to a village in which residents formed patrilineal groups and had the same occupation. Unlike the northern *vạn*, which consisted exclusively of those who lived on the water in boats, the *vạn* in central Vietnam was established by those living on the sandy dunes; it was modelled on the social structure of the land-oriented village, but was a looser and more open entity.

While the *làng* had its *đình*, the *vạn* also had its own communal temple (*lăng*). There fishers venerated their guardian spirit and discussed public matters. According to Nguyễn Duy Thiệu (2002: 334–335), the charters (*sắc phong*) granted to the fishermen's temples by the Nguyễn dynasty (1802–1945) indicate that the *vạn* was a religious organization. The common feature of these charters, which certified the *vạn*, was a royal title conferred upon whales by King Gia Long: 'High-ranking Spirit of the Southern Sea' (*Nam Hải Cự Tộc Ngọc Lân Thượng Đẳng Thần*) or 'Great General of the Southern Sea' (*Nam Hải Đại tướng quân*) (see the vignette at the beginning of the chapter). However, Nguyễn Duy Thiệu's argument about the *vạn* as a religious organization could also be applied to the *làng*, which acquired the legitimate rank of village in a similar way, through a royal charter recognizing the cult of the guardian spirit in the local *đình*.

Another important aspect of the *vạn* in Sa Huỳnh and Lý Sơn was the non-hereditary position of the head of the *vạn* (*chủ vạn*), a kind of professional leader and ritual master elected every three years from among the most experienced and prosperous fishermen. This institution has survived in Sa Huỳnh and Lý Sơn almost unchanged through the present day. Xướng (born in 1933), a head of Vĩnh Thạnh *vạn* (Lý Sơn), stressed that for as long as anyone could remember, the election of the head fisherman had always been conducted according to egalitarian principles:

> This position cannot be kept for long. The fishermen's chief has to resign from the post, and the next chief arises to continue the plans, projects, and much work; thanks to them, all matters are discussed again, materials are purchased, everything for the people.

The chief's wealth or lineage status had never been a determining criterion; more important was his moral conduct and authority among fishermen. His unblemished reputation and nomination was 'spiritually' approved by the Whale Spirit through the spirit medium *séance* held in a local temple. For Sa Huỳnh and Lý Sơn fishers, the function of the head of the *vạn* had far-reaching significance because he could facilitate or constrain their relationship with the sea. A chief's breach of good manners or corrupt behaviour might prevent the entire *vạn* from enjoying good catches or could even cause accidents. As Xướng described it:

> The head of the *vạn* is responsible and takes care of the profession and the people working at sea. For example, at the beginning of a year he prays for a good season at sea and for the fishermen who go to sea. If they do not have any accidents, it is because of him. If the head of the *vạn* acts contrary to the regulation of the divine (*thần linh giao*), then the working people run into difficulties – something terrible might happen, for example bad weather, and people would die. The head of the *vạn* has

to take responsibility before the divine and the people. ... He is elected by fellow villagers, but it is the Whale Spirit who decides whether he has enough merit. Most important are his authority and reputation; to be selected to be the head, he has to have a sincere heart (*có tâm*) and he has to serve the Whale Spirit. He would be elected for the first, the second, and the third year if he had a sincere heart and was virtuous in his service to the people making a living. Second, he has to have merit (*công*) with the local community, like me when I am doing social works. A good service allows one to be promoted to the head of the *vạn* position, to supervise the 'private office' [i.e., the Whale Spirit temple] of the divinity (*coi sở tự cho thần linh*), to be responsible, to contribute ideas and opinions, and to resolve problems when something goes wrong.

The proper conduct of the head of the *vạn* assured the generosity of the sea and the well-being of the entire fishing community. The fishermen and their families respected him and benefited from his knowledge, experience, advice, and his 'spiritual' relationship with the Whale Spirit. Xướng's interpretation captured certain aspects of the genesis of the *vạn* in central Vietnam as a religious, professional, and more egalitarian organization than the *làng*, and to some extent confirms Nguyễn Duy Thiệu's view.

The fishing settlements of Thạch By and Thạnh Đức are called in vernacular Vietnamese *vạn chày* or simply *vạn*, which literally means 'floating fishing community'. In the context of Sa Huỳnh, the term denotes the fishers who are clustered along the beach in separate hamlets. In Sa Huỳnh, the *vạn* of Thạch By and Thạnh Đức traditionally employed diverse fishing techniques. In Thạch By there are two territorially distinct sub-hamlets with different methods of catching fish. Each of these two settlements owns an individual Spirit Whale Temple, forms a distinct *vạn*, and has its own chief. Using a different fishing technique, the third hamlet of Thạnh Đức represents a separate *vạn* and has its own temple. These three *vạn*s are divided and referred to on the basis of their traditional fishing tools and techniques – the net *vạn*, the hook *vạn*, and the lift net *vạn* – but, at the same time, they are bound together through ritual and seafaring ceremonies. However, on Lý Sơn Island the two *vạn*s – Vĩnh Thạnh and An Phú – formed neither clusters nor occupied a territory separate from that of An Vĩnh and An Hải villages in a manner similar to that found in Sa Huỳnh. Their members never made distinctions among themselves on the basis of fishing techniques; rather, they differentiated themselves on the basis of the *làng* to which their *vạn* belonged.

When compared with the *làng*, the *vạn* appears to be a more egalitarian organization due to the nature of the fishing profession, which often involves considerable hazard. Work at sea requires cooperation, mutual trust, and equal investment of labour from the whole crew on board, regardless of whether one is a captain or a 'common' fisherman. However, it does not mean that within the *vạn* there were no hierarchical relations; indeed, even there the land–sea dichotomy was firmly established and at times contested. The *vạns* of Thạch By and Thạnh Đức provide a good example of such shifting spatial imaginaries. Up to the present day, the 'net *vạn*' (*vạn lưới*), Thạch By, claims to be the leading organization and the leading territorial unit because of its direct access to Sa Huỳnh port, which was located directly off its shore. The superior status of the 'net *vạn*' is contested from time to time by the inhabitants of the big sandbar adjacent to Thạch By, who claimed to be more experienced and skilful in the art of fishing. Territorially, this big sandbar, a sort of island enclosed by Sa Huỳnh Peninsula, was part of Thạch By, but it formed a separate small fishing 'guild' called the 'hook *vạn*' (*vạn câu bủa*), which operated in the open sea, in contrast to the 'net *vạn*', which preferred to fish close to the shore. Thạnh Đức constituted the 'lift net *vạn*' (*vạn lưới giả cào*) – representing the third type of fishing device that was also used close to the shore. Although Thạnh Đức considered itself an independent *vạn*, it had a duty to show up at the ceremony devoted to the Whale Spirit's anniversary in Thạch By. Moreover, during the Lunar New Year it was the chief of Thạch By *vạn* who represented the entire community of fishers in Sa Huỳnh and opened the new sea season. U, who was forty-five years old at the time I interviewed him and who spent most of his life at sea, compared the structure of the three *vạn* of Thạch By and Thạnh Đức to an office:

> The *vạn* is ruled by the chiefs. Each craft village [*làng nghệ* – here referring to the 'hook', the 'net', and the 'lift net *vạn*'] has a different specialization. The head of the 'net *vạn*' of Thạch By is like a director; the individual chiefs of the two others are like vice-directors – something like the personnel in an office. On the third day of a new year, the head of the *vạn* is the first to go to sea in the new season.

U also used the phrase 'craft village', the term usually applied to villages that specialize in a particular profession in addition to agriculture. In U's speech the two categories of 'occupational' and 'territorial' overlapped. This suggests that for U the *vạn* was both a 'hamlet' and a 'professional organization'.

In this sense, a loose analogy could be made between the *vạn* and a 'guild' – such as those of medieval Europe, which were established as professional associations and sanctioned by secular and religious authority. The European guilds were also religious fraternities and, under the patronage of specific saints, carried out feasts and ceremonies. As I noted earlier, the *vạn* was certified by the royal charter, which recognized the religious character of the fishing organization. In some cases, the king granted selected fishing communities the right to salvage goods from wrecked ships, as was the case for Lý Sơn. Similarly, the medieval guild, comprised of experts trained in a given craft, was established by a city charter or a ruler and held a monopoly on trade in its craft within the city where it operated (Grafe and Gelderblom 2010).

Another loose comparison could also be drawn concerning certain rules that the medieval guild in Europe imposed on its members. First of all, the guilds in Europe had their own statutes. According to these statutes, the members were under oath to use the craft techniques that were standardized and controlled by their guild. Additionally, the statutes regulated feasting, religious ceremonies dedicated to the guild's patron saint, funerals, and contributions to a common fund for mutual assistance in times of distress. In the case of Vietnam, the self-ruled *vạn* remained outside of the (agricultural) village and regulated its matters through its own 'convention'. Administered by a chief of the *vạn*, this convention allowed outsiders to join the *vạn* and become members after contributing a small amount of money. The main issues regulated by the convention concerned the duty of mutual assistance in the profession, especially in case of storms and typhoons at sea; indicating where boats of the individual *vạn* had a right to anchor and to catch fish; specifying the fishing season; and prohibiting the catching of certain species of poisonous fish. Furthermore, the convention regulated religious festivals, life-cycle rituals such as births, weddings, and funerals, and work for the restoration of temples (Nguyễn Duy Thiệu 2002: 135–137).

From what has been said thus far, it should be clear that the *vạn* – whether professional or religious organization or territorial unit – was not a static institution with clearly defined boundaries, but was, rather, a flexible strategy of controlling marine resources and providing mutual support to its members. Far from being absolute and independent, *vạns* were often situated within the control of and in relation to a larger land-oriented village system. The following section says a few words about the hierarchical *làng*, which has ceased to exist, in contrast to the *vạn*, which have survived to the present day.

Làng system

'Our village lost its sanctity!' This was the bitter sentiment of seventy-year-old Hập (born 1937) of Lý Sơn when I asked him about changes in the structure of the land-oriented village. He was a descendant of one of the founding lineages and he kept the memory of his great-grandfather, who had held the position of village senior and ritual master in the local *đình* of An Hải village and was proficient in demotic Hán-Nôm (Sino-Vietnamese) script. When Hập explained in more detail the dramatic changes that were occurring in the village politics, I could sense a note of nostalgia for an old moral world and tradition that had faded and then vanished in the tumultuous history of Vietnam. Hập himself was a respected architect and a consultant for the state in reconstructing the communal house in An Vĩnh village, which had been neglected during the antisuperstition campaigns and finally collapsed. Hập's statement captures the changes in the nature of village ritual practice in Lý Sơn, a practice that was embodied in an array of hierarchical and political relations and expressed in terms of both material and spiritual resources:

> Before [1975] our *đình* had the Council of Notables. The village senior of the council managed the *đình* and conducted ceremonies. Some years after the liberation, the state restored beliefs (*tín ngưỡng*), but there is nothing left of the previous forces (*lực lượng*) of the *đình*. The chief of the hamlet (*xóm*) of the temple [of the goddess ThiênY A Na] had to move up to run the *đình*...
>
> Our village has lost its soul (*mất tâm linh*) because in these days the representation in rituals does not come from the apex as it did in the past, but from below. ... The chairman of the commune (*chủ tịch xã*) took over the position of the village head (*lý trưởng*), and nowadays it has nothing to do with religion.

Hập underscored the present-day separation of politics and religion and how village space, in which the village headman (*lý trưởng*) and the

Five Notables used to represent the apex of the politico-administrative hierarchy, has been restructured. Nghị (born 1922), another descendent of a founding lineage on Lý Sơn, clearly remembered that before 1975, performing rites as a ritual master of high sacrifice was the most important ceremonial function of the village senior, who spiritually represented the *làng* before the divinity in the *đình*. He was required to be a descendent of one of the village's founding lineages. Although nominally this position was not included in the official administrative apparatus, the village senior was held in high regard by both village and *vạn*, even though the latter was outside of the *đình* system. Below the village senior was the village headman, whose power was authorized and legitimated in the local *đình*. Nghị described who, at that time, ran the village:

> Before the village headman occupied a position in the administrative apparatus, the village senior held the highest position in the village. He was bound to the divine (*thần linh*) and he could contact the sacred (*linh thiêng*). As regards the system of power, the administrative apparatus included the village headman, who managed village affairs; at that time he was like [today's] chairman of the commune (*chủ tịch xã*). At the top of the village stood the village senior; below him was the village headman, who managed staff including the village officials: the keeper of hygiene (*hương dịch*), the guardian of public works (*hương mục*), the head night-watchman [policeman – *hương kiểm*], the treasurer (*hương bổn*), the registrar (*hương bộ*), and the group running various works (*ban chấp sự*). ... The guardian of public works managed procurement [buying offerings for ceremonies], the registrar kept the records, and the *ban chấp sự* was responsible for invitations and supplies.

Like Hập, Nghị emphasized that the position of village senior had lost a lot of its former political power in the spiritual sense, but for him and many representatives of the older generations, the village senior still remains superior to the secular post of chairman. As Nghị put it,

> Today there is no treasurer or village headman – the village dignitaries – anymore. ... The positions were abolished in the time of the 'state distribution economy' (*thời bao cấp*);[7] the old system was eliminated by

---

7. Vietnamese people often use euphemisms that cannot be translated into English directly. In this case the expression *thời bao cấp* – literally 'subsidy era' – in a loose translation means 'the state distribution economy' and denotes the time of collectivization and dependence on the state's handouts. 'The state distribution economy' lasted from 1977 to 1986.

the state administration. ... After the liberation [in 1975], everything was gone; only the position of village senior remained. ... [Nowadays], the village senior has two duties: to keep the financial contributions of the village and to record them. He stands higher than the chairman of the commune; he is the one who communicates with the divine [in the communal house].

Actually, in the South the break in the relationship between religion and politics occurred long before the socialist procedures definitively separated the two domains. Referring to Francophone scholar Lê Văn Hảo, Thien Do (2003: 60) reported that the southern *đình* served a solely religious purpose. The distinctive character of the southern *đình* was the consequence of changes in the village's social structure applied by the French administration in 1904. The *đình*'s decision-making model was split into 'two unequal parts': the ceremonial function and secular administrative activities (ibid.). In their booklet *Geography of Quảng Ngãi Province* (*Địa Dư tỉnh Quảng Ngãi*), Nguyễn Đóa and Nguyễn Đạt Nhơn (1939) provide evidence of the colonial division of administrative and religious spheres in the province in the form of two separate formations: the Assistant District Chief (*Quan Bang Tá*) and the Festive Committee (*Ban Khánh Tiết*). According to this division, the notables who were responsible for performing rites in the *đình* were, in theory, not allowed to take part in any administrative affairs of the village, which were subsequently reserved for a committee of officials.

However, my further conversations with Lý Sơn villagers indicate that the religion–politics binary was not absolute, as village notables and elders who were theoretically left out of village politics due to the colonial regulation still had significant influence over the village officials to whom they ascribed ritual roles during the communal ceremonies. These officials often participated in such formal religious procedures in order to increase their authority. This old pattern of village power was still intact in Lý Sơn on the early 1960s even though the southern authorities abolished the institutions of village headmen and the Five Notables and introduced new forms of village administration. After 1975, the Office of the People's Committee and the Administrative Committee were established on the island, and the *đình* system was ultimately abolished.

Fishers' retribution during the antisuperstition campaigns

In contrast to Hập and Nghị (Lý Sơn), Thoại, a fisherman from Sa Huỳnh, did not lament the decline of the *đình* hierarchical order or the socialist restructuring of local village politics. He offered his own explanation for the separation of politics and religion:

> In the old days, the village senior, the village headman (*lý trưởng*), and the vice village chief (*phó lý*) all took part in religious ceremonies. At that time, there was little social work to do. ... But now, there is a great need for public service in the society. In the old days, with the *feudal* order, they were called *lý trưởng* and *phó lý*, but now their positions have changed and no one uses these titles anymore. ... In the present society, there is much need for public service, so the authorities are busy with other matters, while the work concerning 'spirituality' is done by the elders, who serve the divinities these days.

Thoại's opinion is more interesting if we take into consideration the fact that he himself was assigned by the elders of the inland village of La Vân to lead the organization of annual rituals in the Thanh Minh Temple (Temple for the Dead), which replaced the hierarchical *đình* in Sa Huỳnh. Note that Thoại called the old system 'feudal', suggesting its non-egalitarian character and the fact that fishers depended on the *làng* in many ways, for example, to obtain permission to bury their family members or to buy rice. In Thoại's eyes, today's authorities have much more important matters to deal with than supervising rituals in local temples. In his statement regarding fishers as 'stateless' people (quoted earlier in the chapter), he said that the hierarchical division between the village and the fishing community, as well as the subordinate position of the latter, were 'the custom of the forefathers of the poverty-stricken northern people who came here [to Sa Huỳnh] to work'.

In Sa Huỳnh the *đình* suffered extensive damage during the resistance struggle against the French in 1945, but the final destruction did not take place until the period of post-unification and collectivization, providing an interesting example of the purification of religious spaces by both state officials and fishers. As in other parts of Vietnam, in Sa Huỳnh local officials were determined to wipe out all forms of social differentiation in terms of class and gender restrictions, seating order, ritual functions, and food distribution that the *đình* reproduced (see Luong 1992; Endres 2001; Malarney 2002). Being excluded from the local

đình system and its symbolic communal house, in which village founders were worshipped and which represented and reinforced a hierarchy
of social inequality derived from agriculture, some fishers felt justified in
tearing down the *đình* and using the building materials to construct their
own houses. While the *đình* of Sa Huỳnh was never rebuilt, the Whale
Spirit Temple was enlarged, with the tacit agreement of local cadres,
even during the time of the antisuperstition campaigns. The Sa Huỳnh
authorities allowed the *vạn* to function because it was inherently more
egalitarian due to the nature of the fishing profession, which, as noted
before, often involves considerable hazard and requires cooperation,
mutual trust, and equal investment of labour from the entire crew on
board. Thus, in the view of those authorities, the occupational character
of the *vạn* superseded its religious function, enabling both fishers and
state agents to move beyond the religion–politics binary and upend the
old hierarchical relationship between farmers and fishers.

Growing status of the *vạn*

Times had changed, old rules had lost their power, and the new administrative structure of rural units, *thôn*, to some extent erased the social
differences between the *làng* and the *vạn* in Sa Huỳnh and Lý Sơn.
Moreover, fish had become a lucrative commodity, especially in contrast
to rice, which had become cheap and widely available. A conversation I
had with a forty-three-year-old woman (born in 1964) from Sa Huỳnh,
a neighbour of my landlady, nicely illustrates this process. On one occasion I heard her expressing regret that she and her husband had moved
away from the sandy dunes to the other side of Highway A-1. She explained that at the beginning of the 1990s her husband gave up fishing,
sold their small plot of 'land' next to the highway, and bought an arable
plot for rice cultivation. They had hoped to improve their material situation by switching to farming. Things did not work out as expected, however, and they found themselves unable to earn a living from growing
rice. The wife was forced to open a small shop and supported her family
selling basic foodstuffs and various commodities for home use. During
our conversation, she pointed to the other side of the highway where a
solid, three-storey building with a sea view stood. She wistfully noted
that she and her family had lived on that land in the 1990s. The new
owners apparently made a much better investment, buying the land on

the sea side of the highway and building a hotel where passing travellers can rent a room to stay overnight and treat themselves to freshly caught seafood.

At present, the cultivation of rice no longer guarantees a good income, and the negative attitude towards fishing has become less pronounced. Fishers have ceased to be as dependent on farmers as they were in the past. Furthermore, the national attention to the South China Sea and new state cultural and socioeconomic initiatives have brought about some positive changes in fishers' social and material status. While their economic prosperity and 'civilizational' (*văn minh*) progress are evident in better houses, modern mobile phones, TV sets, new motorbikes, and so on, the fishers' financial 'recovery' becomes most apparent in their lavish sacrifices and increasing financial contributions and to the 'agriculture' village temples and participation in their seasonal ceremonies. Both Sa Huỳnh and Lý Sơn authorities have acknowledged that in recent times the *vạn* has gained a stronger economic position within the village than the *làng*. They base such statements on their observations of money contributed to offerings and ceremonies in the temples. The villagers of La Vân confirmed this, revealing that most of the money for the reconstruction of the Thanh Minh Temple came from Thạch By's two *vạns*, which, as the villagers put it, showed 'sentiment' (*tình cảm*) towards and 'solidarity' (*tình đoàn kết*) with the village. In 2007, for the New Year ritual in one of the village temples in An Hải (Lý Sơn), several captains of fishing crews contributed a total of 44 million VND (about €2,000).

The example of Thiên Y A Na – a Vietization of the Cham goddess Pô Nagar, who is believed to secure the livelihood of both farmers and fishers – well illustrates this phenomenon.[8] In An Hải village (Lý Sơn), the elders were responsible for carrying out an important ritual in the temple of Thiên Y A Na to ensure the fertility of the land. When I attended one such ceremony, I saw a large number of fishers who offered the goddess three fine pigs. Fishers stated that whenever the goddess blessed them with good catches or they managed to escape from a Chinese coastguard ship, they gave her back more than was expected.

---

8. I use the term 'Vietization' to refer to the process in which Việt people adopted Pô Nagar's cult and integrated her into the Việt spirit pantheon. The integration of Cham spirits and gods was simultaneously accompanied by the assimilation of Champa by the successive dynasties of Đại Việt.

The ceremony took place in the late evening, lasted many hours, and ended with a feast before the sun broke the darkness.

Historically, the right to make the more prestigious sacrifice of pigs was reserved for the farming villages, as fishing communities were kept outside *đình* system. During the ceremonies in the *đình*, the master of high sacrifice received 'a first cup of sacrificial drink' (*ẩm phước*) as a blessing from the divinity, which was extended to the entire community in the form of the feast (Nguyễn Văn Huyên 1995 [1945]). This also included the *kiếng* – 'presenting of sacrificial meat' – which was a common practice following the royal model of offering the sacrificial cuts from the pig to the notables after the ceremony, in accordance with their rank. In Lý Sơn and Sa Huỳnh, both *ẩm phước* and *kiếng* survive today, and the practices have been adopted by the *vạn*. I witnessed that the *ẩm phước*, in the form of a cup of alcohol, and the pig's head and entrails were offered to the chief of the fishing community, who held the position of Master of the High Sacrifices in the ceremony in honour of the Whale Spirit. For the duration of the ritual he loudly chanted invitations to the tutelary spirits and all divinities from the neighbouring temples to taste the offerings. After the sacrifice, he and his assistant received half of the pig's head.

However, the *làng* was not always happy with the *vạns*' attempts to elevate themselves through ostentatious sacrifices, and in some cases it tried to regulate this matter. The vignette at the beginning of this chapter gives us a snapshot of the internal dispute between the *làng* and the *vạn* in Lý Sơn about the rights to the Spirit Whale. I noted that this dispute was solved by building two separate temples marking the ritual, territorial, and social boundary between farmers and fishers. The *làng* assigned two different dates for the Whale Spirit anniversary. In June 2007 I had the opportunity to take part in the ceremony organized by the *vạn*. I witnessed that in this particular case the *vạn* was not allowed to offer a pig, as this more prestigious sacrifice was reserved for the *làng*; members of the *vạn* were only permitted to present a chicken to the divinity, a sign of the *vạn*'s subordinate position vis-à-vis the *làng*.

The foregoing discussion of *vạn* members' aspirations to perform *đình*-style ceremonies raises the question of the fishers' motivations for making lavish sacrifices of pigs in agricultural temples, a practice that for a long time was reserved only for the *làng*. Referring to Edmund Leach's

(1954) study of the political systems and social structures of Highland Burma, Thomas A. Kirsch (1973: 3) argued that it was impossible to state what units such as 'village', 'villagers', or 'a village cluster' meant to the Kachin society without referring to their religious ideas (1973: 9). He emphasized that these various units were ordered on the basis of 'shared religious ritual and *right* to this ritual' (Kirsch 1973: 9, emphasis added). More precisely, Leach (1954) presented Kachin society as oscillating between the extreme poles of two social organizations: the *gumsa* and the *gumlao*. The basis of *gumsa*, or 'autocratic' political power, was a 'chief's ritual rights to sacrifice to the spirits controlling fertility of the domain' (Kirsch 1973: 11). This right was acquired by establishing separate 'sacred groves' for each of the village groups, a process that could be seen as analogous to the *làng* erecting a *đình*. According to Kirsch, the formation of the counterpart to *gumsa*, the *gumlao* – which, because of its more 'rebellious' and 'egalitarian' type, could be compared to the *vạn* – was a struggle for greater 'religious freedom' and a 'repudiation of exclusive ritual control by a chief' (1973: 11). Furthermore, Kirsch (1973: 14) showed that in the Kachin *gumsa*, the 'chief' had exclusive rights to make sacrifices to the spirits and to make the 'land of the dead' fertile. However, if his sacrifice turned out to be ineffective, his position could be threatened by somebody else who wished to overthrow him and usurp his prestige (1973: 16). Kirsch argued that in Kachin society the economic ability to give the feast raised the ritual status of sponsors. Therefore, the 'prestige' was not given, but had to be earned by giving feasts; through such feasts the giver proved his 'potency' and 'virtue', which qualified him for prestige (ibid.). I believe that a very similar dynamic underpins *vạn* members' engagement in *đình*-style ceremonies.

Coastal people's sense of territoriality and, closely associated with it, hierarchy is not enshrined in a permanent and immutable situation and structure (cf. Kirsch 1973: 35), but is undergoing a continuous process of change along with the ever-changing ecological, political, and social conditions. Just as rice is the main staple of Vietnamese cuisine but fish sauce (*nước mắm*) its characteristic flavour (Avieli 2012: 31), so the land and the sea, and farmers and fishers, are inextricably bound up in a hierarchical relationship that is mutually constitutive rather than absolute. Fish sauce is both a cultural marker of Vietnamese cuisine and a 'mediating agent that breaks the binary oppositions' (Avieli 2012: 32);

it reconciles the salt with the starch and the sea with the land. Nir Avieli (2012: 32) explains that the mediating quality of fish sauce stems from its 'liminal, "betwixt and between" position: two "solids' (salt and fish) are processed into a liquid, which is an extract and essence of both'. If rice is the core, fish sauce is the 'cementing agent' of the different dishes that make up a Vietnamese meal and for the people, who dip 'their morsels of food into a shared saucer of *nước mắm* before putting them into their mouths' (Avieli 2012: 32).

The relationship between rice and fish sauce thus captures the core message of this chapter, namely that the social structures represented by the *làng* and the *vạn* in Sa Huỳnh and Lý Sơn are far from permanent, static, or absolute, and that the categorical opposites *làng–vạn* are both ongoing, living, and changing hierarchies and relationships. With a growing global demand for marine products and the global consequences of the South China Sea dispute, fishers have started to play a more important role in the village ritual domain to which the *vạn* had no previous access. As in the past, when the feast in the *đình* served to highlight inequalities and status differences within the village, today the *vạn*s use the same means to earn 'permanent prestige and status relations', as well as social recognition (see Kirsch 1973: 17; Malarney 2002). Renovating temples, appropriating the traditional right of the agricultural village to sacrifice pigs, and sponsoring village agricultural rituals became means of displaying fishers' ritual 'potency' and thus their growing status in the community. Each lavish sacrifice made by fishers in agricultural temples served as evidence of their good catches, their material well-being and, hence, their spiritual 'reward'. By challenging the exclusive ritual control of the *làng*, they turned the tables on the old hierarchy. This recent enhancement of the fishers' economic position vis-à-vis the farmers and their ritual investment in agricultural temples show the complexity of local territorial imaginaries and the dichotomies of land and sea. Fishers are not merely a disadvantaged group; they manage to exploit the situation in a way that helps them to demonstrate and cultivate their prestige in response to the changing political and economic context. The next chapter takes this point further as it explores how fishers use their agency to reach compromises with state officials and religious modernizers over what constitutes 'proper' religion.

Figure 5: Head of the fishing community worshipping Quan Âm, Sa Huỳnh.

CHAPTER 4

Discipline, Purification, and Indiscipline among State Agents, Religious Modernizers, and Fishers

On a hot summer day in 1978 the district police arrived at Từ Phước pagoda in Sa Huỳnh and confiscated all statues and Buddhist objects – with the exception of a two-metre-tall image of the Buddhist bodhisattva Quan Âm that stood outside and was too heavy and unwieldy to take to the district People's Committee in Đức Phổ. The policemen who carried out the task of vacating the local pagoda had to decide on the spot what to do with the troublesome object. Reluctant to destroy the statue themselves, they ordered villagers to smash the figure. Taking advantage of this situation, a group of Sa Huỳnh fishers intervened. The Buddhist bodhisattva Quan Âm is particularly worshipped there by fishers, who believe that she is the creator of the Whale Spirit and offers them protection during storms. Risking punishment by the police, the fishers transported the statue by boat to the Forbidden Hill (Cấm Núi) where the waters of the South China Sea push through a channel into a small bay known as the 'sea gate' of Sa Huỳnh. This dangerously rocky section of coastline, separating the community from the sea, was considered very treacherous for passing junks and other boats and for a long time was symbolically made safer by the configuration of yin (âm) and yang (dương) in the form of the divine couple – the goddess Thiên Y A Na, a Vietization of the Cham deity (usually addressed as Bà, 'Lady'), and the Whale Spirit (Ông, 'Sir') – whose temples were right next to each other on the cliff (see Nguyen The Anh 1995; Salemink 2015). As in Chinese thought, for Vietnamese people âm and dương constitute a binary hierarchical opposition. Dương symbolizes the principle of order, while *âm* is associated with the production, reproduction, and restoration of order (Sangren 1987). Each is incomplete in and of itself, and only together do they constitute the balance (Jamieson 1993). The cosmic order represented by a male and female spirit on the Forbidden Hill was, however, challenged during the Second Indochina War. The access to the spirits' temples became more difficult when the U.S. Army appropriated the Forbidden Hill to be used as a military base. In order to be able to continue worshipping their seafaring guardian spirit, in the late 1960s fishers separated the divine pair by moving the Whale Spirit temple to the village proper, while keeping the temple of Thiên Y A Na on the cliff.

To the fishers, the police intervention at Từ Phước pagoda in 1978 came as an unexpected opportunity to fill a spiritual void left on the cliff by the removal of the temple of the Whale Spirit. The men quickly seized the opportunity, but the whole operation first was made possible by a subtle tactic on the part of the head of the fishing community, who negotiated with the police for the rescue of the Quan Âm statue. Reluctant to destroy the Buddhist statue themselves, the policemen welcomed the fishers' offer to dispose of it, which gave them the sense that they had properly executed their task. Both sides saw Quan Âm's translocation as an opportunity to act in accordance with state policies and their own personal preferences. However, twenty-eight years later, the presence of Quan Âm on the Forbidden Hill created a problem for the new head monk of the Từ Phước pagoda, who found it inappropriate that the Buddhist object had been placed in non-Buddhist space and demanded that fishers return the statue to its original location. Neither villagers nor representatives of the Commune People's Committee had anything against the village monk's aspiration to promote the ethics of modern Buddhism, but they also did not share his reformist zeal to suppress local devotional practices.

While the vignette above showcases encounters between state and Buddhist authorities and between the state and fishers, its particular focus is really the encounter between religious authority and fishers. These different confrontations create a theoretical problem because they refer to binaries that are experienced as real, but are neither mutually exclusive nor stable. This chapter approaches binary oppositions not as absolute, eternal, or even inherently antagonistic, but rather as constantly changing and shifting in unpredictable ways within and across triadic relationships between the state, villagers, and more or less institutionalized versions of religion. I first situate the Forbidden Hill in the context of the state's semiotic ideology and the villagers' cosmology. I then discuss the villagers' response to the state policy and their strategy to defend the local gods. In the final section, I complicate the picture of confrontation between the two sides – state and village – as I focus on a religious modernizer, the monk Thích Giác Đức.

Forbidden Hill and Gia's defence of the Quan Âm statue

Before 1975, Sa Huỳnh was a part of the Republic of Vietnam – commonly known as South Vietnam – and served as a base for the U.S. Army. The U.S. forces had been stationed on the Forbidden Hill near the Thiên Y A Na Goddess temple because of its strategic location; no junk or other type of fishing boat could come into or leave the seaport unnoticed. In the beginning the U.S. Army did not permit incense offerings, but the situation eased by 1967–68, when they started to allow people to perform simple rituals, burn incense and votive paper, and make modest offerings to the goddess on the first and fifteenth day of every lunar month. After the unification of the country in 1975, the Forbidden Hill was appropriated by the Border Police as a military observation post, and access to the place was completely restricted until 1990, when the state relaxed its enforcement of antisuperstition laws.

When I arrived in Sa Huỳnh in the mid-autumn of 2006, the climate surrounding religion in Vietnam was totally different from 1978. The Đổi Mới economic reforms initiated in 1986 by the Communist Party brought not only economic but also religious liberalization. Highlighting the national aspect of culture, the Party-state reinterpreted 'folk beliefs' (*tín ngưỡng dân gian*) as 'culture' and, above all, 'national heritage' – a process I described in detail in Chapter 2.

The Forbidden Hill is an example of such a process in which local worship of the Buddhist deity Quan Âm and seafaring gods such as Thiên Y A Na and the Whale Spirit was re-interpreted by Sa Huỳnh state representatives in terms of traditional 'culture'. The Forbidden Hill was the very first place where Lợi, a representative of the Commune People's Committee, took me to explain this beautiful Vietnamese culture. Pointing at the two-metre-tall statue of the female bodhisattva Quan Âm that stood at the foot of a cement replica of the Bodhi tree, Lợi praised the new use of the sacred space which, in accordance with the state's concerns, was properly developed as a place of scenic beauty. With the confidence of someone who is knowledgeable about coastal culture, Lợi pointed out the precarious location of the port and the hazards of the sea and argued that the presence of the statue had a positive psychological effect on fishers who were pinning their faith on the Buddhist goddess. For Lợi, who was a young, energetic, and devoted office worker in the Department of Culture, the Forbidden Hill was the epitome of a scenic place enriched with a beautiful cultural blend of 'folk' beliefs and Buddhism.

For fishers the place was beautiful too, but for a different reason. In Thạch By the last vestiges of the *đình* were wiped out when the general secondary school was built on its foundations. The old world of symbolic hierarchy and village status epitomized in the *đình* was gone forever, abolished and simplified by the Party-state administration. Although fishers tried to recreate the balance of *yin* and *yang* by moving the Whale Temple close to Từ Phước pagoda, the traditional asymmetry had been disrupted and was in urgent need of a new rearrangement. First, the old order and the hierarchical relationship between the *đình* (the male and agriculture ritual domain), the Buddhist pagoda (primarily a female religious domain), and the Whale Temple (the fishers' ritual centre) collapsed along with the last walls of the *đình*. Second, when the Whale Temple was moved from the cliff, the divinities coupled as *Ông* (Sir) and *Bà* (Lady) were separated. Consequently, the cliff was stripped of its masculine aspect and male ritual activity ceased, leaving only the goddess Thiên Y A Na, who was losing her power to control the sea. This situation created a spiritual vacuum that called for a creative reconfiguration of the local cosmology.

The solution came unexpectedly with the threat of violent action against the Buddhist deity. The people of Sa Huỳnh did not hesitate over what to do with the troubling figure of Quan Âm and they knew precisely where she belonged. By placing the Quan Âm statue on the cliff in 1978, the fishers were confident that the place had become both sacred and beautiful. They were aware that according to Buddhist doctrine Quan Âm was a man who had taken a female form. The androgynous Quan Âm perfectly filled the void left by the removal of the Whale Spirit and, in the absence of a strong female deity, grew in popularity. Since Quan Âm was moved to the Forbidden Hill, the narratives about the transformation of the goddess Thiên Y A Na from a fierce to a benevolent spirit started to circulate among villagers. In the past men did not allow women to perform rituals or any other devotional activities to the goddess out of fear that they would offend her with their earthly female 'uncleanliness' such as menstruation and childbirth (see Chapter 6). Men themselves were afraid to approach her directly in the temple because she was considered a fierce deity, quick to punish even minor unintentional misconduct. Passing the Forbidden Hill on board their vessels, fishers would bow their heads from afar out of respect and ask for safe passage. In the early 1990s, fishers recorded that, inspired by the compassionate and merciful nature of Quan Âm, the goddess went through Buddhist 'self-cultivation' (*đi tu*), lost her power to control the sea, and finally left the temple to become a bodhisattva. At that time women began to approach the goddess and make offerings of fruit and sweets in her temple every month during the new and full moon. In consequence, the previously male domain of the Forbidden Hill was appropriated by women, becoming a symbol of their local vision of religiosity.

☰

According to the villagers, the activities of geomancers and various ritual masters were strictly banned after 1975. Gia (born in 1947) was well known in Sa Huỳnh not only as a gifted healer and exorcist (see Endres 2008; Kwon 2009), but also as the saviour of the Buddhist statue. During my visit to Gia's house, I learned that in the late 1970s fishers chose him to be the head of the *vạn*. Villagers later confirmed that he was held in high esteem by most people in the village and that he was 'talented and virtuous' (*có tài có đức*). He led an ordinary life until the age of twenty-five, when he fell ill. During our conversation he recalled that at that time an 'invisible' (*vô hình*), 'spectral' (*huyền bí*) being entered his body, controlled him, threatened him, and prevented him from working or going fishing for one hundred days. When these hundred days had passed, the spirit allowed him to resume his daily chores and eat meat again, but on every first and fifteenth day of the lunar month Gia was obliged to serve the spirit and cure people. At the time of the antisuperstition campaigns in 1978, Gia was arrested several times and accused of spreading superstitious practices. He was banned from healing and carrying out exorcisms. He recalled,

> I cannot count how many times the police came here and said that I was spreading superstition and the occult (*huyền bí*), that I was uneducated and lacking consciousness (*vô trí vô giác*).[1] I wanted to save people. I have never taken a single penny; I have been helping the people at large. You, young lady, know the people's level here; they have only finished elementary school and even this cannot be certain. During the war, they just learned to spell, that was all. And that was why they called it occult practice!

Gia smiled and continued:

> Once, the provincial police sent a letter and summoned me to the commune office. They detained me for two days. During this time, people gathered, around 300 people from Sa Huỳnh alone. The police officer misunderstood it; he thought that I had alerted them. I answered him: 'Honourable officer, I have been sitting here for two days working with the cadres. How could I have asked the people to come here?' Their presence reflected that I worked in their interest and it cost nothing. I wanted to stop healing but the village and the neighbourhood did not let me stop. People came in crowds! I had a lot of work to do, [I could not refuse] you know... a sense of community spirit (*tình làng nghĩa xóm*).

Gia bridged political and religious domains and knew how to use the semiotic ideology of the state to blur the opposing categories in the triadic relationship of state–religion–society. He made himself publicly visible through his healing rituals, his service to the fishing organization (*vạn*), and his ability to deploy various tactics of indiscipline, a capacity that made it possible for him to shift identities and represent himself politically and professionally as a different persona in official and unofficial situations. When arrested and detained in the People's Committee office, Gia politely mocked local authorities, referring to his detention for political reasons as 'work' (*làm việc*) with 'honourable cadres', thereby reproducing conventional political language. Blurring the state–village binary, he revealed the irrationality of the local authorities who accused

---

1. The antonym of *vô giác* (lacking consciousness) is *giác ngộ*, a Buddhist term used to describe 'Buddhist enlightenment', which has been adopted in Vietnamese Marxist discourse to denote 'class consciousness'.

him of mobilizing the masses while he was in fact in detention, preoccupied with 'raising his socialist moral standards'. The presence of a group of villagers in front of the People's Committee building may have looked like subversion, but Gia offered it as proof that his conduct had not been exploitative of his fellow villagers.

He earned credit not only among his co-villagers as a ritual master and head of the *vạn*, but also demonstrated his capabilities by devising a solution for the Buddhist statue. Gia clearly remembered that it was a hot summer day in 1978 when the district police arrived at the pagoda and ordered villagers to smash the figure of Quan Âm, which stood outside and was too big to transport elsewhere. He recounted:

> During the subsidy period (*thời bao cấp*) revolutionaries did not rely on any religion (*tín ngưỡng*), any superstitions (*mê tín dị đoan*). They were in the process of eradicating all of them. ... I had the opportunity that year to represent the fishers of Sa Huỳnh and gained the people's trust and confidence. Hence, I came to the pagoda and stood face to face with the police. I showed comradely spirit (*tính đồng chí*) and said, 'This is a statue, in fact, cement and plaster only. If you want to smash the statue, you will have to hire people. Instead, please give it to me. I will take it to the hill to beautify the place!'

'Did the police agree?' I asked. He answered:

> The police were unanimous in their decision. They said that it was urgent that I transport the statue as soon as possible. I called folks together and, first, we transported it close to the Whale Temple. Then we took a boat, crossed the channel, and carried the statue up the cliff. I also planted a small Bodhi tree in the place where the statue was erected. It took five to ten years to grow. But it withered and later people made an artificial tree of cement. They wanted the Quan Âm statue to look important and older and to make it more dignified.

When Gia used the semiotic ideology of the state to defend the Buddhist statue, it was not the act of resistance against state rule that was important to him and his co-villagers, but rather the desire to participate in local religious life. As other villagers stated very clearly to me, 'If Gia had not interceded for the statue, if it had remained without worshippers, all of us would have been guilty (*mang tội*).'

If indiscipline brings into play a kind of rationalism, it is both an 'art of thinking' and an 'art of using' (Certeau 1984: xv; see also Mbembe

1992).[2] Gia's manipulation of the state's semiotic ideology was a tactic of indiscipline that allowed both the fishers and the police to escape this overarching state purification project and avoid the destruction of the Buddhist statue by blurring religious and political distinctions. Gia's strategic blend of protestations and simulation of 'comradely spirit' (*tính đồng chí*) presented the police with a dilemma. According to Hồ Chí Minh, 'comradely spirit' was a crucial part of the critique and 'self-critique' practised among members of the Party, whose aim was 'self-improvement'. Pushed to his limits, Gia played with this expression in order to convince the policemen to give him the statue. The local authorities were also reluctant to reject Gia's argument on account of his position as the head of the fishing organization. He *practically* represented the fishers – not just ritually – and because of this status it was difficult to counter him. Assigned the task of desecrating the local pagoda, the police had to decide what to do with the troublesome object, which was too cumbersome to take to the People's Committee. Caught in a web of state discipline, the officials could not just leave the statue because they had received an order to cleanse the village of 'superstition', but neither were they keen to dirty their hands by destroying it. Displaying their own indiscipline towards the state's semiotic ideology by accepting Gia's proposition, they entered into a form of silent collaboration. The policemen ordered Gia to remove the statue as soon as possible and, loading the remaining statues onto their truck, they left the pagoda empty, maintaining the appearance that their task had been carried out properly.

Keane (2008) observes that semiotic ideologies respond to the materiality of such practices and objects as texts, offerings, altars, statues, temples, and rituals, and are conditioned by social actors' experiences. To 'purify' the local pagoda by dispelling its sacred aura and showing that Quan Âm was nothing more than a powerless effigy, the policemen first had to identify the meaning of the statue with reference to the state's semiotic ideology. Once the statue was defined as a *religious* and therefore *superstitious* object according to the Marxist-Leninist principles that inspired the antisuperstition campaigns of 1978, it could be removed and destroyed. Although Gia regarded the purifying actions of

---

2. Certeau does not use the term 'indiscipline', but he speaks about antidiscipline, which he contrasts with discipline (1984: xv).

the police as sacrilege, he blurred the categorical boundaries by publicly using the political rhetoric and confirming the legitimacy of the state to save the statue, which he felt obliged to protect. Aware of the state policy of preserving places of historical, cultural, or aesthetic interest and of the 'socialist beautification programme' (Harms 2012), he used the argument that the Quan Âm statue would beautify the local landscape. By planting the Bodhi tree, he was acting accordance with the new political tradition of 'National Planting Day' – inaugurated by Hồ Chí Minh during the Land Reform with his famous saying, 'The forest is gold if one knows how to protect it.'[3]

In this way, Gia carried out his own counter-purification action in which he chose to foreground the aesthetic value of the statue while downplaying its religious value. Moving between the opposing poles of a secular–religious binary, he displayed his 'secular' rationality by pointing out that, in fact, the statue was matter out of place and nothing more than a plaster effigy, not worth the effort of smashing and, for that reason, it belonged to a secular space. Purification is never a finished project, not because of resistance but because it creates endless 'hybrids' across different social fields, mixing objects and categories (Keane 2008: 289; see also Latour 1993; Douglas 2001). Gia's work of counter-purification created such a hybrid object of beauty, culture, and religion; it shifted the function of the statue from religious to aesthetic and hence moral by using Communist semiotic ideology to ensure that the Buddhist statue remained in the local village landscape, albeit outside the pagoda grounds. In this sense, the Quan Âm statue on Forbidden Hill became a hybrid by-product of the state's semiotic ideology that prescribed the cleansing of inappropriate elements from the village space (Douglas 2001: 36).

Buddhist purifying discipline

I often witnessed Lợi (born in 1975) authoritatively instructing villagers on religious policy and superstitious practices. But when I, in the company of Lợi, visited the Buddhist pagoda Từ Phước and met the head monk Thích Giác Đức (born in 1945), the roles of 'instructor' and 'instructed'

---

3. The Party-state sought to replace local village traditions with more profane celebrations. Hồ Chí Minh invented the new tradition of a National Planting Day in order to replace more traditional festive occasions in village ritual life (Kleinen 1999a; McElwee 2016).

were reversed. 'What's your name, *chú?*' asked Lợi, using, as usual, the term meaning 'junior uncle'. At this the monk became indignant:

> *Anh* (you) call me *chú*. That's wrong. You call me 'uncle', meaning that I'm an ordinary person, don't you? In [Christian] religion, if you go to church you must call a priest 'Reverend Father' (*cha đạo*). You are working on culture but you come to a Buddhist pagoda and you call me 'uncle'. You cannot address me properly, huh? If you come to the pagoda you must respect the social status and the religious title of the person here. For example, if one is a Venerable (*đại đức*), then call him 'Venerable'; if one is a Master (*thầy*), call him 'Master'.

Vietnamese kinship terminology is usually used to establish hierarchy, but in certain contexts it might also be used to circumvent a system of asymmetry (Sidnell and Shohet 2013; see also Luong 1988). Being thirty years younger than the head monk, Lợi initially used a respectful kin term to address the monk. The monk viewed this as a violation of the proper hierarchical order not because Lợi used the wrong kin term, but because he dared to use a kin term in the first place. Yet this was not the encounter of a young man who was intentionally misbehaving, as he later shifted to the term 'Master', although for most of the time he strategically avoided directly addressing the monk with personal pronouns. Rather, it was an encounter between a 'political official' representing secular authority and a Buddhist monk representing religious authority. Framing their interaction differently, the monk claimed a higher status than the state official, while Lợi sought to circumvent this confrontation by refusing to use the surname *Thích*, which is reserved for Buddhist clergy, or the even more proper term in this context, *Thầy* ('Master') (see Sidnell and Shohet 2013). To diminish the monk's religious authority, Lợi strategically started out using the kin term 'junior uncle', which implied more proximity and familiarity than the monk was willing to tolerate.

In his study of discursive practices and power structures, Hy Van Luong (1988: 251) shows that the diverse use of linguistic forms is not 'a passive reflection on the social differentiation', but 'an active part of the historically specific and power-embedded construction of reality'. This is why the monk admonished the young official, reminding him that he was in a sacred place and that he was obliged to recognize religious authority. However, instead of seeing this relationship as an example of the antagonism between state and religion in Vietnam, I look at the two sides as representing semiotic ideologies enacted through different power-embedded disciplines of state and religious authority. In the previous section I analysed an example of confrontation between state, religion, and society, and the tactics Gia used to position himself within and across this triadic relationship. The binary opposition is not limited to state versus religion or state versus village, but can also be extended to the encounter between villagers and religious authorities.

During the period of High Socialism, some pagodas were considered historically significant and for that reason villagers and cadres refrained from destroying them (Malarney 2002: 46). According to official directives, these pagodas qualified as sites of historical interest or scenic beauty and came under the direct management of local authorities, which decided on their possible renovation. Like many village pagodas in Vietnam, Từ Phước was situated in the vicinity of a local market; well located, it attracted people and spread Buddhism among the entire Sa Huỳnh community. The former bonze (*trụ trì*, 'head of the pagoda'), who established the pagoda in this place in 1956, selected the location on the basis of its proximity of the communal house (*đình*), the freshwater stream flowing down the mountains, and ponds suitable for growing water spinach (*rau muống*). However, despite its scenic location, Từ Phước pagoda did not have the good fortune of being rated as a place of historical importance, nor could the local authorities discern any aesthetic qualities.

In the southern parts of Vietnam, the new communist government considered Buddhist pagodas belonging to the Unified Buddhist Church of Vietnam (UBCV)[4] to be dissident and shut them down. In most cases, their clergy were arrested and defrocked, and Từ Phước pagoda and its monks, who belonged to the UBCV, shared a similar fate in 1978. From Từ Phước pagoda's chronicle, to which the head monk kindly gave me access, I learned that there were no clergy in the pagoda

---

4. In the 1960s the conflict between Buddhists and Catholics unified Buddhists to emulate the highly institutionalized organization of the Catholic Church. As a result, the Unified Buddhist Church of Vietnam was established at the An Quang pagoda in Saigon in 1963 (Soucy 2012). After 1975, it was suppressed as a dissident Buddhist sect.

from 1980 until 1999, when the current monk was appointed.[5] In 1981, the Vietnamese Party-state formed the Buddhist Association of Vietnam to displace the UBCV. In 1984, Từ Phước pagoda was officially admitted into the Vietnamese Buddhist Association, which remains the only official Buddhist umbrella organization with legal status in Vietnam (Soucy 2012). The UBCV is still present in Central and Southern Vietnam, although not in Sa Huỳnh proper.

After the reforms, the People's Committee of the district returned all confiscated statues to the pagoda, with the notable exception of the statue of Quan Âm. Thích Giác Đức has ever since sought to return the Quan Âm statue to the pagoda, but the villagers have insisted on leaving it on the hill. The monk was aware of the official state policy of protecting places of historical and cultural interest, beautifying the landscape, and promoting tourism, which Buddhist clergy were expected to support, but he was nevertheless more interested in advocating so-called 'reformed Buddhism' – a modern version of Buddhism cleansed of non-Buddhist elements and propagating ascetic forms of self-cultivation. The monk explained that when he came to Sa Huỳnh, the village pagoda did not have a qualified monk. A layperson was in charge of the building, and the only Buddhist practice taking place was the chanting of the *sutra*, which could not take the place of the teaching of a qualified monk. Thích Giác Đức described his role as follows:

> The war was over, but after the miserable time of restrictions and at the hands of people who damaged the building, the temple ultimately fell into ruin. Then came the years in which the state expanded religious freedom and Buddhist activities could spread in the region. Without a monk there cannot be any development. … Since I have been here, the pagoda has been renovated and become spacious. There are facilities to accommodate any group of Buddhist pilgrims who are passing by. I mean, they come to bring relief to flood-hit central regions; doing their duty, they stop over here. This is the point where the South and the North meet. That is why I need to have a place for them when they are on their return journey. The purpose of Buddhism is to bring prosperity and peace to all people; this is what the Buddha teaches.

---

5. See Tiểu sử chùa Từ Phước. (n.d.). Thạch By, xã Phổ Thạnh, tỉnh Quảng Ngãi [Từ Phước Pagoda's Chronicle. Thạch By, Phổ Thạnh commune, Quảng Ngãi Province].

The monk did not share Lợi's interest in the state's effort to convert temples into places of historical and cultural importance or into tourist sites. Such a policy aroused reluctance rather than enthusiasm. Instead, he stressed his role in reinstating the secular notions of Buddhist practice that underpin meditation and spirituality by emphasizing personal development of the individual rather than a relationship with a god. Eloquently and carefully constructing his critique of the presence of the Quan Âm statue on Forbidden Hill, the head monk sought to purify not just the Buddhist pagoda but also the village landscape by ridding them of non-Buddhist elements.

Alexander Soucy (2007: 361) argues that criticism of local practices and the desire to purify Buddhism by eradicating superstitions was part of a larger movement of Buddhist reform that took place throughout Asia in the twentieth century, a 'self-conscious reformation process' in which the encounter with Western colonial powers played a role. This modernizing trend was not unique to Buddhism, but also affected other world religions, such as Islam in Indonesia. Many Javanese religious reformists who were strongly influenced by modern ideas coming from the Middle East emphasized the importance of original scripture and decried local practices that they regarded as non-Islamic (Hefner 1997). In the Vietnamese context, both the Đổi Mới programme of political and economic changes and the normalization of diplomatic relations with the United States in 1995 have significantly increased interaction between overseas Vietnamese and Vietnamese in Vietnam and have, at the same time, influenced Buddhism there.[6] For example, Thích Nhất Hạnh imported a 'purified' version of Buddhism that was more in line with his Buddhist doctrine developed in exile and which influenced Buddhist practice in Vietnam more generally (Chapman 2007).[7] Another example of this trend that dismisses non-Buddhist elements is a local Vietnamese Buddhist sect which constitutes a religious 'resurrection' of an old and short-lived Zen school known as Bamboo Grove Zen

---

6. The increasing interaction between overseas Vietnamese and Vietnamese in Vietnam is not limited to Buddhism but includes other religions, such as spirit possession or Caodaism. For transnational spirit possession see Fjelstad and Nguyen Thi Hien (2006) and for transpacific Caodaism see Hoskins (2015).

7. Thích Nhất Hạnh is the world's most famous Buddhist leader after the Dalai Lama (see Chapman 2007).

(*Trúc Lâm Thiền Tong*), established by the Vietnamese king Trần Nhân Tông (1278–1293) in the thirteenth century. The sect was re-established in the late 1960s in the South by Thích Thanh Từ, a monk who 'discovered' meditative Zen and modified it in his resurrected Bamboo Grove Zen school. However, what matters here is that both Thích Nhất Hạnh and Thích Thanh Từ emphasized meditation and greater spirituality in their attempts to cleanse Vietnamese Buddhism of alien, non-Buddhist elements and to create new orthodoxies and orthopraxes.

The monk Thích Giác Đức did not explicitly state that he belonged to the Bamboo Grove Zen school, but he shared the school's emphasis on meditation in contrast to the more liturgical Buddhist practices of northern Vietnam (see Soucy 2007; Taylor 2004). Listening to the monk, Lợi asked him whether he considered the Vietnam Buddhist Association (headquartered at the Quán Sứ pagoda in Hanoi) to be the administrative head of all Buddhist sects in the country.[8] Lợi was aware of existing Buddhist pagodas around Sa Huỳnh which belonged to the 'unofficial' UBCV and was discreetly testing the monk. The monk answered directly that, in his opinion, the Quán Sứ pagoda was not a place of Buddhist devotion, but was, rather, simply a central secretariat in which the state monitored the religious congregation, approving and publicizing new administrative rules.

The monk continued his critique of northern pagodas by claiming that they remained under strong Chinese cultural influence, which is why people selfishly prayed for wealth, health, passing exams, and the like instead of engaging in self-cultivation, as is practised in the South. He then more overtly expressed his disapproval of those northern pagodas which, according to the state's vision, had become 'beauty spots' and destinations for sightseeing tours and conducting business rather than places for practising Buddhism – a criticism also shared by the UBCV. Lợi listened patiently, but in more awkward moments tried to interrupt the monk and asked me to switch off the recorder. However, the monk continued his tirade, stating that for him many temples had nothing to do with the cultivation of Buddhism and only pretended to be places of Buddhist practice; in reality they were simply earning money from

---

8. The Vietnamese Party-state mandated that all activities of the Sangha's Body, which is the Buddhist Association, be centrally located in the Quán Sứ pagoda (see Soucy 2012).

tourism. The monk believed that such places could not develop as sites for Buddhist religious cultivation, similar to Từ Phước pagoda which, left without clergy, was doomed to decline.

Eventually, Lợi changed the subject and brought up the issue of the Quan Âm statue and its current location above Sa Huỳnh port. Although both Lợi and Thích Giác Đức must have known why the statue had been moved to the top of the cliff instead of remaining in the grounds of the pagoda, neither of them mentioned the issue. Instead, Lợi talked about the villagers' beautification and decoration of the place on the cliff and the role of Quan Âm in granting fishers peaceful passage at sea and safe return. Describing Quan Âm as simultaneously representing 'Buddhist beliefs' (*tín ngưỡng Phật giáo*) and 'folk beliefs' (*tín ngưỡng dân gian*), he stressed that the two sides not only did not clash, but in fact complemented each other. At the same time, by not using the term 'religion' (*tôn giáo*) with reference to institutionalized Buddhism and emphasizing 'beautiful Vietnamese customs', Lợi undermined the Buddhist monk's authority to decide on the future of the statue.

For the monk, Quan Âm in the non-Buddhist space of Forbidden Hill was matter out of place, but in Lợi's view the statue was an example of the merging of 'beautiful Vietnamese traditions' and Buddhism that – enriched with local flavour – entered the reality of everyday life and expressed itself in daily practices. Lợi declared that he did not identify with any of the main religions (*tôn giáo*), including Buddhism, and in his view, as a 'worker of the state', he ought to represent a secular orientation. However, he disclosed that this had not prevented him from honouring his wife's ancestors during his wedding. In Lợi's discussions with the monk Thích Giác Đức, he stressed that he saw no contradiction in claiming to be secular and following ancestor worship (*thờ ông bà*), which for him was a 'beautiful Vietnamese tradition'. When Lợi asked the monk for his opinion on the beautification of the cliff and whether he identified himself with the people's project, the monk replied curtly that whatever the villagers were doing had nothing to do with him. In this way the monk drew a clear distinction between the villagers' *tín ngưỡng* (religious beliefs) and Buddhist *tôn giáo* (religion).

Lợi decided to delve further into the subject and asked the monk if he would be willing to conduct a ceremony on the cliff, given that people might consider him better qualified to perform rituals. In making this invitation, Lợi, who was knowledgeable about local culture, granted a form of authority to the monk who, in his view, understood religious procedures better than the villagers. The monk diplomatically answered that he did not have a clear understanding of the matter, but in the last two years he had consistently refused to lead village ceremonies for local gods because he found them to be in contradiction to Buddhist teaching, especially as the villagers butchered pigs and prepared elaborate feasts. He then used pre-Đổi Mới rhetoric that associated superstition with the peasant class, thereby distancing himself from the official agenda that prioritizes 'folk' religious beliefs as 'pure and authentic Vietnamese traditions'. Playing with the political language of the state's semiotic ideology, he called the 'folk' beliefs 'superstition' (*mê tín gọi là tín ngưỡng dân gian*) and contrary to Buddhist religion (*tôn giáo chỉ là Phật giáo*). In doing so, he quite directly contradicted Lợi's vision of a productive cultural merging of 'folk' beliefs and Buddhism. In contrast to the local state official, Thích Giác Đức sought a radical break from local traditions and, in that sense, he was more dismissive of the villagers' beliefs and practices as heterodox and heteropractic than Lợi. Note that when he stressed his role in reinstating 'pure' Buddhism, he mentioned pilgrims and North–South reconciliation as his project, but not the villagers, who, apparently, remained outside of his main concern.

In his insistence on a hardline Buddhist doctrine of personal development, Thích Giác Đức sought to purify the villagers' everyday ritual life and space. The monk's efforts to redirect his followers from devotional to more sophisticated practices such as self-cultivation and meditation resulted in Sa Huỳnh villagers being sidelined from ritual control over the village pagoda. However, they were not willing to surrender their ritual control over the cliff which – 'enchanted' by the rescued statue of Quan Âm – had become even more potent. Circumventing the monk's purifying discipline, they commissioned a new statue of Quan Âm so that the old one could remain atop the cliff where, they felt, it was better suited, even though the monk considered the local pagoda to be the more appropriate place for the Buddhist statue. Here we need to consider the semiotic ideologies of state and religion together with their competing disciplines aiming to control local religious practices. The monk's attack on Lợi undermined the office worker's authority and beat the state at its own game of wielding its doctrine as the only legitimate one. The monk implicitly sought to prove that the Buddhist discipline that he had propagated since he came to Sa Huỳnh was doctrinally more correct than that of the state-sanctioned Buddhist Association. His protest against the state's appropriation of Buddhist spaces for tourism rather than for Buddhist pilgrimages reflected the wider struggle of the modernizing movement to bring Buddhism back to its imagined original core (Soucy 2012).

Somewhat paradoxically, the monk's efforts provided fuel for heterodox rites, as villagers continuously re-enacted their religious practices in a more unpredictable way than the monk wished, making the work of purification unfinished business – just like the state's efforts in 1978. On the first and fifteenth day of the lunar month, Sa Huỳnh fisherwomen usually made offerings first to the deities on Forbidden Hill and afterwards at Từ Phước pagoda, where they listened to sermons given by the monk, prepared vegetarian meals, and chanted sutras together with other villagers. Knowing the monk's rigid views on their religious practices on Forbidden Hill, the fisherwomen were careful not to mention to the monk their prior visit to the cliff. Despite Thích Giác Đức's orthodox ideas, these fisherwomen saw nothing contradictory in leaving the Quan Âm statue on top of the cliff in the vicinity of the goddess Thiên Y A Na. Similarly, fishers felt that they had fulfilled their moral obligations by saving the statue from destruction and, following Hồ Chí Minh's instructions, beautifying the local landscape. For them the Quan Âm statue made the cliff – a transitional point between Sa Huỳnh and the open sea – more sacred and powerful.

Vernacular religions are never rigid or predetermined, nor, as I learned, is the gender of gods entirely defined. The local worldview was continuously modified, negotiated, and reinterpreted across and within the triadic relationship between state agents, religious modernizers, and diverse categories of villagers. Even though fishers in Sa Huỳnh considered Quan Âm a female deity, they were also aware of her old symbolic form as a man. By placing her statue on the cliff, men were confident that it would not threaten the *dương* order. But women have their own commentary on changes on the Forbidden Hill. For them, Quan Âm radically transformed the fierce nature of Thiên Y A Na, who in the past only tolerated male devotional practices and did not allow females on the cliff at all. Women rendered this transformation with the witty words, 'Even the goddesses have to acknowledge the higher position of women and follow the progress of modern society!' In this way, they defeated the men's religious semiotic ideology with their own version of religious practice and subtly shifted the ground of male ritual hegemony – a theme I will continue to explore in Chapter 6.

Shifting binary oppositions

By underlining the modes in which the binary poles of diverse contestations come to the fore and shift in the intersections of community, state, and religion, I have suggested that these binaries are not entirely determined by the matrix of purifying disciplines to which they are subjected (Certeau 1984). The ethnographic examples of Gia and the monk Thích Giác Đức show that there were real confrontations, but also temporary and pragmatic coalitions and manipulations of semiotic ideologies that allowed various categories of actors to achieve often contradictory goals within the same ideological frame. If the defence of the Quan Âm statue in 1978 put the fishers and policemen at opposite poles of the state–society binary, the state-initiated process of purifying the religious domain and beautifying local landscapes made them 'move between those poles' as they explored the situation with an eye to 'maximiz[ing] their positional advantages' (Harms 2012: 6).

Nearly thirty years later, both the state official and the monk asserted their competing purifying disciplines and modernist rationalities. While the effects of this divide extended further to involve villagers, those like Gia did not identify themselves with either form of this top-down modernist discipline. As I have shown, the villagers' attachment to spirits and their insistence on leaving the statue on the top of the cliff was a deviation from the monk's version of Buddhist orthodoxy and orthopraxy. While the villagers shared Thích Giác Đức's belief in the importance of a pagoda, they did not share his doctrinal view, according to which their local cosmologies and devotional practices had little to do with Buddhism. In that sense they oddly allied themselves with the state official Lợi, who declared himself to be secular. Still, this required that they learn how to use political language that would be difficult for the other side to refute. In this sense, the shifting contest between the Buddhist purists like Thích Giác Đức and the state agents like Lợi for control over sacred places was an ideological struggle between their competing purifying disciplines. Villagers were the ones who had to navigate these disciplines and rework their religious practices and cosmology to accord with the present realities of post-socialist Vietnam and those who asserted that neither cultural interest nor local customs had any place in 'pure' Buddhism. State and religious semiotic ideologies exist simultaneously and do not exclude each other, but index continuing tensions between villagers, state representatives, and religious authorities which are experienced as real binaries that proliferate, shift, and blur over time.

Figure 6: Paracel (Hoàng Sa) Memorial erected by Quảng Ngãi Province on Lý Sơn Island.

CHAPTER 5

Making the Paracels and Spratlys Vietnamese through Commemoration

In May 2007, I had a conversation with a member of one of the founding lineages of Lý Sơn Island, who accused a prominent and well-known Hanoi historian of secretly selling historical documents about the Paracel (Hoàng Sa) and Spratly (Trường Sa) islands to the Chinese 'enemy'. These documents were part of his family annals (*gia phả*), which he had taken to Hanoi for translation into modern Vietnamese. He believed that only some of them had been returned and declared that, if not for this loss, today his lineage could present valuable evidence supporting Vietnam's claims to the Paracels and Spratlys. In 2008, the Vietnamese Communist Party was confronted with strikingly similar accusations, lodged by Vietnamese nationalists inside and outside the country, of 'selling' out Vietnam's territory to China and hence of failing to defend national sovereignty. Many Vietnamese in the country and abroad alleged that a diplomatic note sent by the former prime minister Phạm Văn Đồng to the Chinese premier Zhou Enlai on 14 September 1958 could be interpreted as ceding the Paracels and Spratlys to China.[1]

In August 2007 I finished my ethnographic field research and returned to Europe. The villagers from Lý Sơn Island phoned me several times. I was astonished to hear their thanks for my help in elevating Âm

---

1. See 'China has no reason when citing the 1958 Diplomatic Note', http://vovworld. vn/en-US/current-affairs/china-has-no-reason-when-citing-the-1958-diplo-matic-note-250365, accessed 12 September 2018. For a defence of Phạm Văn Đồng by Lưu Văn Lợi, a retired Vietnamese diplomat, see http://www.bbc.co.uk/ vietnamese/vietnam/story/2008/09/080917_luuvanloi_inv.shtml, accessed 22 February 2018.

Linh Tự Temple (Temple of the Dead) to the rank of 'national heritage'. Although I protested and tried to explain that I had not played a part in this process, they had their own interpretation of the matter. They came to the conclusion that the presence of a foreign researcher on the island added legitimacy to provincial authorities' endeavours to obtain a 'National Certificate of Designation of Historical and Cultural Relic', issued by the Ministry of Culture, Sport, and Tourism.

〰〰

Taken together, these two seemingly unconnected events serve to illustrate how inhabitants of Lý Sơn Island, 30 km off the coast of Quảng Ngãi Province in central Vietnam, project their island as an imagined centre of a revised map of the nation's territory in the context of the conflict between China and Vietnam over the Paracels and Spratlys, with repercussions at the local, national, and international levels. The map of Vietnam has been redrawn to include much of the South China Sea, stretching as far as the Paracel and Spratly archipelagos, thereby effectively situating Lý Sơn Island in the middle of Vietnam's combined land and sea territory. The state's appropriation of Lý Sơn's legacy encouraged villagers on the island to rework some of their local narratives in such a way that they simultaneously support the state's claims and their individual, lineage, and communal interests. In this way, I focus on the island community's dual processes appropriating and reworking national narratives that build on such presumably binary categories as *local* and *national*, *individual* and *lineage*, *ancestor* and *ghost*. The process in which the Lý Sơn community inscribes itself at the centre of Vietnam's history and geography cannot be fully grasped without an analysis of the state's narratives themselves (Trouillot 1995).

In Vietnam, the state not only appoints gods and heroes, assigns sacred spaces, and grants certificates in order to nationalize and institutionalize them, but also sees religious traditions as one of many possible ways to achieve national unity. The fact that most of the island's religious structures survived the two Indochina Wars, which barely touched Lý Sơn, added legitimacy to both the provincial authorities' and the local community's endeavours to reinstate the local commemoration of Paracel and Spratly sailors and to apply for national recognition of this ceremony.

128

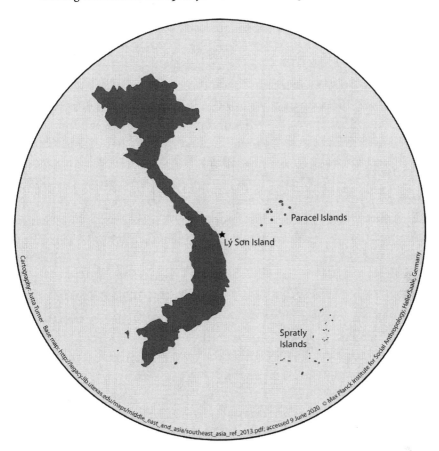

Figure 7: Imaginary map of Vietnam's land and the sea with Lý Sơn in the middle.

In this chapter I describe how local commemorative projects on Lý Sơn are employed to add legitimacy to the territorial claims of the central Party-state and hence strengthen its arguments in the South China Sea dispute. I stress that commemorative practices are not exclusively the purview of the state, but also of the people who hold a stake in them. By looking at various state and local initiatives, I go beyond 'simplistic polarities' and 'static binarism' (see Herzfeld 2016: 24) that reduce state–society relations to straightforward antagonism. In this way I show that not only do 'state' and 'village' come to be treated as highly personalized actors that strategically mediate different positions of authority and the 'rationalizing logic of the nation-state' (ibid.), but also that the commemorations become a space where the two poles of the state-society binary collapse into each other even as they are held onto by people as distinct categories. Thus, this chapter demonstrates that, while the islanders construe their locality in terms of a 'unique seafaring tradition', they also realize that its recognition largely depends on their participation in wider visions of the past, translated into 'cultural' and 'national heritage'. This reflection provides background for a more in-depth analysis of strategies undertaken by various lineages to have the figures of two local sailors – Phạm Hữu Nhật and Võ Văn Khiết – recognized within the provincial pantheon of heroes of the Paracels. I focus particularly on the female ancestor of Phạm's kin group and their attempt to present her as a local heroine rather than as a ghost that is potentially dangerous to her kinsmen and villagers due to her premature and violent death.

Islanders as guardians of the Paracels and Spratlys

Although the small atoll of Lý Sơn lies much closer to present-day Quảng Ngãi Province on Vietnam's mainland than it does to the Paracel Islands, which are some 300 km to the east, in eighteenth-century historical documents the atoll's proximity to the Paracels was often noted (see Chapter 3). The historian Lê Quý Đôn estimated the distance to the Paracels as roughly one day's sailing from Lý Sơn (Lê Quý Đôn 1972 [1776]: 203). Despite competing claims to the Paracels and Spratlys, up until the 1990s most East and Southeast Asian fishers considered the South China Sea open seas and its fishing grounds common property. This has changed as China, Vietnam, the Philippines, and Taiwan have all taken more assertive stances (Sheng-Ti Gau 2012). With the discovery of offshore deposits of oil and natural gas in the early 1970s, the rival states began to extend their claims over the sea in an effort to gain greater control over its mineral and marine resources. Open conflict broke out in 1974 when Chinese forces overran a South Vietnamese military garrison on the Paracels. In 1988 it broke out again in the Spratlys, resulting in the sinking of three Vietnamese naval ships by Chinese forces (Amer 2002).

As the economic, political, and military powerhouse in the region, China's assertion of its claims to the territorial waters around the Paracels resulted in the enforcement of a fishing ban, the capture and detention of Vietnamese fishermen, and the confiscation of their vessels by the

Chinese coastguard. The already difficult economic situation of Lý Sơn Island, lagging behind the mainland in terms of healthcare, education, and infrastructure, worsened after Lý Sơn fishermen were denied rights to use fishing grounds that had for generations been considered their own. Because of Lý Sơn's proximity to and historical association with the Paracels and Spratlys, Vietnamese authorities designated Lý Sơn a restricted border zone and prohibited international and domestic tourism. This changed when the island became a putative symbol of the 'defence of sovereignty' over the 'East Sea' (i.e., the South China Sea) and was developed into a destination for tourists eager to show their solidarity with the islanders, who were bearing the brunt of defending the nation's sovereignty.

China's seizure of Vietnamese vessels and the arrest and months-long detention of Lý Sơn fishermen have been widely covered in Vietnam's mass media, adding fuel to a heated, mostly media-driven debate about the disputed areas of the South China Sea and to the dissident-driven allegation that the Vietnamese state is weak in its dealings with China. Opinions about what constitutes a genuine threat to the country's national interests suggest that economic considerations prevail in Vietnam's overall strategy. While Vietnam is obviously concerned about the potential loss of control over offshore oil and gas deposits as well as other natural resources, the Vietnamese state simultaneously has a stake in maintaining good diplomatic and political relations with its main trading partner and the region's dominant military force, China. The state, however, appears to be doing little to create other job opportunities for Lý Sơn fishers who are denied access to the fishing grounds on which they depend. Consequently, Lý Sơn fishers feel abandoned by the central state and left to their own devices.

In his analysis of the local consequences of the international conflict on Jinmen Island – known as the Taiwan Strait Crisis of the 1950s – Michael Szonyi (2008) vividly illustrates how militarization is slipping into the daily lives of people and into individual imaginations. In this sense, militarization not only refers to the state's capacity to exercise military power, but also becomes a vehicle for producing and exercising political power. It creates new spaces for interaction between state and society and provides a multitude of ways for people to respond to global economic and political discourses (2008: 246). To shore up its legitimacy, in the early 1990s the Vietnamese state turned its attention towards Lý Sơn Island as a valuable source of information about the history of the Paracel and Spratly flotillas. Many of the Paracel soldiers died at sea and their bodies were never returned to their relatives, giving rise to special ritual and memorial practices on Lý Sơn. Some of their names, however, were preserved in place-names, such as two small islets in the Paracel archipelago that bear the names of Captain Phạm Quang Ảnh and Captain Phạm Hữu Nhật, who stood out from others because of their skills and expertise (Sơn Hồng Đức 1975). In 1994 and 1995, a group of scholars from the Faculty of History at Hanoi National University visited Lý Sơn several times and inquired about the history of the island and the Paracel navy. In the context of a large-scale project for the preservation of cultural and national 'heritage', these scholars visited a number of families, collecting various documents and family records and recording oral histories. The results of the investigations were published by Nguyễn Quang Ngọc and Vũ Văn Quân (1998), who wrote about the role and activities of the Paracel navy in an article entitled 'Sources on the Origin, Tasks and Activities of the Paracel Army'. At the beginning of the publication, they praise the feudal monarchs for their deep awareness of the significance of the 'East Sea' and their efforts to protect and extend their possession over the entire region of the two archipelagos. The Paracel navy, which operated in the Paracel and Spratly regions, became an example of Vietnamese control and thus served to legitimate claims to these islands.

Therefore, it is no surprise that, on 3 August 2001, the Vietnamese prime minister issued a directive establishing and reconstructing a 'zone with historical sites' (*khu di tích lịch sử*) related to the Paracels and Spratlys. The purpose was to preserve all places of historical significance regarding the heritage of the forefathers, which supported Vietnam's claims to the Paracel and Spratly archipelagos (Nguyễn Đăng Vũ 2001). Facing competition from several states, including China, for control over the Paracels and Spratlys, the Vietnamese Party-state chose to frame their claims to sovereignty over the archipelagos not in economic terms, but with reference to the historical trajectory of the 'nation' and to the emotional ties of the Vietnamese people to their soil, which, according to this directive, includes not only the land but also the sea. In early October of the same year, representatives of the National Border

Defence Committee and the Ministry of Culture and Information visited the Lý Sơn District in order to 'explore the current situation of all places of historical value' connected with the flotillas of the two archipelagos (2001: 31). In the days that followed, a conference was organized in close collaboration with local authorities, including members of the Quảng Ngãi People's Committee, local researchers, and scholars from Hanoi National University. Although the anniversary celebration of the Paracel and Spratly soldiers was included in commemorative projects, the state preferred to maintain a low profile for these ceremonies, as the whole issue of contested archipelagos was highly politicized. Indeed, at the time of my fieldwork in 2007, the Paracel and Spratly ceremonies on Lý Sơn still had a low profile, and Lý Sơn Island itself hardly ever appeared on official maps, which did include the Paracels and Spratlys, despite the efforts of Quảng Ngãi provincial authorities to present the island not only as a historical treasure trove, but also as a potential tourist destination. Although local commemorative traditions attracted the attention of regional media, including Đà Nẵng television, which produced several documentary films about the individual lineages' religious observances, I could hardly find at that time any information about Lý Sơn on the Internet.

However, in 2009, with the heating up of the South China Sea dispute, the situation changed dramatically as the island became the topic of many Internet debates regarding the unexpected 'rediscovery' of a cultural and historical legacy 'preserved for centuries' by islanders.[2] Widely publicized in the context of the dispute over the Paracels and Spratlys, Lý Sơn became a symbol of an imagined, age-old consciousness of the 'ancestral lands' in the South China Sea and the struggle to protect them, provoking a newfound patriotism, especially among students and intellectuals, who staged several peace rallies, tinged with anti-Chinese sentiment, to demonstrate their national devotion. In 2013 Lý Sơn welcomed guided tour groups from the mainland for the first time. Considered a historic and contemporary stepping stone to the far-flung Paracels, Lý Sơn has become a destination for thousands of Vietnamese tourists from all over the country. Just as it did for Lý Sơn residents and provincial authorities, for many Vietnamese from the

---

2. See https://en.vietnam.com/news/article/ly-son-island-of-history-and-economy. html, accessed 12 September 2018.

mainland the island came to represent the centre of a re-imagined map of the nation's territory that now included both the land and the sea.

Paradoxically, the state's various commemorative projects as well as the national and international attention on the Paracels and Spratlys dispute opened up new possibilities and space for creativity for both provincial authorities and the marginalized community of Lý Sơn fishers. What drew my attention during my fieldwork in 2006 and 2007 was that the Vietnamese state had to face not only international but also local contestations, as local officials and islanders introduced their own accounts of this emotionally charged issue. In this way, the encounters between local and central state authorities were bound up with the competition between different lineages. The head of the Quảng Ngãi Journalists' Association, along with local historians, archaeologists, and authorities, became officially and personally engaged in the process of recovering historical materials. Some of the local authorities encouraged their kin and fellow villagers to collect all existing written documents that might have historical value and contribute to the reconstruction of patriotic traditions on the island. Confronted with a large-scale campaign and the tremendous amount of effort that had been put into the task, many lineages did not remain indifferent towards the official initiatives; however, the outpouring of genealogies and documents from competing lineages was not always congruent with an official vision of the Paracel–Spratly commemorations. I will return to this point in the next section of this chapter when I take a closer look at the efforts of one of the founding lineages to reaffirm the meritorious service of their female ancestor. But let me first turn to the role of commemorations in the state's cultural project.

Commemoration and ancestor worship

Commemorations, due to their capacity to shape national memory, powerfully represent the past in modern Vietnam. Claims of continuity with the past distinguish commemorations from other ritual forms and secure them a special position among official symbolic imagery (Connerton 1999). Kertzer (1988) argues that contemporary political leaders are eager to use religious rituals and symbols to legitimize their power and engage people in institutionalized and emotional forms of action. In Vietnam, the commemoration of death anniversaries has become a potent tool for politicians and historians to create the past, write narratives about national and revolutionary martyrs, and teach 'proper' Vietnamese religious tradition. However, the state deliberately prevents the majority of local commemorations from turning into national-level events (see Malarney 2007). Instead, state officials keep the number of attendees relatively small, while at the same time playing their role as patrons of national/local tradition under the umbrella of national progress. The state controls and influences commemorations in a number of ways: through articles in academic journals, through provincial conferences, by mapping out commemorative locations, and by designing the events themselves (Ho Tai 1995, 2001; Malarney 2001; Pelley 2002: 164; Schwenkel 2009). This process involves selecting and reshaping certain narratives of the past, while silencing others.

In her inspiring essay, Hue Tam Ho Tai (1995) asserts that the Vietnamese state exercises complete control over the location, planning, and budgeting of commemorative projects, without any participation or input from the people. Decisions regarding national monuments result not from shared visions or confrontations between ordinary citizens and the state, but from multivocality originating within the state apparatus itself. In reference to the Vietnam-America War, Christina Schwenkel (2009) persuasively demonstrates that, indeed, the state is not a monolithic actor and national history is far from a homogeneous experience. State memorials and commemorations in Vietnam are also the result of transnational confrontations that take place in museums, cemeteries, wartime photography exhibits, former battlefields turned into tourist sites, and among American veterans (Schwenkel 2009: 5-9). Yet both Ho Tai and Schwenkel are mostly concerned with contestations over historical and national representation played out in state commemorative practices. By contrast, I map a different landscape of commemoration, providing a window into the local history of the South China Sea. I argue that such confrontations between the state's and the people's views do occur at the local level, where commemorations of the past are contested and therefore are not the exclusive purview of the state. The local narratives can become open to negotiation, as they are products of multivocality originating within various competing state and non-state groups of Vietnamese, including local officials, lineage representatives, descendants, and other individuals. As Kwon (2006,

2009) has demonstrated in his study of commemoration in Vietnam, the bereavement of families of civilians killed in military operations has not been acknowledged in national remembrance ceremonies, but it has produced a variety of patterns in the domestic cult of ancestors. Modern warfare's power to totally destroy bodies and the subsequent painful impossibility of proper burial has created all sorts of ghosts who have to be reunited with the living through family commemorative rites (Kwon 2006). National history and heroism only have meaning for the people when they are integrated with local history and the genealogical heritage of the community (Kwon 2006: 117). It is precisely this space of commemorative practice where the binary opposites of state and society collapse into each other, drawing religion into the centre.

The Paracel–Spratly commemorative projects are inscribed in the Vietnamese discourse on culture and religion. This discourse, initiated by the state, concerns ancestor worship, which is one of those religious practices that have received state recognition as 'national religious traditions'. According to the definition by Đặng Nghiêm Vạn (1998: 246), ancestor worship is 'the veneration of those passed away who deserve credit for the generation and nurture of their descendants ... or who have achieved merit in service to their commune or country'. Ancestor worship, he observes, is a long-standing religious tradition of the Vietnamese people that is deeply rooted in their consciousness, especially as it represents national custom and is 'imbued with a sense of duty' (ibid.: 247). Kwon (2006: 104) notes that 'the traditional religious institution became the technology of national integration. Imagining the nation-state became a matter of thinking about dead war heroes within the familiar system of ancestor worship.' In this light, the traditional cult of ancestor worship has recurred as a 'hero-centered political culture' because the state's focus is on the exemplary service of the ancestors rather than on a peaceful afterlife (ibid.). Nevertheless, Vietnamese people take a more egalitarian approach to the dead: the spirits of all ancestors, regardless of their merit or contribution, and even the ghosts of strangers, deserve acknowledgement. Therefore, those who are not recognized by the state have not necessarily been forgotten; rather, lo-cal officials, communities, and individuals often speak on their behalf. These groups engage in contestations over memory as they subtly shift the ground and, thus, turn their kin or fellow villagers – the 'unknown dead', the 'wandering souls' – into heroic and meritorious members of their locality.

Local contestations – The competition between lineages

The prestige associated with historical records of the Paracel and Spratly sailors resulted in a 'commemorative fever' among various lineages in Lý Sơn, which began to compete with each other in demonstrating the meritorious and patriotic services of their ancestors and obtaining the official recognition known as the 'Certificate of Designation of Historical and Cultural Relic' (see Ho Tai 2001: 1). Such a certificate not only provides state recognition allowing people to worship their divinities in any way they wish, but it can also bring in public funding for restoration and promotion of a particular site as a tourist attraction. In Lý Sơn some of the founding lineages employed scholars to write letters to the Provincial Office of Culture, Sport, and Tourism in support of claims regarding the cultural and historical value of their legacies.

One of the most revealing competitions took place between two lineages, Võ and Phạm. Both lineages trace their origins to the first families of migrants who today are venerated in the village communal house as 'pioneers' and as 'those who first broke the land' (*tiền hiền*). The two lineages, both from An Vĩnh village, were proud that their family annals (*gia phả*), which had been preserved, handed down for centuries, and re-edited in the process, were taken to Hanoi by scholars and sent to the Institute of Sino-Vietnamese Studies for translation. The originals, containing descriptions of local events, names, and information about the lives of respected ancestors, were later returned to the owners after copies were made for the Institute's library. Whereas the Võ lineage had the support of their kinsman – a provincial official devoted to cultural studies – the Phạm established good connections with well-known historians and local authorities through the lineage's representative, the fifty-eight-year-old Anh (in 2007).

The growing attention of intellectuals and officials helped the Võ lineage restore their sacred places. In 1997, An Vĩnh villagers put all their efforts into collecting money and rebuilding the temple that the ancestor of the Võ lineage had originally built for the village. Villagers installed altars there devoted to worshipping the founder of the temple, the tutelary spirit, the spirit of the soil, the spirit of *Bạch Mã* (White

Horse), and to the Paracel officer Võ Văn Khiết, just to name a few. To obtain the 'Certification of Designation of Historical and Cultural Relic', one has to prove the artistic and historical value of a place or the merit of the ancestor worshipped (Endres 2001: 88). Võ Văn Khiết seemed a perfect fit for all official requirements, and the Võ lineage had all the necessary documents to prove Võ Văn Khiết's meritorious service to the village as well as to the country. In the Võ family record, dated 1803, we can read that, due to Võ Văn Khiết's virtues, he was appointed head of the *đình* by the villagers of An Vĩnh (Nguyễn Quang Ngọc and Vũ Văn Quân 1998). He was described as a straightforward, honest, diligent, and knowledgeable person. The lineage, together with villagers and with the help of their kin and other local authorities from Quảng Ngãi, prepared the necessary petition. In 2001, the temple was listed in the official report of the Provincial Office of Culture among other monuments for the commemoration of the Paracel flotilla. The document lists Võ Văn Khiết's temple as a historical site of the Paracels (UBND Tỉnh Quảng Ngãi and Sở văn hoá Thông Tin 2001).

At the same time, members of the Phạm lineage began their efforts to reaffirm the meritorious service of their female ancestor, Lady Roi, and her historical value. Although they had not been backed by the villagers like the Võ kin group had been, in 2003 the Phạm lineage received official permission and support from local authorities of the district People's Committee to apply for recognition of Lady Roi's temple as a historic site. A year later, while collecting materials for the Quảng Ngãi Museum, the members of the lineage unexpectedly came across additional documents preserved in their ancestral house. The newly discovered credentials included a genealogy (*phổ hệ*), the family record, a charter (*sắc phong*), and altar tablets that not only shed new light on Lady Roi herself, but also on one of the lineage's ancestors, captain of the Paracel flotilla Phạm Hữu Nhật, after whom one of the islets of the Paracel archipelago is named. With the help of the head of the Quảng Ngãi Journalists' Association, archaeologists from the local museum, historians, and authorities from the province and district, celebrations were held in March 2005 for the unveiling of a commemorative plaque in honour of Phạm Hữu Nhật, who was then officially recognized as a respected ancestor of the Phạm lineage and a soldier of the Paracel navy. However, the struggle for the certificate was not yet concluded. The lineage continued to count on the support of well-known historians and journalists and even of Đà Nẵng television, hoping that, with such powerful and unquestioning supporters, success would quickly follow.

While there was no contestation concerning the heroism of Phạm Hữu Nhật, the efforts of the Phạm lineage to recognize their second ancestor, Lady Roi, met with strong opposition from the members of the Võ lineage, who felt that the Phạm wanted to elevate their lineage over others through the deification and official recognition of their female ancestor. By acknowledging Võ Văn Khiết as a collective ancestor of the whole village, Võ lineage members stressed their self-effacement, which contrasted, they believed, with the more individualistic aspirations of the Phạm lineage, which sought only its own glory. They stressed that Võ Văn Khiết's temple had been handed over to the village a long time ago and it was communal rather than lineage property. Consequently, by projecting themselves in relation to the larger entity of the village, Võ members were able to align themselves with the 'collective' position while accusing other lineages of 'individual' and hence fractious tendencies. However, it would be difficult to deny that this more collective aspect of the official recognition of Võ Văn Khiết had in fact elevated the Võ lineage status within the local community.

The above narrative illustrates that power struggles between the lineages represent another dimension of the process of recovering local memories. Both the Phạm and the Võ lineages first sought local and genealogical continuity, as they wanted to point out that their family members, as well as the Lý Sơn people more generally, though spatially distanced from the mainland, had always contributed to the defence of the nation. National continuity was meaningful for them only when incorporated into their lineages' concerns.

By way of comparison, the Chinese example shows that in the volatile post-socialist environment, rural Chinese communities began to rebuild their identity around clan, lineage, or religious affiliation (Hillman 2004). Susanne Brandtstädter (2003) explains that where a state is unable to create trust and state institutions have failed to reproduce the moral world of a community, new forms of individual and collective morality appear. Investment in gifts, kinship rituals, ancestral halls, and cultural inventiveness connected with temple reconstruction became an intrinsic part of the process of the restoration of community pride and identity and, above all, of prestige and 'kinship relatedness' (Brandtstädter 2003: 435; Hillman 2004). Referring to northern Vietnam, Hy Van Luong (2003: 216) observes a similar phenomenon when he reports that by the end of the 1990s Vietnamese people had actively established formal organizations to strengthen their own social networks and to fill the vacuum left by the Communist state, which in the post-socialist era had partially withdrawn from social domains such as health care, education, and welfare. Many of those organizations, such as patrilineages and the exclusively male same-age associations, have been recently reinvented.[3] My own data are in accord with this statement. As Siu (1989), Brandtstädter (2003), and Hillman (2004) rightly point out in the case of China, the ritual revitalization represents a re-cycling of cultural fragments in a rural society rather than a resurgence of traditional practices. At the same time, however, it is intrinsically connected with kinship conflicts, rural politics, and strategies of status maintenance and prestige building that play out across and within the triadic relationship of state–village–religion. In this process, re-enacted village rituals articulated with official state categories. Although all part of the state semiotic ideology, these state categories mean different things to different people (see Siu 1989), as I argue in the case of Lý Sơn.

With reference to Vietnam, while many recent ethnographic studies highlight the re-emergence of village 'collective identity' through the revivification of village rituals, they reject the romantic image of the village as a homogeneous, cooperative, and autonomous entity (e.g., Luong 1992; Kleinen 1999b; Truong Huyen Chi 2001, 2004; DiGregorio 2007). The 'collective identity' and 'collective response' to the state's

---

3. In Sa Huỳnh and Lý Sơn I came across not only lineage associations, but also new organizations such as the Association of Elders (*Hội người cao tuổi*), known in pre-revolutionary times as the Association of Longevity (*Hội bảo thọ*), the Association of Vietnam War Veterans (*Hội cựu chiến binh*), and the Committee of Grave-visiting Rites (*Ban lễ Thanh Minh*), just to mention a few of them. The head of the Association of Elders in Sa Huỳnh stated that these organizations had been formed in the late 1990s, and their main purpose was to organize financial and moral assistance for the members' families in case of sickness or death. Luong (2003: 216) explains that, '[i]n its selective emphasis on tradition as an integral part of Vietnamese identity in an age of globalization, the Vietnamese state also became more tolerant of the proliferation or nonpolitical *reinvention* of traditional organizational forms' (emphasis added).

changing political, economic, and cultural policies result not only from tensions and interfaces between the villagers and the local state, but also from debates and contestations between villagers themselves (Truong Huyen Chi 2004: 25). Following the relaxation in cultural policy and the revival of traditional religious practices in Vietnam, it became common for lineage representatives to compete over ritual space, to invent or reinterpret life stories of spirits, and to hire scholars to help prepare petitions and ensure good connections with staff at the Ministry of Culture, who might facilitate the process of applying for state recognition (Truong Huyen Chi 2001, 2004; see also Endres 2001; DiGregorio 2007; Ho Tai Hue Tam and Lê Hồng Lý 2008). Most of the lineages seek to formulate their efforts to recover and restore rituals and religious sites as reconstitution of community space, but it would be misleading to ignore individual interests that lie behind such endeavours.

Truong Huyen Chi (2004: 24) insists that without an in-depth understanding of the particular historical process of a local setting and the relationship between lineages, one could hardly comprehend the complexity of the 'deep play' between different groups. Analogically, I argue that we can learn how Lý Sơn people judge the validity of local histories and try to promote their own lineage's interests by the way they use their family records to argue their cases. Genealogies not only validate present relationships, but they are often modelled on the forms of actual relationships (Bohannan 1952). Vietnamese family annals are written records, but even in this 'rigid form' they remain fluid and change substance in response to current situations. As the example of Lý Sơn community well illustrates, for villagers, obtaining the certificate not only became a source of communal pride, but also served as an occasion to display the 'meritorious past' of individual lineages and gain financial support for the renovation of their temples, which could become tourist attractions in the future.

Provincial authorities and their incentives

Parallel to the competition between various lineages on Lý Sơn Island, provincial authorities saw a chance to promote their own province and elevate themselves to higher state positions by catering to Hanoi's 'official interest' in patriotic traditions on the island. For instance, it is not a coincidence that the former head of the Quảng Ngãi Journalists'

Association, and the most active person in the Paracel project, was given at least two promotions over the last few years, finally reaching a top position in provincial administration. He sought to present Lý Sơn as a crucial source of historical documentation supporting Vietnam's claims to sovereignty over the Paracels and Spratlys. As a result, Quảng Ngãi authorities have invested thirteen billion VND (about 500,000 euros) since 2007 to build the Paracel and Spratly memorial on Lý Sơn Island, a project that includes a museum, a restored communal house, and a monument dedicated to the Paracel flotilla. Furthermore, the Provincial Cultural Office decided to 'recover' local traditions connected with the Paracel sailors and even petitioned the Ministry of Culture to give the commemoration ceremonies the status of 'national festival'. The Quảng Ngãi provincial officials became directly engaged in helping the Võ and Phạm lineages restore their temples, and provided funds for organizing traditional ceremonies related to Paracel sailors (see Nguyễn Đăng Vũ 2002). In the same year, the authorities took over all responsibility for preparing the Paracel Tribute Rituals (*Lễ khao lề thế lính Hoàng Sa*) from the Lý Sơn villagers, who complained that they were deprived of the opportunity to shape the ceremony according to their local views.

On the other hand, the Quảng Ngãi provincial authorities did not shun expressing national devotion and, additionally, fanned the flames of a new-found patriotism among islanders by appealing to their sense of pride regarding the protection of the ancestral lands of the South China Sea. During the preparatory work for the Paracel Tribute Ritual Ceremony in April 2010, banners were stretched across the streets of the provincial capital that announced, 'Preserving sovereignty over all islands of the South China Sea'. The banners were intended as a reference to the Paracel Islands, but could also be understood as a reference to Lý Sơn itself, as China, according to local views, claims all islands of the South China Sea.[4] Three years later the Quảng Ngãi Province went even further and organized an international conference, 'Việt Nam's sovereignty over Hoàng Sa and Trường Sa Archipelagos – legal and

---

4. Personal communication from Andrew Hardy, April 2010. China claims over 80 per cent of the South China Sea; see for example Michael Richardson, 'Territorial Claims in South China: LNG deal with KL shows Beijing may be easing off', *Strait Times*, 22 March 2010 http://www.iseas.edu.sg/viewpoint/mr22mar10.pdf, accessed 26 August 2010. See also Carlyle A. Thayer (2010).

historical aspects', which served as a platform for presenting historical evidence in the dispute over territories in the South China Sea. The foreign participants who attended the conference visited all temples on Lý Sơn Island related to the Paracel and Spratly navy and watched the Paracel Tribute Ritual, which was carefully prearranged by the province and district authorities. The strategy of connecting local commemorations with the global dispute paid off when in 2014 the Vietnamese Ministry of Culture, Sport, and Tourism selected Lý Sơn Island to host the national exhibition of Vietnam's and China's historical maps, under the slogan 'Paracels and Spratlys belong to Vietnam – legal and historical evidence'. With the aim of raising morale among local fishers and local soldiers stationed on the island, the exhibition on Lý Sơn was marked by the attendance of representatives from the Vietnam Naval Forces and central and local state authorities.

Adam Chau (2006) observes that in the post-socialist context, the Chinese local state had increased its power and autonomy noticeably vis-à-vis the central state, though this trend has been dramatically reversed in the last few years as the strong political leadership of President Xi Jinping expanded central control over local officials. In Chapter 2, focusing on the antisuperstition campaign of the late 1970s, I noted that the official authorities had more space within which they could contest, modify, or even ignore central government policies. With new means of communication such as the Internet, cell phones, better roads, and off-road vehicles, I shall argue that the Vietnamese central state is, as in China, gaining a stronger grip on local government. Therefore, even if the interests of local governmental authorities are vested in the local, and the local government might behave differently from the central state as Chau argued (2006: 213), the local state agents in Vietnam are in no position to ignore the central government's directives. As in China, in Vietnam local agents not only take on the role of patron of village rituals and practices, but also facilitate the re-emergence of specific places as important cultural and historical sites, guaranteeing that these sites are not perceived by the central government as promoting superstitious cults. In this sense, villagers interact not with the local state per se, but rather with individual state agents who have a certain degree of autonomy. Chau draws attention to the *guanxi* (reciprocal social relations based on gift-giving and patronage, in Vietnamese called *quan hệ*), referring to them as 'rhizomatic networks' capable of subverting the 'mono-organizational' state (ibid: 238). The 'guanxi-pulling' relations are like rhizomes of a tree that grow inside and alongside the channels between local state agencies and civic organizations. Thus, it is up to communities and individuals to work out the 'channeling zone' through which they can pay their tributes and respect 'upward' – to the local state – and win official recognition and legitimacy 'downward' – for their local ritual spaces (ibid.). This process, which Chau vividly describes, has been observed by many anthropologists working on Vietnam, who have noted that local communities are eager to establish good connections with authorities and engage scholars in order to back their specific legacies (see Endres 2001; DiGregorio 2007; Ho Tai and Le Hong Ly 2008). As I have shown, in Lý Sơn the competing lineages tried to establish their networks of social relationships through kinsmen who happened to be in the local government or were well-known historians or journalists.

Earlier in this chapter I mentioned that Lý Sơn villagers had attributed at least part of their success in obtaining national recognition for their village temple to my presence in the village. Apparently, I was seen as someone who had access to provincial and even central authorities. However, I was also seen as someone who might constrain or even jeopardize their efforts to get the state certificate. When I asked An Vĩnh villagers if I could see a spirit possession organized in Âm Linh Tự Temple, they debated for weeks about my request, called me from time to time, and informed me of the 'progress' of negotiations between them and village elders. In the end, I learned that the elders had decided not to show me any religious practices that could be construed as 'superstitious'. Couching their words in pre-Đổi Mới semiotic ideology and displaying their own deference towards the state rules, they explained that if reports of 'superstitions' and 'outdated practices' taking place in a village temple listed as a 'national heritage' were to reach the authorities in Hanoi, their petition would be rejected. While my presence on the island was useful in promoting the 'unique local spiritual culture', Lý Sơn people still felt the need to exercise some control over the production of the 'ideal' Vietnamese culture (Harms 2011a: 25). The elders had to carefully calculate the 'supposed benefit' of allowing me, as a foreign researcher, to witness their rituals.

Ancestors and ghosts of Lý Sơn

In Vietnam, as in China (see Wolf 1974), the ancestors of one kin group can be dangerous to members of other kin groups, who may view the ancestors (*tổ tiên*) simply as 'ghosts' (*tà ma, hồn ma, hồn người chết*). Other potentially dangerous ghosts who may threaten not only non-kinsmen but their own family members as well include those whose lives were interrupted unexpectedly and brutally. They cause a particularly serious problem if their deaths occurred in an unfamiliar place, out of 'the domain of domestic security' and at a distance from the ancestral altar (Kwon 2009: 89). To calm such spirits, Vietnamese people in central Vietnam usually erect a small shrine, altar, or gravestone in secluded areas such as the Forbidden Hill in Sa Huỳnh, where the grave of Bà Lao is located. Typically, the seacoast in the southern part of central Vietnam is dotted with elevated platforms, called *nghĩa trủng* or *nghĩa tự*, that serve as graveyards for those who died violently, away from their homes, but who had merit within the village or the country. Because they 'did good' (*làm việc nghĩa*), people fulfil their duties to them just as they do to their ancestors (Nguyễn Đăng Vũ 2006). The soldiers of the Paracel navy who never returned to their natal villages and whose bodies presumably sank into the deep waters of the South China Sea could be included in this category.

As Lý Sơn people explained, to be ready for the possibility of dying away from home, the Paracel soldiers going to sea would prepare a straw mat, rattan rope, bamboo poles and a small wooden tablet noting their name, age, native village, and designation of their unit. When a man died, his comrades would wrap his body in the mat, attach it to the poles and lower it from the boat into the waters in the hope that some of the living would find the beached corpse and give it a proper burial. Most of the time, however, the bodies of soldiers never returned to their kin. The Lý Sơn people did not want to leave their loved ones unburied, so they would make mannequins and bury them in fake graves in order to console the 'wandering souls' of those who had died tragic deaths (Nguyễn Quang Ngọc and Vũ Văn Quán 1998: 14; Phan Đình Độ n.d.). According to local accounts, a 'village ritual master' or 'master of the Dharma' (*thầy pháp*) would mould mannequins out of clay that were supposed to substitute for the bodies of the Paracel sailors.

Located in the yard of the Âm Linh Tự temple in An Vĩnh village, the burial mounds of the Paracel sailors are still preserved on the island and represent an integral part of the community's collective memory (Đoàn Ngọc Khôi 2004). Following surviving oral tradition and family annals, every second month of the lunar year villagers organized the Paracel Tribute Rituals (*lễ khao lề thế lính Hoàng Sa*) in the Âm Linh Tự temple. In the past, the ceremony was dedicated to both the living and the dead soldiers. The elders and families of the Paracel sailors who were assigned by imperial authorities to replace those who died during naval operations offered a leaving feast just before the sailors embarked. In the framework of the ceremony, a master of the Dharma would build a miniature ship with images of sailors, place offerings on its deck, and launch the ship into the sea in the hope that the sailors would return safely (Nguyễn Đăng Vũ 2002: 56–57).

Finally, a potentially dangerous category of ghosts includes the spirits of virgin girls who died violent and untimely deaths. They are thought to be burdened with memories, unfulfilled desires, and unrequited lust (Taylor 2004: 201), which make them want to remain among the living. They pose a problem in terms of ancestor worship because they have no descendants to venerate them. If forgotten, they can turn into angry ghosts and harm the living. Thus, the premature deaths of these young unmarried girls blur the binary distinction between ghosts and ancestors. It is believed that they are especially envious of motherhood and therefore can cause the death of children in their patrilineage or even in the whole village. In turn, worshipped with care, they may also earn reputations for responsiveness and efficacy. Without heeding whether the wishes and requests of the living are good or bad, these spirits grant all of them in return for the satisfaction of their needs (ibid.). Thus, the closest relatives of the dead usually set a separate altar outside the house or even build a small shrine where they commemorate and honour these women by burning incense and offering food in order to achieve peaceful coexistence.

The female ancestor of the Phạm lineage was not the only young woman in Lý Sơn who died accidentally. There was another lineage that, like the Phạm, stressed its direct relationship with the founders of An Vĩnh and had an ambition to elevate its female ancestor to the position of village goddess. However, only the Phạm lineage was able to back their statements with a written genealogy when submitting the life story (*lý lịch*) of their female ancestor to the provincial authorities (see Chapter 2). As noted earlier, in Lý Sơn, the Phạm lineage tried to obtain recognition not only for its ancestor Phạm Hữu Nhật – the soldier of the Paracel flotilla who died violently and whom the Vietnamese state ultimately acknowledged – but also for its female ancestor, Lady Roi. I found that the individual Phạm family members had different versions of her story. One of them in particular riveted my attention: the version that Anh, the representative of the Phạm Lineage Association, told me, based on 'recently discovered' annals. Originally written in Sino-Vietnamese characters, the annals date back to the seventeenth century. The transcribed document, dated 1900, was translated into vernacular Vietnamese by a local specialist in the Sino-Vietnamese language (*Hán-Nôm*) only in 2004, the same year the document was authorized by an official of the Lý Sơn People's Committee. A lacquered box containing the sacred annals was displayed on an ancestor altar of the lineage temple, protected from unauthorized persons. However, Anh prepared several paper copies of a new modernized version, and he gladly showed them to anyone who expressed an interest.[5] According to these annals, which Anh unexpectedly discovered in the Phạm's ancestor halls in 2004, Lady Roi was a second-generation descendant of the first migrants and founders of the village who settled on the island in the early seventeenth century. In those times the coastal regions of Vietnam, including Lý Sơn Island, were allegedly being harassed by 'Chinese' pirates who plundered the villages, raped the women, and killed the villagers. Lady Roi, only sixteen years old at the time, was a victim of these invasions.

Anh emphasized supernatural events in his story, noting that Lady Roi died on the fifteenth day of the fifth lunar month of 1645. The moon on the night of the fifteenth day of lunar months is always a full moon (*răm*), and on that day Buddhist adherents visit pagodas, burn incense on the Buddha's altar, make offerings to hungry ghosts, and refrain from eating meat. Emily Ahern (1975: 206) observed that in Chinese culture, on the first and fifteenth day of each month, every household performed a modest ceremony for ghosts. Women took responsibility for worshipping spirits that might cause sickness and other misfortunes

---

5. *Gia Phả – Hộ Phạm Văn* (*Family annals – Hộ Phạm Văn*), kept by the Phạm Văn lineage, An Vĩnh commune, Lý Sơn District, Quảng Ngãi Province.

if they were not propitiated (1975: 206). In Sa Huỳnh and Lý Sơn, I often witnessed such ceremonies performed by women in front of their houses. However, in his story, Anh kept silent about his female ancestor's problematic nature as a potentially harmful ghost and, instead, emphasized those aspects of Lady Roi's character that are in keeping with Buddhist tradition, such as being a devoted daughter and a symbol of purity and self-sacrifice. Highlighting particular aspects of ideal Vietnamese womanhood constituted one of Anh's first attempts to shift the terms of the ghost–ancestor hero binary to achieve state recognition for Lady Roi.

According to Chinese and Vietnamese tradition, filial piety is an essential female virtue (see Yü 2001: 466). For example, the goddess Quan Âm represents the Buddhist ideal of filial piety and self-sacrifice motivated by pure compassion for all beings (2001: 312–347). In popular stories, she often takes on the appearance of a faithful daughter who sacrifices her own body in order to rescue or cure her parents. Anh adapted this motif in the *lý lịch* of his female ancestor:

> She [Lady Roi] came to the shore to look for her father, whom she had tried to warn of the approaching enemy. Surrounded by Chinese pirates, she chose death to maintain her virginity and threw herself into the sea.

Anh said that after her death, Lady Roi appeared in dreams, sitting in the lotus position similar to Bodhisattva Quan Âm, and informed the village of her tragic death by suicide. Quan Âm is believed to save women from sexual attacks; in the case of Lady Roi the suicide served as an escape. In this way, Anh wanted to emphasize that in a critical moment his female ancestor, like Quan Âm, who is considered a 'veritable heroine', sacrificed herself for her parent and did not give up long-standing values related to filial piety, the most important components of which are care, obedience, and moral vigilance.

In his study on popular religion, Taylor (2004: 252) notes that many tales about female spirits in Vietnam describe them as loyal daughters and as virgins who commit suicide when threatened with rape, resist marriage when obliged to marry a stranger, and remain faithful to their parents, their husbands (if they had one), or their country even after death. Margery Wolf (1975: 112), who studied women and suicide in China, notes that suicide was highly honoured by the upper-class

Chinese. She gives an example of a woman who took her life because a thief had taken refuge under her sleeping couch. She was awarded a posthumous tablet for 'the nobility of her mind' – a common encomium given to unmarried women and placed outside their houses, usually in temples (ibid.). In the context of Vietnam, Taylor (2004: 209) points out that the undefined nature of such women allowed them to be venerated as 'spiritual protectors of the sovereign or bearers of the "national essence"'. In scholarly discourse on culture, these female spirits are understood as maintaining and representing the core values of the Vietnamese nation, including patriotism and heroism (2004: 252). As depicted in popular Vietnamese tales, their encounters with enemies or corrupt state officials usually led them to heroic deaths.

Thus, in addition to traditional morality, which glorifies virginity and honour, patriotism and heroism were other important elements of Anh's narratives in the *lý lịch* of his female ancestor. He demonstrated that by choosing death, Lady Roi not only displayed such enduring virtues of a Vietnamese woman as chastity and purity, but she also became an 'indomitable heroine' (*anh hùng bất khuất*) who exhibited 'awareness of protecting the dear island' (*ý thức bảo vệ hòn đảo yêu quý*). In his narrative, Anh eloquently combined the supernatural and the real and used notions of violent death to show how his female ancestor, the young virgin, proved to be an efficacious and protective spirit during the Second Indochina War, when her grave served as a hiding place for stolen weapons. In this sense, she not only heroically confronted 'Chinese pirates', but also gave her protection to the communist guerrillas. Through the simultaneous process of hybridization and purging of those elements that were not congruent with the desired political biography, Anh redefined the dubious 'ghostly' aspect of his female ancestor into a form of patriotic heroism befitting the state's official semiotic ideology.

In his analysis of the potential positions of women in the militarized society of Jinmen, Szonyi (2008: 178) argues that women were expected to sacrifice themselves for the sake of the nation. Self-sacrifice either as a wife-mother, a soldier, or a prostitute comforting the army in order to protect civilian women became a 'defining element of womanhood' (ibid.). In Vietnam the national heroines – the Hai Bà Trưng sisters, who fought against the Chinese – were also introduced as defenders of the 'sacred land' of Vietnam in postcolonial narratives. Their bravery and 'indomitable spirit' passing from one generation to the next provide, according to official interpretation, an inspiration for Vietnamese women to revolt against the enemy (Pelley 2002: 181). Taylor (2004: 252) notes that the Second Indochina War brought a new image of women as 'longhaired guerrillas' (*du tích tóc dài*) according to which schoolgirls were seen as patriotic revolutionaries, mothers were considered heroes (*mẹ anh hùng*) because they sacrificed their sons for the revolution, and wives were described as virtuous because they stayed faithful to their husbands who had fallen in action. Ngo Thi Ngan Binh (2004: 52) reports that Hồ Chí Minh, praising southern women's revolutionary ability and their contribution to the national struggle, rewarded them with the 'eight golden words': *anh hùng* (heroic), *bất khuất* (indomitable), *trung hậu* (loyal), *đảm đang* (resourceful). Anh's narratives inevitably drew on these evocative hybrid images of the Vietnamese woman: active and courageous on the front lines. Szonyi (2008: 149) argues that militarization contributes to changing ideas of what kind of identities and behaviour are appropriate for men and for women. In this light we can see ancestor worship not only as politicized and militarized, but also in its gendered dimensions. However, on Lý Sơn Island, it is the state that ultimately determines which local heroes best suit the national narratives.

Local contestations of the Phạm's female ancestor

Between 2002 and 2006, a number of articles about Lady Roi, the Paracel soldier Phạm Hữu Nhật, and the lineage itself appeared in local newspapers and magazines. Moreover, Đà Nẵng television produced several short films about the Phạm lineage's family rituals. A large campaign promoting the Phạm ancestors in the local press and TV would not have been possible without Anh's diplomatic skills, eloquence, and good connections. Although he was neither head of his lineage nor in charge of fulfilling ritual obligations in the ancestral hall, he took on the role of lineage spokesman. His revolutionary past helped him win the support of, among others, local officials and well-known public figures such as the late historian Trần Quốc Vượng.

Anh told me that among the members of his lineage there were those who had sacrificed their lives in the two recent Indochina Wars as well as in the remote past. He had collected all the available materials about his ancestors, including the annals, newspaper clippings, photographs, letters, and petitions from famous professors and local district- and province-level authorities who supported his efforts to gain government recognition. Additionally, the bulky collection *The Dossier of Historical Sites of the Phạm Lineage* included entries of those who had visited him in recent years.[6] Anh also asked me to make an entry in his visitors' book. As a keepsake of my visit, a photo was taken and added to his document collection. I had unintentionally become the foreign researcher who took note of the 'meritorious past' of his family. In his detailed dossier, a copy of which was later given to me, I read:

> Generations of the Phạm lineage and of the people of Lý Sơn are all the more suffused with the significance of history; history is a witness of the era, a candle wick of the truth. The vital power of remembrance enlightens people's lives with the memory and awareness of the past.

In the letters and applications for government recognition of Lady Roi's temple as a historical site, submitted by the lineage to the local authorities and to the chairman of Vietnam's Association of Historians in Hanoi, Lady Roi is, above all, cited as a 'virtuous' example (*có đạo đức*) 'showing filial piety' (*có hiếu*), and a 'symbol of unifying patriotism' (*biểu tượng của thương yêu nước đoàn kết*) 'having merit with the nation' (*có công với nước*). One of Anh's main motivations was to show that members of his family had cultivated a 'national character' and patriotic traditions for generations. The other aim was to demonstrate the historical and communal value of the temple where his female ancestor was worshipped. He referred to local solidarity by indicating Lady Roi's 'merit with her hamlet' when she 'spiritually supported' her fellows during the boat festival competition, which was recreated on the island by the Quảng Ngãi Office of Culture in 2004. Anh maintained that, since Lady Roi was respected by the entire community, over time the temple developed into a public space for the entire village rather than for the lineage. According to his story, the place was converted from a small shrine into a proper temple by the members of the Phạm lineage and some of the villagers in 1897. He believed that the temple, at more than a hundred years old, deserved the rank of historical heritage site. With the assistance of local authorities, Anh turned for help to a well-known

6. *Hồ sơ di tích lịch sử - họ Phạm Văn* (2005). Tộc họ Phạm Văn. Vĩnh Commune, Lý Sơn district, Quảng Ngãi Province.

historian, Trần Quốc Vượng, who expressed his support by writing petitions and even taking part in the celebration of the 359th anniversary of the death of Lady Roi in 2004.

However, by 2007, local officials' and scholars' interest in Lady Roi had faded. Although there was no contestation concerning Phạm Hữu Nhật, they gradually withdrew their support for Lady Roi as a local heroine and her temple as a commemorative site when questions were raised regarding Anh's documentation, leading to uncertainty and hesitation. I was invited to take part in the anniversary commemoration of Lady Roi's death (*giỗ bà*) on the night of the fifteenth into the sixteenth day of the fifth lunar month in 2007, and I found it to be much simpler and more modest than I had expected based on the description of the celebration three years earlier. There were no guests at all from the province. I was warmly welcomed as a foreign researcher by the Phạm kin group. As I talked with family members, I discovered that they had different, sometimes contrary, versions of her story. Whereas some of them claimed that she had died during her encounter with Chinese pirates, others argued that she simply drowned in the sea while collecting seaweed.

Anh's efforts and the great interest in his family on the part of local state agents, intellectuals, journalists, and even television in previous years were seen differently by the villagers. Some of them were disappointed, such as those belonging to the other founding lineage that has its own claims through a female ancestor who was a contemporary of Lady Roi. They thought that I could authenticate their claims for governmental recognition and asked if I could intercede for them with the Provincial Office of Culture, Sport, and Tourism in Quảng Ngãi. Others, like members of the Võ lineage, one of whom was working as an official in Quảng Ngãi, were sceptical of the accounts of the Phạm lineage. When I asked why they were so suspicious, they gave an enigmatic reply that there appeared to be strong doubts about the accuracy and authenticity of the Phạm's family annals with respect to Lady Roi, and that even provincial authorities had to revise their knowledge on the matter. They also expressed their concern over the consequences of potential acknowledgement of the Phạm's female ancestor as a divine heroine. They believed that it would embolden the descendants of other lineages to claim a right to the same status for their female ancestors.

The villagers I talked to considered Lady Roi to be merely a Phạm female ancestor rather than a local heroine and said that they never went to her shrine to pray. They also questioned whether Lady Roi had really lived at the beginning of the seventeenth century, even if there was no doubt among them that she had indeed existed. They claimed that their very old grandparents remembered her from the time they were children. One member of the Võ lineage asserted that Chinese pirates had not yet been operating along the South China Sea coast in 1645, the year of the supposed death of Lady Roi. To convince me of his point of view, he took me to the head of the Võ lineage, who showed me their family annals in which the first mention of pirates on the island was dated 1789 – 144 years later than the Phạm documents suggested.[7] The document was translated from Sino-Vietnamese to Vietnamese and authorized by the Institute of Hán-Nôm in Hanoi. The Võ members gave me the annals and pointed to a paragraph, where I read:

> Until the sixth day of the tenth month of the Kỷ Dậu year (1789), the year when fifteen vessels of Chinese pirates plundered this quarter, the *cụ* [old man] kept all copies of acts. Although all copies of acts were soaked and ragged, the *cụ* even so brought and stored them.[8]

They refuted Anh's version about Lady Roi's reputed death at the hands of the Chinese, claiming instead that she had died accidentally at sea while she was collecting seaweed. In their eyes, rather than being a heroine, she was just the ghostly spirit of a young and childless girl who might pose a threat to the luck of her descendants if she was not worshiped. Moreover, they believed that their own forms of proof constituted the only valid history, one which could challenge Anh's narratives and annals.

---

7. According to Murray (1987), piracy emerged in the South China Sea only in the late eighteenth century. Most Cantonese-speaking fishermen, who over time intermingled with the Vietnamese, operated as pirates along the border of Guangdong and Fukien provinces around Hainan Island and in the Gulf of Tonkin. In 1773, the Tây Sơn Rebellion established its rule in Quảng Nam, Quảng Ngãi, and Bình Định provinces and recruited Chinese pirates, who supported the Vietnamese rebels (see also Kleinen and Osseweijer 2010). It is very likely that those pirates had reached the island of Lý Sơn in 1789, as the Võ lineage argued.

8. *Gia Phả – Hộ Võ Văn (Family annals – The Võ Văn Lineage)* kept by the Võ Văn lineage, An Vĩnh Commune, Lý Sơn District, Quảng Ngãi Province.

A local heroine or ghostly spirit?

The question arises as to why Anh's narratives, unlike those of the Võ lineage, failed to win the support of the village. Before I try to answer, let me first refer to an article by Charles Keyes (2002) in which he analyses what is in many respects a similar story. Keyes reports that in March 1996, thousands of local people from Khorat in north-eastern Thailand gathered around a monument honouring the memory of Thao Suranari. They wanted to publicly express their outrage against an 'insult' to her memory. This hostile reaction from local people, officials, and even military officers was provoked by the publication of a book by a teacher at a local university. The author shows in her book that the national cult of Thao Suranari arose due to a political agenda aimed at making the people of north-eastern Thailand identify themselves as Thai rather than Lao. What is interesting about this story, according to Keyes, is that the Thai author explained in her book how, over the years, the additional meanings of patriotism, regional loyalty, and gender equality were generated within the political framework, and actually eclipsed the spiritual import of the original story found in archival documents. The author called for remembering Thao Suranari as a spirit rather than as a national heroine. However, such a postulate was unacceptable to those who wanted to recall the past 'only in the service of national unity' (Keyes, 2002: 128).

The narrative of Lady Roi seems to be a mirror image of the Thai story. As I have shown, by constructing the narratives about Lady Roi's efforts to protect the island and its inhabitants in all times, the Phạm lineage manipulated religious and political categories in order to turn her potentially disconcerting ghostly spirit into a respected divinity and a local heroine for the entire community of Lý Sơn and even beyond. Lady Roi, who tried to warn her father about the Chinese and, in a critical moment, chose a heroic death, can be interpreted as a metaphor for Vietnam: a victim that always has to defend its sovereignty and independence. In his story, Anh used the Chinese plot, which was analogous to the contemporary tensions between China and Vietnam and the Vietnamese struggle to prove their claims over the Paracel and Spratly archipelagos. The Chinese pirates symbolize China's greedy desires for Vietnamese ancestral land. When Anh described his female ancestor as an indomitable heroine who has 'awareness of protecting the dear island', he was referring to the centuries-old tradition of resisting foreign invaders. In this way, the *lý lịch* of Lady Roi served him and his lineage by crafting and documenting their own moral and patriotic identity (cf. Leshkowich 2014).

Therefore, the question about why the Phạm patrilineage failed in its attempt to elevate its female ancestor to the position of heroine should be followed by the question: Can women in Vietnam 'stand for' the patrilineage, community, and nation? Ancient Vietnamese history offers a few isolated examples of women who became national heroines, such as the Hai Bà Trưng sisters and Bà Triệu, but their heroism refers to the distant past when Vietnam was not yet 'Confucianized' and did not yet conform to the Chinese moral and social organizational model.[9] On the other hand, later, when Vietnam adopted Confucian ethics, popular legends recorded many examples of women who broke rigid Confucian rules and gained autonomous and high positions in society. Recent ethnographic accounts report that many female spirits became increasingly popular among people precisely because of their ambiguous and undefined nature as young, unmarried women who had died violently (see, e.g., Dror 2002a; Taylor 2004; Endres 2008). However, what really matters here is that most of them were accepted by the state as 'goddesses' representing Vietnamese identity rather than as 'national heroines'.

Nguyên Van Ky (2002) notes that during the Second Indochina War hundreds of thousands of Vietnamese women sacrificed their youth and responded to the revolutionary call to fight against Americans. Many of them died and had no time to 'savour the taste of love, falling instead into the oblivion of history'. In turn, those 'female warriors' who survived lost the chance for marriage and found themselves 'in such a state of moral and material abandonment that they have often had to form a community within the community (village) to cope with the general indifference' (ibid: 87). While the sacrifice and heroism of these women were never officially acknowledged, the Vietnamese state recognized the sacrifice of mothers whose children were martyrs in the Second Indochina War by giving them the honorary title 'Heroic Vietnamese Mothers' (*Mẹ Anh Hùng Việt Nam*). In this way the state emphasizes the important

---

9. For more information about the Hai Bà Trưng sisters and Bà Triệu, see Taylor (1983).

role of Vietnamese women as mothers and their highest sacrifice for the country – the idealistic, militaristic understanding of womanhood glorified by the contemporary Vietnamese state (see Chapter 6). As we can see, the state also determines which female heroines would best suit the national narratives.

Despite Anh's efforts, Lady Roi's experience did not lie within the Paracel and Spratly commemorations' ambit and did not fit into the state's semiotic ideology of national heritage. Ultimately, she did not chase away the Chinese; she was not accepted by provincial authorities and villagers as a local heroine because 'she did not do anything'; 'she just died', as the villagers said. She behaved according to gender expectations and Confucian ideology, which was 'normal' rather than 'extraordinary' behaviour. By committing suicide she avoided rape and saved the honour of her lineage, but it was not enough to consider her act a 'heroic and meritorious death' for the sake of the collective. Thus, Lady Roi's death was seen by villagers rather as a sacrifice for the lineage than for the village or the nation.

In contrast to the 'problematic' sexuality of women which, from the viewpoint of Confucian ethics, if not carefully controlled and guided might bring shame upon a family and even an entire lineage, men conform more easily to the cultural ideal of the 'meritorious dead' and can thus become the embodied model for celebrating the nation. Anh's ultimate failure in his campaign to seek recognition for Lady Roi shows that only male ancestors of the Võ and Phạm lineages were accepted and acceptable as national heroes. In Vietnam's neo-Confucian kinship model, only men can be full-fledged members of the patrilineage – girls were expected to leave their paternal patrilineage and marry into their husband's patrilineage while remaining marginal at best in the public sphere. Hence only male figures can embody not only the lineage's interests, but potentially also the broader interests of the community, at least in the eyes of those who wished to recentre marginal Lý Sơn Island in Vietnam's imagined 'geo-body', composed of both territory and nation (Winichakul 1994). By integrating the familiar, gendered system of ancestor worship with reference to the sacrificed Paracel sailors into the national narrative, Lý Sơn villagers as well provincial authorities sought to restore the version of 'collective identity' of the community that better fitted into the frame of 'national heritage'.

Conclusion

In the end, the question is not whether Anh's narratives about Lady Roi are truthful, but what his narratives say about the past and the present, and how the past is remembered, preserved, and reconstructed in the present. As we have seen, the people of Lý Sơn did not remain indifferent to official politics and international dimensions of controversial disputes, but stretched them through the subtle tactics of indiscipline to produce rationalized ancestor worship practices that serve their desired ends. They constructed autonomous spaces for their vernacular religious practices not at the margins, but in the heart of territories occupied by state and religious ideologies (Mbembe 1992: 127). They outwardly adopted political language to promote their vision of religion without challenging the official rules. They exploit established ideologies, seeking to escape the state discipline without fully leaving it (Certeau 1984: xiii).

The state notions did not clash with the people's view, but rather provoked reconstruction of their memory in terms that were more acceptable to both sides. The process of constructing the present and the past was not about 'what happened', but about how 'it may be understood' (Toren 1988: 696). Local officials often played a crucial role in the course of 'historical production', as they were also members of the village and lineages. Moreover, despite their attempts to follow official ideological directives, villagers had personal preferences and prejudices that affected the process of restoring local memorials. Villagers rethought, subverted, and manipulated national and local narratives according to their own culturally constituted desires. Reinstating the credentials of various lineages shows that villagers were able to selectively and tactically deploy signs and symbols across authoritative languages such as ancestor worship and state semiotic ideology to further their own interests (see Keane 2007). Yet the examples of the Võ and Phạm lineages show that remaking the past is not a peaceful process that invariably strengthens local or national unity. It is, rather, a process in which conflicts and antagonisms cut within and through the state–village binary, as various groups and individuals confront one another with variable and potentially contradictory memories, understandings, and interpretations of history. However, such confrontations are strategically restricted to specific fields of negotiation, defined by both the state and local initiatives, while other parts of ancient and more recent history are passed over in silence.

Moreover, in this process ancestor worship is not only historically and politically constructed, but also *gendered*. In Lý Sơn, the multifaceted interaction between modern cultural policies of the state and traditional customs generated a creative array of encounters with the ghosts of those who died as Paracel sailors or, like Lady Roi, just as young, childless women. By integrating the familiar system of ancestor worship with reference to the sacrificed Paracel sailors into the national narrative (see Kwon 2006), Lý Sơn islanders attempted to relocate their marginal island to the centre of Vietnam's land–sea map. At the same time, they sought to rework their narratives in such a way that they backed their lineage claims. Anh adapted his narratives about the 'heroine' Lady Roi to official versions and gave them their own meaning. He emphasized the continuity with the past, which plays such an important role in the state discourse. But the continuity, he stressed, refers to his lineage, his village, and his island. In terms of blood relations, he shows that the 'revolutionary spirit' dates back to the origins of his family and has been maintained over generations. His ancestors came to Vietnam's defence whenever the country called them. Moreover, service to the fatherland was not only a male matter; exceptional courage also characterized the women of Anh's family. However, as we have seen, in contrast to his male ancestor Phạm Hữu Nhật, who was acknowledged by the state as a 'hero of the Paracels', Anh's female ancestor Lady Roi did not gain this honourable status. According to neo-Confucian ideology, she was no more than a ghostly spirit whose experience did not serve to broaden the official agenda of 'national and cultural heritage'.

Provincial officials' earlier support and later reservations regarding the inclusion of Lady Roi and her temple into the commemorative project of the Paracel navy shows how the central state, which faces international and local challenges, tries to control and shape the commemorations by keeping them small. These commemorations underline the connection of the modern state with the glorious rulers, with the history of 'resistance', and with the struggle over Vietnam's sovereignty and autonomy rather than their continuity with the lineage, village, or the island. Similarly, the state makes a selection of those narratives of heroism and chooses those figures whose celebration best suits the dominant history. The state, aware of the social power of commemorative rituals, did not allow female spirits to become a part of national anniversaries. On the other hand, local state agents have an influence on the state project. In the case of the Paracel and Spratly anniversaries, following both the official political line and their own preferences, they deliberately select oral histories, publish articles, hold conferences, and assign spaces that, taken together, recover and reconstruct the remote past in a way that promotes their interests. Nevertheless, narratives of women's heroism continue to be relegated to specific fields that do not gain public recognition. The state commemorations are supposed to collectively venerate those whose bodies were lost in the South China Sea, whose names sank into oblivion while their bravery and heroism are still worth remembering. However, as we have seen, for those who live in the present this is not enough. They want the ghostly spirits to become the flesh and blood of their kin – both male and female – and to have their names carved into stone forever. This calls for a separate analysis of how in real life women deal with male claims to exclusive authority in the religious domain, which is the focus of the next chapter.

Figure 8: Women on the way to Thiên Y A Na temple, Sa Huỳnh.

CHAPTER 6

Women and New Gendered Ritual Divisions

One incident that happened during the local ceremony for the goddess Thiên Y A Na confused me for a long time. Before going into the field as an ethnographer, I had prepared myself with extensive reading on ritual intensification and the growing role of religion in rural areas of Vietnam and China. But what I witnessed on the Forbidden Hill in Sa Huỳnh contradicted all my dry knowledge on ritual intensification and by no means resembled what, in my naivety, I had expected to find in my field setting.

In my field notes for the last day of the lunar year, I recorded a description of the Chicken Ceremony (*lễ cúng gà*) performed by six men in the Thiên Y A Na temple in Sa Huỳnh. I noted that although the men were accompanied by one woman, the forty-two-year-old Hảo, it was largely a male affair. Some of the men performing the ritual were summoned by the head of the *vạn* just before the ceremony started. Their familiarity with the ritual procedures was limited, which was a source of worry for the head of the *vạn*, who could not carry out the ritual due to a recent death in his family. According to local beliefs, death is one of the most polluting events – second only to female menstruation – and can disrupt human relations with the gods.

The whole ceremony took place before the Lunar New Year with the intention of thanking the goddess for the passing year and ensuring 'good weather and wind' for the year to come. Although she was believed to have left the temple and lost her power, fishers still held the main ceremony according to the old tradition. Men sometimes called her the 'Goddess of the Past', referring to her previous powerful status.

In my field notes, I scrupulously listed ritual offerings prepared by women: sticky rice (*xôi gạo*), boiled chicken (*gà luộc*), plain rice gruel (*cháo*), bananas (*chuối*), sweets (*kẹo*), dry pancake (*bánh tráng*), sugar (*đường*), rice liquor (*rượu*), betel (*trầu*), cigarettes (*thuốc lá*), incense (*hương*), and gold foil (*vàng mã*). The last note in my field notes, 'no flowers' (*không có hoa*), referred to the disappointment of the head of the *vạn*, who complained that the women had forgotten about this important item. He expressed his worry that the goddess would not be willing to listen to their prayers without flowers. Having no other choice, the old caretaker of the temple left an empty vase on her altar.

Finally, in my field notes I noted 'avian flu chicken' (*gà cúm*), which was a coded reference to the most confusing incident, which at that time I did not know how to interpret. Soon after the men started to arrange the offerings on the altar, they found that something was wrong with the chicken prepared by the women. Instead of fresh shiny yellow, the skin color was matte and blue. The men examined the chicken carefully and reached the conclusion that, apparently, the chicken was spoiled. It was most likely sick at the time it was killed and cooked. They looked at each other with astonished expressions on their faces and, after a brief moment of hesitation and some hushed conversation, put the chicken on the altar and started the ceremony. When the ceremony was finished, Hảo took the offerings from the altar, put them on the plates and distributed them among the men. However, the suspicious chicken was put aside.

I was sitting in the boat on the way back through the channel when the old caretaker, along with other men, took the spoiled chicken out of the plastic bag and threw it with disgust into the water. They did not want to comment on it, but told me that the chicken was not fresh and it was better not to eat the meat. It seemed that the men did not attach great significance to the event, but for me it was the first time I had ever seen Vietnamese people throw away offerings, which generally were believed to be sacred after the worship. At that time, I thought that the ceremony was a parody. In my head I played with Vietnamese words: '*Cúng gà* [literally, worship with chicken] ... *gà cúm* [flu chicken] ... *cúng gà cúm* [the ceremony for the flu chicken] ...', but I did not dare say them out loud.

Initially, I did not know how to link 'flu chicken' either with the villagers' stories about their alleged fear of the goddess's punishment or with the concern of the head of the *vạn*, who was so careful not to offend the deity with his 'polluting' condition, even refraining from performing the ritual himself. Nor could I make any sense of how the 'flu chicken' fit into ethnographic accounts of growing expenditures during the ritual intensification in Vietnam. How could women be so careless and choose a sick chicken to offer the goddess? Were they not afraid of her punishment? These thoughts raced through my mind as I sat in the boat.

The answer came later when I spent more time with women. Gradually, I started to understand that they had their own vision of what constitutes a proper ritual for the goddess Thiên Y A Na. Women were confident that it was inappropriate to offer Thiên Y A Na pork or chicken meat – so called 'salty offerings' – since the goddess abstains from 'non-Buddhist' practices in her self-cultivation (*đi tu*). In that sense, women shared the monk Thích Giác Đức's disdain for elaborated village feasts that required slaughtering pigs and chickens (Chapter 4). However, in contrast to the monk, for whom all local gods were outside of 'pure' Buddhism, women claimed that Thiên Y A Na had gone through a spiritual metamorphosis – largely initiated by Quan Âm, who had joined the female pantheon on the Forbidden Hill in the late 1970s – and had herself become a Buddhist bodhisattva. Consequently, women felt a moral obligation to do everything they could to respect her Buddhahood achieved through self-cultivation and accumulation of merit. To avoid openly confronting the men or questioning their ritual legitimacy, the women had provided a chicken to satisfy the symbolic requirements of the old male religious authority, but in practice its spoiled condition made it impossible to consume the meaty offerings on the goddess's premises. In this manner, the women subtly undermined the men's power and defended their own vision of the Forbidden Hill – now dominated by female religious activity and Buddhist ideas.

~~~

This chapter is intended as an in-depth analysis of women's religiosity as it is played out against a backdrop of exclusively male claims to religious practices in the coastal society. I offer some ethnographic vignettes from female perspectives and present religious activities as seen by women. Male hegemony in the coastal society is not monolithic; it is contested by women who challenge gender conventions and navigate their own way through repressive discourses on traditional morality and 'local productions' of femininity and masculinity (Rydstrøm and Drummond 2004:

6). Up to this point in my study, women have appeared in the individual chapters only briefly and incidentally, as petty traders and as the wives of men who played important political roles in the local community. If a woman occupied a central position in my analysis, it was only due to her ambiguous status either as a goddess or a ghost. In the male perspective, such women were confined to the orthodox Confucian ethic and depicted as 'virgins' and 'virtuous', 'loyal', and 'obedient' daughters and wives. In the previous chapter, I showed that although Phạm's female ancestor, Lady Roi, proved to have all the desirable female virtues and conduct required by Confucian ideology, ultimately that was not enough to earn her recognition as a local heroine. She was *just* behaving according to gendered expectations. Her death by suicide saved her lineage's honour, but did not equate to actions deserving of the title 'hero of the collective' at the village or national level.

This chapter aims to deconstruct the conventional imaginary that portrays a woman as an 'example of virtue' but denies her any agency and power to decide her future (see Ortner 1995, 2001, 2006). Instead of virtuous daughters, I offer alternative narratives of 'flesh and blood' women engaged in confrontation with local standards of sexuality and gendered ritual roles. By presenting women as important actors in the local arena of village affairs, I want to give them the last word in my analysis of multi-faceted contestations over religious practices. At the same time, I cannot escape the fact that some of the female experiences were part of my own experience. Thus, writing about women and analysing their perspectives, a female anthropologist is forced to write about her own experiences (see, e.g., Tsing 1993).

Exploring vernacular expressions of religion through the political, historical, and economic aspects of male activities, as I have done thus far, might give the impression that I fell into the trap of accepting the public ritual hegemony of men and their dominant role in the religious landscape of the coastal society. Indeed, for the entire duration of my fieldwork in Sa Huỳnh and Lý Sơn, it was men who guided me through the local landscape of village affairs, who had an interest in me as a foreign researcher, and with whom I spent many hours discussing local events, politics, and religious matters. Women simply assumed that it was the men's job – as those who held the knowledge of the place – to familiarize me with the local landscape.

Women did not consider themselves inferior, but in comparison to northern Vietnam they remain socially and 'religiously disadvantaged' vis-à-vis men who hold important political positions and perform community-level rituals (see Kirsch 1985: 304). As we observed in the previous chapters, men in Sa Huỳnh and Lý Sơn monopolized the most prestigious religious roles in village temples, carried out ancestral and communal house rites, and reserved for themselves the role of defining religious orthodoxy. While male descendants of the lineages were acknowledged, Lady Roi was not recognized as a heroine. Women neither claimed the rights to these posts nor showed that they felt excluded or disrespected. However, it would be wrong to think that they sat by quietly and remained silent and obedient. From their marginal position, women added their sharp and witty commentaries on male authority. These commentaries in a subtle way disrupted male narratives and grabbed my attention because they transgressed the limitations imposed on the women by the men.

Although in Sa Huỳnh and Lý Sơn male ritual practices represented the 'most articulate, codified and commendable aspects' of local religious life, should we assume that men are more religious than women and thus deny women's religious agency (Kendall 1985: 30; see also Ortner 1995, 2001, 2006)? According to my observations, women actively entered – though to a limited extent – the public religious domain with their own interpretations of conventionally accepted religious beliefs (see Kendall 1985: 24–25). However, there were important limitations that I wish to point out. Lý Sơn Island, with its impressive legacy of village temples, including the village communal house, with 'lenient' cadres and a historically 'mild' antisuperstition campaign, preserved a much stronger gender division of ritual roles than mainland villages of Sa Huỳnh. While women indeed contributed significantly to the reconstruction of the ritual economy, Lý Sơn men continued to define communal house orthodoxy, and I never encountered a Lý Sơn woman crossing the doorstep of communal village temples. In Sa Huỳnh, on the other hand, the no-female taboo was broken by women who took advantage of male notions of the spiritual impotency of the goddess Thiên Y A Na and entered her temple to make simple Buddhist offerings and burn incense. As the vignette above suggests, women did not try to rigorously follow the men's 'ritual offering protocol', as for them the male ritual performance referred to the goddess's violent nature from the past and missed her ongoing Buddhist transformation and new vegetarian diet regime. That is why in this chapter I chiefly focus on Sa Huỳnh. The religious activities of women in Sa Huỳnh shed an interesting light on the ongoing process of redefining ritual gender roles in this coastal society and give us a more complex picture of various dynamics of ritual life in post-socialist Vietnam.

The event described in the vignette gives us a sense of women's varied possibilities for influencing men's affairs, possibilities that men could hardly predict or comprehend (see Tsing 1993: 205). In the process of defining local orthodoxy through subtle indiscipline and refusal to accept of male domination, women seek to give voice to their visions of religious practice (cf. Mbembe 1992a; Tsing 1993; Malarney 2002: 207; DiGregorio 2007). However, I do not see women's transgressions in terms of overt resistance to male-dominated religious ideology and practice because women did not usurp the space of the men's ritual performance. By examining various strategies women adopted to challenge local conventions, I argue that instead of actively resisting, women inserted their religious practices and notions into the male-dominated religious domain. As Tsing (1993) showed in her ethnography of Meratus, women rework the structure of dominant male discourses, reconfigure conventional local knowledge of the world, humans, and gods, and destabilize those who remained in the centres.

In the following analysis I explore from two different perspectives the question of how women counter male domination, escape from difficult social situations, and resolve the mental and emotional consequences of conflicts they face in everyday life. First, I will look at the pre-revolutionary division of ritual roles in order to provide a historical and political background for the subsequent analysis, which deals with a post-revolutionary redefinition of women's status. The second perspective focuses on Sa Huỳnh women's interpretation of gender and religious practices and their subtle strategies to cope with their marginal status and daily concerns. The 'polarities' of social status, gender, and spiritual hierarchy are not monolithic categories; rather, in everyday practice, they intersect and shape each other (cf. Tsing 1993; Kirsch 1985).

Pre-revolutionary gender divisions in ritual life

In the case of the Thai society, Kirsch (1985) argues that there was a notable gendered division of labour: men performed political–bureaucratic roles, while women specialized in economic–entrepreneurial activities that did not have a positive Buddhist valence. In the light of Buddhist ideology, women were seen as much more attached to the worldly domain than men, not only due to their gender roles as 'lovers' and 'mothers', but also to their contact with money (see also Keyes 1984).[1] Like in Thailand, in Vietnam women focused on economic–entrepreneurial activities that not only sustained their households' budgets, but often enabled men to concentrate on studying in pursuit of political–bureaucratic careers (Luong 1998, 2003). Luong (2003) notes that Vietnamese women historically played a fundamental role in the Vietnamese economy and in generating substantial household incomes through commerce, handicraft production and agriculture. The observation by an astonished seventeenth-century Chinese traveller to Hanoi that 'even wives of high-ranking mandarins were not concerned about losing face [through their trading activities]' (in Luong 2003: 202) well illustrates the fact that trade was a domain of women.

Following Malarney (2002), it is correct to say that the position of women in the Vietnamese family is similar to that of families in Southeast Asia, as women have always been engaged in production and responsible for the household finances. Yet despite women's major roles in economic–entrepreneurial activities and contributions to the family budget (Leshkowich 2014), Vietnamese public life, kinship, and household systems remained strongly male-oriented (Luong 2003: 202). Women's lives were controlled by the Confucian ideology that guided women in terms of 'housework', 'appearance', 'speech', and 'conduct' (Ngo Thi Ngan Binh 2004: 50). The orthodox Confucian texts acted as 'practical tools to assist parents in teaching daughters appropriate feminine behaviour' and instructed women regarding desirable female virtues and conduct (ibid.). A woman's duty was to ensure the happiness and well-being of her family through self-sacrifice and self-cultivation as a devoted and obedient daughter and well-mannered wife.

As in China and Korea, Vietnamese women left their own kinship setting and entered their husbands' patrilineage as strangers. They could

---

1. In contrast to Theravada Buddhism, Buddhism in Vietnam allowed women to enter the monkhood, but it nevertheless reproduced male hierarchy and contributed to the view that women and men were diametrically opposed (see DiGregorio 2001: 193).

secure their position in a family by giving birth to a son who would perpetuate and extend the husband's patrilineage and by raising healthy children who would take care of the parents in their old age. Women were largely denied access to Confucian education and official positions in the national mandarinate or in local village administration, and they were forbidden to enter the village communal house – *đình* – and excluded from local tutelary deity worship (Luong 2003: 202–203; see also DiGregorio 2001, 2007; Malarney 2002). Female religious activities were mainly restricted to local Buddhist pagodas and spirit-medium cults. It should, therefore, not come as a surprise that, to ensure the safe birth and long life of sons, women often turned to the world of spirits for assistance (see Kendall 1985: 35).

Socialist redefinition of women's status and the Party-state's attempt to institutionalize gender equality

In Vietnam, the attack of the Party-state on the village religious domain – in which male-oriented kinship played a major role – was implemented by undermining patrilineages through the collectivization of land, granting equal inheritance rights to both sons and daughters, replacing ancestor worship with national commemorations, and giving women access to education (Luong 2003). Moreover, the Confucian traditional ethics that strictly confined women to the domestic sphere had to be reformulated during the war years. Ngo Thi Ngan Binh (2004: 52) reports that in its efforts to mobilize the masses to serve the cause of national liberation, the Party-state reformulated the values of Vietnamese femininity and encouraged women to break away from the strict Confucian family ideology. The Party initiated movements such as 'moral Education of the New Woman' to educate and transform young women into the 'new socialist woman' (2004: 52). Traditional Confucian values did not mesh with the image of the 'new socialist woman' that the Party promoted in the time of revolutionary zeal, which entailed women's active participation in both production and revolution (ibid.). Ngo Thi Ngan Binh notes that in the context of war, a 'woman with masculine behaviour – loud-spoken, straightforward, self-assertive, competent in fighting, and fearless of risk – was acceptable and even praiseworthy' (ibid.).

However, in the post-war period, and particularly in the period of Đổi Mới, emphasis on female military participation became irrelevant, and women were instead encouraged to contribute to the national economy and development. Paradoxically, in its implementation of the new cultural policy, the Party-state returned to a more traditional Confucian formula. Consequently, the earlier socialist rhetoric glorifying female military participation and women's revolutionary abilities has gradually given way to a discourse of traditional feminine qualities such as loyalty, gentleness, elegance, tactfulness, and resourcefulness that corresponds more closely to the new image of a 'proper contemporary Vietnamese woman' (Ngo Thi Ngan Binh 2004: 53).

Despite the Party-state's self-glorification as a propagator and patron of gender equality, the Vietnamese revolution did not change the fact that women bore the main responsibility for their families' well-being. Women still sought solace in the spirit world and engaged in religious practices like the Mother Goddess cult or Buddhist worship in order to avoid misfortunes and deal with the crises of everyday life (Malarney 2002: 82). Malarney (2002: 102) points out that women preserved religious ideas and practices in spite of the socialist transformation. Many of them rejected the Party's cultural reforms and held Buddhist rites or spirit possessions under the veil of secrecy. As a matter of fact, in contrast to men, who were more integrated into the Party, women remained outside of the political power structure, which allowed them to practice religion without serious repercussions. On one hand, women's strong attachment to religion earned them negative labels such as 'superstitious', 'traditional', and even 'backwards'. On the other hand, as Malarney stressed, in the present day women are considered to be more specialized than men in the ancestor cult, which supports Nguyễn Tuấn Anh's (2010) thesis on significant changes in kinship relations.

Nguyễn Tuấn Anh's (2010: 39) recent research in rural settings of northern Vietnam shows a noteworthy shift in gender roles: ever since the Đổi Mới period, women have crossed the gender divide and have been allowed to sit in patrilineage councils and even to become members of the patrilineage, formerly an exclusively male institution. More importantly, Nguyễn Tuấn Anh (2010: 225) points out that the change in women's position has taken place in relation to the changes in kinship relationships. As I have already noted above, in the pre-socialist period, married women were not formally full members of any patrilineage, hence their position in the kinship structure was marginal. In the socialist transformation period, women gained the same rights to education and participation in the collective system of agriculture and industry as men, while the material and ideological foundations of male-oriented kinship were undermined (see Luong 2003: 204). In the Đổi Mới period, with the resurgence of the kinship system, women gained more economic opportunities that enabled them to become patrilineage members 'in their own right' (Nguyễn Tuấn Anh 2010: 225).

Nevertheless, it would be too optimistic to conclude that the Party-state's efforts to make women equal to men eradicated gender inequality, as the male-oriented kinship model remains powerful in shaping gender relations. In fact, complete equality between men and women 'may hold rhetorically, but less completely in practice' (Rydstrøm and Drummond 2004: 8; see also Luong 2003; Nguyen-vo 2008; Werner 2009). Let me illustrate this with a brief example. During my visit to all 13 districts of Quảng Ngãi Province in 2006, I noted only one instance of a woman holding one of the highest positions in the local administration, namely chairperson of a district (*chủ tịch huyện*). It is worth mentioning that it was a frontier district in the mountainous area, and the woman was of Hrê ethnic background, which might suggest that male dominance in and women's exclusion from politics is largely an ethnic Kinh (Việt) affair. This exception, however, proves the rule that women in Vietnam remain marginal to men and usually do not hold important political positions in local official administrations heavily dominated by men (Malarney 2002).

Women and religious practices in the coastal society

In the previous section I charted changes in women's social status, both within the family and in Vietnamese society at large, brought about by the socialist transformation and the postsocialist reforms (Malarney 2002; Luong 2003; Werner 2009; Nguyễn Tuấn Anh 2010; Leshkowich 2014). Pointing out a significant shift in gender-constructed relation-ships, many authors have drawn heavily upon findings from either northern or southern Vietnam. I do not intend to make generalizations about 'Vietnamese women' here; rather, my aim is to point out the sig-nificance of regional dynamics and differences. In this way, I seek to cast some light on gender relations and women's roles in contestations over religious practices in an understudied part of central Vietnam.

The pre-revolutionary situation of women in Sa Huỳnh and Lý Sơn was much the same as in other parts of Vietnam. In the land-based villages women were excluded from worship in the *đình*. A similar ritual prohibition was maintained in the sea-oriented fishing communities – *vạn chày*. In Sa Huỳnh and Lý Sơn, it was not only the communal houses and the Whale Spirit temples that were typically limited to men, but the Thiên Y A Na temples as well. A male medium's body usually served as a vessel for Thiên Y A Na or other spirits to enter and engage with villagers. Possession by Thiên Y A Na, called *lên đồng*, was an exclusively male affair involving the village master of the Dharma (*thầy pháp*), who was also the one who, through secret formulas, captured and forced a selected spirit – sometimes sent by the goddess – to 'ride' a suitable person during a séance. This village master would not be possessed by the spirits himself, but played the role of mediator between divinity and the spirit medium whose body (*xác*, literally meaning 'corpse') served as a vessel for supernatural beings. The master of the Dharma, sometimes called 'master of magic water' (*thầy phù thủy*), also played the role of spokesman during communal offerings or used his special powers to expel or pacify evil spirits that caused a wide range of diseases and misfortunes in the village.[2] On Lý Sơn Island the tradition of 'sorcery' was handed down from father to the eldest son, who learned the ritual forms, magic charms and incantations, and the craft of making amulets by assisting his father. Women were generally excluded from this circle due to their menstrual cycles or pregnancy, which made them 'unclean'.

The fact that spirit possession for Thiên Y A Na in Sa Huỳnh and Lý Sơn was a male affair stood in sharp contrast to the colourful and cheerful types of possession rituals performed in the majority of cases by women in other parts of Central Vietnam. The cult of the goddess Thiên Y A Na – popular all over Central Vietnam – spread in the imperial period among upper-class women in Huế who acted as spirit mediums for this goddess (Nguyễn Hữu Thông 2001; Salemink 2007, 2008b, 2015). Nguyễn Hữu Thông (2001) explains the great popularity of the cult of the goddess Thiên Y A Na among these women by the fact that this group experienced particular difficulties in traditional Vietnamese society because of the pressure their husbands' families exerted upon

---

2. For more information about the 'master of the Dharma', see Cadière (1955–1957), Hickey (1964), Didier (1996), Do (2003).

them. He sees possession as women's compensation for social deprivation and a way out of the impasse between social expectations of them as women and their personal aspirations, preferences, and interests as individuals (Nguyễn Hữu Thông 2001).[3]

In Sa Huỳnh, the spirit possession cult for Thiên Y A Na was disrupted in the early 1960s when the Forbidden Hill was appropriated by American forces and completely abandoned after 1975 during the antisuperstition campaign launched by the Communist government (see Chapter 4). Apparently, the provincial authorities were aware of the existence of this practice in the past. One of the editors of a cultural magazine published by the Provincial Office of Culture, Sport, and Tourism in Quảng Ngãi City told me that the caretaker of Thiên Y A Na's temple in Sa Huỳnh was a very skilful spirit medium, but under strong pressure from local authorities and in fear of being accused of superstition (and of being sent to a re-education camp), he had already given up the practice by the 1970s and refused the editor's recent request to organize a séance. This is consistent with my own experience in Sa Huỳnh. I have never come across this type of possession performed in the Thiên Y A Na temple. Villagers claimed that it was not practised anymore, which may well be true, given the newly powerless status of the goddess Thiên Y A Na in Sa Huỳnh.

Sa Huỳnh villagers reported that up until 1980s the Thiên Y A Na temple had been reserved exclusively for men. When the goddess still held power, she had such a reputation for fierceness and violence that even men did not have the courage to approach her alone. This had to be done with the assistance of the temple's caretaker or ritual master. Women were believed to be particularly ostracized by the goddess and banished from her temple due to the 'uncleanliness' associated with menstruation and female sexuality.

While in northern Vietnam the beliefs surrounding female 'pollution' are no longer binding, in Sa Huỳnh and Lý Sơn these beliefs still remain strong and sustain male ritual hegemony. Especially in Lý Sơn,

---

3. On spirit possession see, for example, Lewis (1966, 2003); for South Korea, see Kendall (1985, 1996a, 2009), Van de Port (2005); for Vietnam, see Durand (1959), Cadière (1955–1957), Nguyen Thi Hien (2002), Fjelstad and Nguyen Thi Hien (2006), Endres (2007, 2011), Salemink (2007, 2008b, 2008c, 2010, 2015), Norton (2009), and Pham Quynh Phuong (2009).

menstruating and pregnant women are not allowed to approach temples or have contact with the village gods. Consequently, men are the ones who perform the act of worship. The presence of menstruating women is believed to disrupt the rituals to such an extent that mediums might not be possessed and divinities could give misleading information or even cause harm.[4] A similar taboo on women's participation in village rituals existed in China. According to Ahern (1975: 196), pollution beliefs were intimately connected with the Chinese kinship system. Death, birth, and menstruation were seen as pollution because they transgressed the bodily boundaries (see Douglas 1966: 122). Ahern (1975) declares that women were perceived as particularly 'unclean' because they have a boundary position in families. Given that the kinship system focused on male lines of descendants, women were depicted on the boundaries, breaking in as strangers. In this sense, they were perceived as polluting and disrupting the relationship between gods and humans (1975: 204).

Although I was the only woman on the island who was allowed to enter the village temples, take part in rituals, sit on the mat and join communal feasts, every time I was asked by elders whether I was 'clean' (*sạch sẽ*). Men warned me that I should leave the temple if I was not. Understandably, they were troubled by the uncertainty of whether I, as a woman and hence potentially polluting, was telling the truth about my bodily status at the time of the ritual. With the development of massive tourism on the island in the last few years, elders reluctantly allowed female tourists from the mainland to enter selected temples and make modest offerings, but they complained that women's presence and practices 'pollute' (*ô nhiễm*) sacred spaces. To remedy this situation, once a year they performed a special ritual that would chase away the pollution caused by 'mainlanders' in those temples.

At the time of my fieldwork, the only male ritual of spirit possession I was able to witness was one organized specially for me in the Thiên Y A Na temple in An Hải village (Lý Sơn). The performance was quite different from the style I know from northern Vietnam or Huế.[5] In Lý

---

4. For comparative cases, see Wolf (1975), Ahern (1975), Kendall (1985), Yü (2001), and Lhamo (2003).

5. Salemink (2008b: 262) notes that in northern Vietnam the spirit-medium cult, known also as *lên đồng*, has a more individualistic character because it includes one spirit medium and his or her audience. In contrast to northern *lên đồng*, the

Sơn, spirit possession for Thiên Y A Na was devoid of aesthetic elements like music, dance, and sophisticated costumes, and it was a secret business that involved only a few insiders. I discovered that the ritual senior of the Thiên Y A Na temple, who was also a descendant of one of the founding lineages, served as the spirit medium. During a séance held in the temple, he sat in front of the Thiên Y A Na altar and was covered with a red scarf. When the séance started the village master of the Dharma used magical formulas to capture the divinity and have her possess the senior, which was announced by his repeated convulsions. I was instructed that I could ask any question regarding my dissertation, prospects of getting a job, earning money, or travel abroad, but I should not ask about 'love matters' (*vấn đề tình yêu*). Already astonished by the list of 'proper' questions and the unexpected warning, I asked what was wrong with 'love matters'. The men very seriously answered that the goddess might get angry for wasting her time on such 'trivial' problems. Later, from women, I learned about the men's 'serious questions' that did not arouse the goddess's anger. Women revealed to me that in most cases men organized spirit possessions in the local village temples when they wanted to inquire about the lucky number of a lottery draw, the winner of the boat race between hamlets, illegal business ventures carried out by their relatives abroad such as secret cannabis plantations, or to ask the goddess to 'spiritually' ensure fishermen's security while passing through contested waters of the Paracels and Spratlys or using explosive materials during fishing. Apparently, 'love matters' were not on their priority list.

In the context of China, Chün-fang Yü (2001) noted that the presence of a goddess or feminine symbols in a religion does not translate into respect for real women in that culture. Female goddesses such as Mazu (in Vietnamese Thiên Hậu), Guan Yin (Quan Âm), and princess Miao-shan (analogous to the Vietnamese princess Liễu Hạnh)[6] are understood as 'postmenopausal women', free from the 'messiness of childbirth and the problems of sexual desire' (2001: 481). Although they still retain all that is attractive about femininity, they are devoid of 'anything negative which true womanhood entails' (ibid.). Yü (2001:

---

ritual of spirit mediumship in central Vietnam – called *hầu vui* – has a collective character with no sharp distinction between the spirit medium and the audience.

6. For more details see Dror (2002b, 2007).

492) argues that goddesses like Guan Yin and Miao-shan were seen as "'both a virgin and a mother" (Erndl 1993: 144), a condition that no real woman can attain'. Hence, the reluctance of the men of Lý Sơn to approach the goddess Thiên Y A Na with a question about love might be interpreted as an indication that, in the men's perception, the goddess was completely devoid of 'stigma' associated with menstruation, sexual intercourse, death, and childbirth and, hence, sexuality (Yü 2001; see also Sangren 1983). I assume that asking about love would equate the goddess with the earthly female 'uncleanliness' and sexual desires, from which she was believed to be entirely free. It would also contest the idealized pure nature of the goddess Thiên Y A Na, who was assumed to have even achieved Buddhahood, as happened in the case of Thiên Y A Na in Sa Huỳnh (see Chapter 4).

The fact that men in Lý Sơn and Sa Huỳnh performed the spirit possessions for Thiên Y A Na does not mean that women could not be spirit mediums. They did so, however, in the domestic domain and, in contrast to male spirit possession, women did not have the power to expel spirits from people's bodies. Women could heal only certain diseases, read cards, tell futures, and make amulets in the privacy of their houses. Many such female spirit mediums were engaged in some sort of economic–entrepreneurial activities. For example, in Quảng Ngãi City I interviewed a man whose mother moved from Nam Định (northern Vietnam) to Quảng Ngãi in the late 1930s, opened a bakery, and introduced a northern style of spirit possession with dancing, music, and elaborate and expensive attire ordered directly from Hanoi. Quảng Ngãi turned out to be an excellent choice; the new bakery was profitable enough to build a house and make a good living. The woman was convinced that her bakery trade flourished thanks only to her ties with the 'other world'. In Sa Huỳnh, I met another woman who had worked as a driver for American forces during the Second Indochina War. She also acted as a spirit medium and held séances in the privacy of her home.

During the antisuperstition campaign of the late 1970s, these women were forced to abandon their calling as spirit mediums and were threatened with time in re-education camps. Relatives of the woman from Quảng Ngãi recalled that after the state began its anti-superstition campaign, the family burned all her ritual attire for fear of being accused of spreading 'outdated customs'. The woman's son clearly remembered that his father forbade her to invite possession by going into a trance, but he still saw his mother in front of the mirror, dancing and speaking with spirits. In contrast to the men, such as the old caretaker in Sa Huỳnh who was under pressure from the Party, these women resumed their activities as soon as the antisuperstition campaign relaxed its grip.

Women's interpretation of the spirit world

Villagers in central Vietnam make a distinction between an ancestor (*tổ tiên*), a ghost (*tà ma*), and a divine spirit (*thần*). In contrast to ancestors, whose deaths took place at home (*chết nhà*) and who received the proper rituals from their relatives, ghosts are usually wandering spirits of the dead who did not receive proper burials and who do not have filial descendents to propitiate them with regular rites and offerings (see Chapter 5). However, as Kwon (2008: 24) notes, 'ghosts in contemporary Vietnam do not have a coherent existence' because they move between the place of ancestors and the space for ghosts. In the previous chapter I showed that ghosts could inhabit the domain of ancestors or the place of heroes, but these are not the only possible destinations for ghosts. They can turn into a powerful kindred spirits or even gods (*thần*) for a community or an individual (Kwon 2008: 104).

Men in the coastal society often explained that most of the gods (*thần*) had been humans and turned into deities only after their death. During their earthly existence, some of these deities acted as village chiefs or mandarins or performed other important social duties. If they had been upright and honest in their service to people, they would enjoy the merit they had collected through their good acts. A village which had a predestined affinity (*duyên*) with such a god would be blessed with prosperity and peace. However, anyone who offended the divinity would be sure to meet a strict punishment. Not every god was munificent; a number of them could be harmful as well, and it was up to the people to please them, so villagers frequently had to satisfy them with lavish offerings.

Men and women in Sa Huỳnh and Lý Sơn believed that gods did not stay forever on this earth. After some time helping – or causing disruption to – humans, they disappeared unexpectedly, passed to another supreme and invisible world (*siêu lên cõi tầng cao hơn, lên cõi vô hình cao hơn nữa*), or were downgraded to hell (*bị đọa xuống địa ngục*). Men considered that the temple, cave, stone, or tree left by such spirits ceased to be sacred and powerful (*không còn linh nữa*). They stated that at first villagers were usually not aware of the god's travel to the other realm, as some of their wishes could still be fulfilled by the soul of the dead person (*âm hồn*), which followed and helped the deity or who just simply pretended to be a god in order to nibble on some of the offerings made to him. However, the power of these helpers was very limited, and sooner or later villagers had to recognize that the sacredness of the place was gone (*hết linh thiêng*), as was the case with the Thiên Y A Na temple on the Forbidden Hill in Sa Huỳnh. In Chapter 4, I reported that in the early 1980s, Sa Huỳnh fishermen were convinced that the goddess Thiên Y A Na had lost her power and left the temple. As I indicated, this change in the local perception took place in the context of the socialist restructuring of the village political and religious sphere. The *đình*, epitomizing male hegemony, had been destroyed long ago, and the only remaining temples were those dedicated to the dead and to the Whale Spirit. The seasonal rituals in those temples were still conducted by men in a way similar to the celebration of the goddess Thiên Y A Na, which I briefly described in the vignette at the beginning of this chapter.

However, women in Sa Huỳnh had their own explanation and interpreted the goddess's transformation as a natural consequence of Buddhist self-cultivation, through which she turned from a fierce deity into a benevolent spirit. Women, who for a long time remained outside of rituals worshipping her and, therefore, outside of her blessing, projected Buddhist beliefs of compassion and mercy – usually associated with the bodhisattva Quan Âm – onto the goddess Thiên Y A Na, and in the early 1990s began to visit her temple and make regular offerings every month during the new and full moons. They usually combined the trip to the Thiên Y A Na temple on the Forbidden Hill with a visit to Từ Phước pagoda in Thạch By village (Chapter 4). While they were not very concerned about the men's rituals and offerings, as the vignette above illustrated, they never failed to prepare themselves well. Every time they would load a light round bamboo basket that served as a boat with supplies such as flowers, fruit, incense, and fresh water and then, with the help of the old caretaker of the Thiên Y A Na temple, they would cross the channel.

In contrast to the men, for whom the goddess Thiên Y A Na still symbolized protection and securing passage at sea – and hence the past – women perceived the goddess as a 'modern spirit' capable of addressing their female concerns. Among women who visited the Thiên Y A Na temple were middle-aged working women – fish traders, nurses, housewives – as well as women who were in their retirement age and had more time to devote to religious activities. All of these women made offerings to the goddess on behalf of their families, but they also had their private incentives. Some of the women believed that the goddess supported their fish trade and, thanks to her blessings, they were able to make a good living. Some women had been left by husbands and, through the goddess, they hoped to secure their future well-being. Older women who engaged in the Thiên Y A Na cult prayed for health and peace for their families. One of them had lost an adult son in a motorbike accident while her husband, who was also a victim of a similar accident, survived but was paralyzed. This woman wanted to prevent such tragedies in the future.[7]

Women were aware of the official Party policy of equality between men and women, and often used it to justify their religious practices in the Thiên Y A Na temple. They viewed the prohibition on women's participation in village rituals as 'feudal' and 'outdated'. They were aware of the former 'misogyny' felt by the goddess and of the 'no-female' taboo in her temple but, as one of the women commented, not only the men but also the 'goddess has to accept the reality and follow the progress of modern society!' (*Bà phải chấp nhận thức tế và theo tiến bộ xã hội hiện đại!*). Such a statement sends us back to the problem of how modern Sa Huỳnh women resolved tensions intimately connected with their gender. In the next section, I tell of a few women whose stories give a more in-depth picture of the conflicts that

---

7. Unfortunately, one week before I finished my fieldwork in Sa Huỳnh, I learned that her second son was killed in a motorbike accident. When I visited her I could see that the death of her second child was a terrible blow to her, and I am not sure how she dealt with this disaster. Motorbike accidents, mainly among men, happened so often in Sa Huỳnh that it became a real social problem. It was common to meet families who had lost two or three sons in this way. These tragedies badly affected women, who not only lost their husbands and sons, but also were left on their own to try to earn a living.

Sa Huỳnh women face in their everyday lives and the strategies they employ to deal with them.

Negotiating female identity and the quest for divine protection

Despite the governmental policy aimed at abolishing most of the discriminating rules, Sa Huỳnh women were still expected to follow traditional principles according to which a woman gained her status only after marriage and bearing a son. I noted several cases when women were left by their husbands because they gave birth only to girls. Some of the husbands never divorced their wives, but started families with other women in order to have a son. In most of these cases the 'two wives' accepted such an arrangement. They stayed in separate houses and the husband moved between the two families. Men saw nothing wrong with having a second wife and claimed that the situation required them to look for such a solution. Moreover, villagers were quite open about such polygamous relations.[8]

Unmarried women – often called *ế chồng* – were described as 'difficult', 'selfish', or even 'abnormal' (see, e.g., Bélanger 2004: 96). As Danièle Bélanger explains, the Vietnamese term *ế* refers to 'something that does not sell, or something in little demand' or 'a shop deserted by customers. *Chồng* means husband and therefore *ế chồng* means "being on the shelf" or simply being unable to find a husband' (2004: 114ff.). Thus, in public opinion, women gained social recognition upon becoming wives and mothers, while those who remained single and childless defied norms and expectations of femininity as seen from the angle of Confucian ideology (ibid: 96). In Sa Huỳnh, children were thought of as a guarantee that their parents' would not be left alone and that they would be taken care of in old age and after death. In situations where parents could not count on the state pension, having a child gave at least some kind of security and hope that the adult child would provide material support (see also Phinney 2005).

---

8. Since the late 1950s, polygamy has been officially forbidden and illegal in Vietnam. However, there has been a long tradition of second or 'minor' wives (*làm lẽ, vợ lẽ*), which to some extent still survives. Bélanger (2004 114ff) notes that the term 'polygamy' in Vietnam has a different meaning than in other parts of the world. In Vietnam it denotes that the first wife has a superior status, while subsequent wives are inferior and have fewer privileges. She documented that in present times, taking a second wife is a strategy for some men to have a son.

Hảo, who appeared in the vignette at the beginning of this chapter, was a single mother whom I met during my visit to the Thiên Y A Na temple. She worked all day as a fish trader in the district market. She was proud of the new three-storey house that she had just built. She showed me her small altar to the goddess Quan Âm and then said that, thanks to Quan Âm and especially Thiên Y A Na, her trade was going well and she had been able to save money over the years to build her new house. Hảo introduced me to her two sisters and a female friend. Her younger unmarried sister, a thirty-six-year-old woman (in 2007), was in the advanced stages of pregnancy when I met her. During our intimate discussion, Hảo's sister revealed to me her decision, inspired by the desire for a child, to get pregnant. She told the father, a man she met by chance, her purpose and promised him that he would not bear any responsibility for the child.[9] I asked her whether she was stigmatized by villagers because she chose the option of bearing a child out of wedlock. She explained that if she had been a young girl, she would be seen by her neighbours as an immoral person who did not know how to protect (*giữ*) her virginity. However, at the age of thirty-six, she was considered past her prime already and had, in effect, lost her chance to marry. In Sa Huỳnh, people believed that in the late twenties the body of a woman changes, and if she is still unmarried and childless at that time, she will become more silent, capricious, and difficult, not to mention the fact that her 'charm is gone' (*hết duyên*). Hảo's sister talked about herself as 'ugly' and 'old' and apparently saw her unmarried status as her own 'failure' but, at the same time, she sought to be recognized as a mother. She said that her situation was understandable to the villagers, who knew that having a child was the only way for her to gain a bit of security in her old age. She told me, 'Without a child there is no one who will feed me' (*không có con không có ai nuôi mình*).

Bélanger (2004) observed that being childless in Vietnam may be more problematic than being single. As she notes, in Vietnam, '[f]ertility stands as a fundamental marker of femininity; women who have children are thought to be more beautiful, complete, and feminine than childless women' (2004: 108). Due to a shortage of men after the Vietnam War, women who could not marry were encouraged to give

---

9. I came across quite a few cases in Sa Huỳnh where men did not bear any financial responsibility for their children after divorce.

birth to a biological child outside of marriage. Bélanger (ibid.) writes that biological motherhood was seen as 'natural and necessary to all women, regardless of their marital status'. Consequently, the right of older single women to bear children was legitimized by the 1986 Law on Family and Marriage (Phinney 2008). In Bélanger's own surveys among local leaders and community members in two rural settings, participants agreed that the best strategy for older single women to have someone to take care of them in old age was to have a biological child, even outside of wedlock and against the traditional image of a 'proper' Vietnamese woman (2004: 108).

It is hard to judge whether all single women in Sa Huỳnh desired to have children like Hảo's sister did, but for those women I met it was indeed important. Another unmarried middle-aged woman also shared with me her desire to have a child. The woman told me about a dream she had a few years ago that was still very significant for her. In her dream she saw the goddess Thiên Y A Na appearing over a tree. The goddess took her to the Father of Heaven, who held in his hands a small child. She looked down and saw crowds of people begging for this child, but the goddess pointed her out as the mother. Apparently, marriage and motherhood still held deep meaning for this woman, and she looked at her own life through the lens of family. Referring to me as a foreigner, the woman stated that life in Sa Huỳnh must be much simpler than in my country. In the village, she said, 'the peak of happiness is to marry, have children, and earn money'. She said that a free relationship with a man was not an option for her because it would be unacceptable in Sa Huỳnh.

Perhaps the woman was correct that, officially, short-term relationships were not accepted, even though I knew that in practice they existed. Indeed, in the village, a young unmarried woman having an intimate relationship with a man without the prospect of marrying him would be criticized. Nevertheless, through men's jokes and teasing, older women were encouraged to have sexual relationships, especially because, in the male perception, there was no point in these women keeping their virginity since they had passed the age considered appropriate for marriage.[10] Villagers were also more tolerant towards widows. Publicly, it

---

10. On the tradition of teasing women in Vietnamese folk culture and sexual harassment in Vietnam, see Khuat Thu Hong (2004).

was expected that widows would show traditional virtues and faithfulness to their late husbands by avoiding karaoke gatherings, taking care of their children and their husbands' parents. However, villagers turned a blind eye to their possible 'love relations' as long as the women were not too open about them. In turn, a woman who had been abandoned by her husband was in a much worse situation because having an intimate relationship with a man would cast suspicion on her 'proper behaviour' and might suggest that she had given her husband a reason to leave her.

Hảo married early and, already at the age of twenty-two, despite giving birth to a boy, she was abandoned by her husband. She told me that when she was still young there was a man in the village for whom she felt affection, but because she was afraid of what her neighbours would say, she decided not to have an intimate relationship with him and kept her distance. She admitted that if she had not been afraid of gossip, she would probably now be a married woman.

Still, childless status caused much anxiety for married women who feared abandonment by husbands. Hương, a woman of thirty-one, is an example. I become acquainted with her when I visited her simple restaurant where she sold cheap bowls of beef noodles. I ordered my meal and took a table next to a young woman whom I had met during my last visit to the Thiên Y A Na temple. The woman poked me in the ribs, smiled, and reminded me that the next day would be a full moon and proposed that we go together to burn incense on the altar of the goddess. I agreed and we made an appointment to meet at the fishing harbour early the next morning. In the meantime, Hương brought a bowl of steaming soup and joined us at the table. I asked her if she was also planning to visit the temple, but she shook her head. She was busy with her small business, and had to prepare fresh noodles to sell to passing travellers until the late hours of the evening.

Hương asked me how old I was and, upon hearing my answer, smiled with contentment and said that we were the same age. She introduced herself to me as a single woman who was too old to find a husband. Knowing local Sa Huỳnh customs, I knew that at her age it would be extremely difficult for her to find a husband: marriage to a thirty-year-old woman was considered too risky. There was always the danger that she would be too old to give birth to a child. I tried to console Hương, saying that she perhaps still had a chance to find a husband, adding that

I was also unmarried. The woman looked at me carefully and then burst out laughing, probably knowing that I was trying to be nice. The joke was on me – Hương admitted she was married and had been for ten years! Then she excused herself for making fun of me and said that it was probably easier for a foreign woman to find a husband, even later in life – in her thirties – but a local woman had the chance only once, when she was young.

Hương's real worry was about her childless status. She praised her husband for being faithful to her when he could have easily found a younger woman to have children with. Hương tried to be a good wife and daughter-in-law by looking after her husband's parents, who shared their modest house with them. Her husband did not have a stable job; he drove the cows to the pasture every morning, where he stayed until late afternoon. He usually spent his evenings in male company, drinking and discussing village matters while Hương took a short break from work to shop.

After years trying to have a child, Hương and her husband decided to look for medical help in a hospital in Ho Chi Minh City. They took a very long trip by train and waited for several days for an appointment with a gynaecologist. However, the doctor could not find any reason for her infertility. Apparently, other possibilities, such as two 'fertile' people not being able to not have children together because of emotional stress or marital difficulties or the husband being infertile, were not even considered. Having run out of money, they were forced to return to Sa Huỳnh. Hương then turned to local religious specialists, desperate by the time she came across a village healer, Gia (he appeared in Chapter 4 in the context of the Quan Âm statue defence). She started visiting him regularly twice a month.

When I met Hương in her restaurant, she told me that at the new and full moon she usually closed her business early in order to do the washing-up and to prepare everything for the next day. After her chores were done, she went to Gia's house. On one such day I accompanied her. Although it was about ten o'clock in the evening, two rooms were packed with people. Gia was sitting behind a big table right in front of the family ancestral altar, surrounded by fishermen who came to ask him to prepare protective amulets and charms against misfortune at sea. They brought fruits, which were piled up on the table as offerings to the ghost who foretold and healed through Gia. During the séance the fruit was transformed into *lộc*, a kind of gift from the spirit.[11] People believed that consuming this fruit would bring them blessings and could even cure sickness.

In the next room I saw about ten women between 20 and 40 years of age sitting on the wooden bench waiting for a consultation. Hương introduced me and we joined the women on the bench. Soon I learned that all of them hoped that Gia could treat their infertility. Two of them had become pregnant thanks to Gia's magic, but still asked for new amulets out of fear that they might lose their children. We waited about an hour until the healer called Hương. He scrawled mysterious signs with red ink on a sheet of paper and ordered her to burn the charm and to drink its ashes with water. In the meantime, Gia looked at me and proudly emphasized that his scribble originated from the other world and was dictated by the *ngài* ('Excellency') who possessed him.[12] Hương thanked the healer and we left his house.

On the way back, I asked her what she thought about the effectiveness of Gia's magical methods. Hương answered that she hoped that a terrible burden would be taken from her, but if she did not get pregnant before the Lunar New Year (*Tết Nguyên Đán*), she and her husband had decided to adopt a baby. Hương took responsibility for her alleged infertility and tried to cope with this feeling by any and all means available to her. Although she did not really know what to think about Gia's methods, in the regular consultation with the village healer she found consolation and relief in her attempt to change her childless status, and her actions showed her husband and his parents that she was taking some measures to influence her 'fate'.

As I have shown, village expectations that define local standards of femininity and to which women are compelled to conform can provoke conflicts and frustrations. On the other hand, women did not remain passive recipients of their 'fate', but took the initiative to face such challenges and to go beyond local conventions. At the same time, we can see that family and motherhood are still important points of reference in their lives, and women are ready to use any means to fulfil their roles

11. For a good discussion of *lộc*, see Soucy (2012).

12. *Ngài*, or Excellency, refers to deities and persons of high status. Here, however, Gia used the term *Ngài* to describe the spirit that possessed him.

as mothers. Religion plays an important role in this process, as it allows them to articulate their specific needs and negotiate their conditions with gods. Moreover, religion offers women ways of transforming the divine power into protection and turning it to their own purpose (Ortner 1997; see Leshkowich 2014). In the next part I analyse in greater detail spirit possession as one strategy women sometimes adopt in critical situations.

Quest for authority as a gendered process

Súng was one of the persons in Sa Huỳnh with whom the various spirits established contact. She did not look for it to happen; it just did. Three days before the Lunar New Year in 2007, the people in Sa Huỳnh saw Súng spreading water in a magic spell (known as *xin phép*; literally 'asking for permission') around the yard of her restaurant. Then her neighbours, to their surprise, witnessed a mass of cars parking in front of the usually deserted restaurant. Guests heading from north to south or vice versa on the main road were stopping in greater numbers than ever before and choosing Súng's restaurant from among dozens of others. Súng's was one of the many roadside restaurants that had sprung up in the late 1990s. Located next to each other, they fiercely compete to attract passing travellers with fresh seafood and the offer of rooms to stay overnight. However, at that time even the well-known and popular roadhouse owned by my landlady could not attract such crowds of people as Súng's did.

The Lunar New Year's Eve was a special night for Súng because that was when she discovered her new abilities. When the clock struck midnight she started to hear voices reaching her from the other world and then she saw many divinities (*thần*), who entered her body simultaneously. She called this particular state *nhập vào* (literally 'being entered'), which means in this context 'lending one's body to the spirit'. She recognized one of them: the Buddha Mother (*Bà Phật Mẫu*).

The Buddha Mother continued to appear every afternoon between 1:00 and 5:00 pm. After some time she introduced her younger sister, several other goddesses including Thiên Y A Na, and even fairies (*tiên*). In turn, the newly introduced divinities sent their servants to solve particular problems for people who turned to Súng for help. Rumours about Súng's abilities circulated not only among the people of Sa Huỳnh, but also in neighbouring villages. People came from all over the area to Súng's house to get help from the Buddha Mother. The goddess was very precise; she never appeared before lunch and always left Súng by dinner time, and this gave Súng some space to prepare meals for passing guests. People who were unfamiliar with the timetable of the goddess arrived in the morning and, having already spent the money for the journey, had to wait for hours until she appeared.

In July 2007 Súng's daughter, who was studying in Ho Chi Minh City, came home for the summer holidays. She could not recognize her mother during her encounters with the Buddha Mother. During possession Súng's voice became completely different, her eyes blurred and she seemed to be a stranger to her daughter. Indeed, Súng spoke with authority and power. During this time, visitors, whom she called 'heads of family' (*gia chủ*), had to be careful with their queries. Sometimes, they were scolded for addressing inappropriate matters, such as a lucky combination for the lottery or gambling, which contrasted, for example, with the questions approved by elders in the spirit possession on Lý Sơn Island.

Súng's possession caused confusion and consternation among some of her neighbours, especially men. Gia was a recognized and respected healer in the village who was regularly visited by rich ship owners and other notable men. Súng's practices of healing and expelling ghosts – usually reserved for male ritual specialists – challenged the established male authority and destabilized their monopoly over sacred power. Men in the village called her practices 'superstitious' (*mê tín dị đoan*), though each had his own understanding of the term. A man living in the immediate vicinity of Súng's house associated superstition with lack of education. He was sure that only education would give Súng the strength to abandon her profession as a spirit medium. Another neighbour emphasized a slightly different aspect. He interpreted superstition not in the terms of 'backwardness', 'ignorance', or a 'painful legacy' of the feudal era, as the State-party suggested, but in terms of authenticity and authority. He tried to get a clear answer from me about whether I believed in her supernatural abilities. He could not accept my reply that as a scholar I was more interested in learning about people's practices than verifying their legitimacy. It is noteworthy that none of these men contested Gia's authority.

Mattijs van de Port (2011: 75) describes 'authenticity' as 'the "cultural production of the real": the rhetorical, performative and aesthetic practices through which people seek to upgrade the reality calibre of the stories-they-live-by'. He points out that 'the cultural production of the real tends to bring irrefutable facts ("incontestable") into play, which have powerful reality effect' (2011: 75). In Chapter 5, I showed that family records turned out to be insufficient to authenticate the 'meritorious death' of a female member of the Phạm lineage. By emphasizing supernatural events in its story, the lineage tried to 'produce' evidence for its female ancestor, Lady Roi, which could authenticate her as a local heroine. However, provincial authorities were more willing to accept male ancestors of Lý Sơn lineages as potential heroes of the Paracel and Spratly flotilla than their female kin, because men fit better into national narratives about the 'meritorious and heroic dead'. Male ancestors satisfied not only the interests of their lineage, but also the broader interests of those who sought to reconstruct Lý Sơn's history and prestige. To put my argument in a nutshell, women were not credible because their conduct and sexuality were tied and limited to their own lineages, which they, as women, could not perpetuate.

In the previous chapter I observed that religious practices were gendered. Let me take this point further by returning to the case of Súng. In Sa Huỳnh, whatever men did in the spiritual realm was seen as valid, whereas women's spiritual practices were perceived as superstitious and inauthentic. In order to authenticate herself as a spirit medium vis-à-vis men's religious practices, Súng sought ways to challenge, contest, and negotiate male ritual hegemony through the creative appropriation of beliefs and practices. Birgit Meyer (2006) analyses how Pentecostal pastors use mass media as a form of mediation between this and the 'other world' to present religious vision practices as authentic and credible (see also Ngô 2016). She observes that 'belief is no longer opposed to visual evidence and hence has lost its grounding in the invisible' (2006: 433). Although Súng did not go so far as to use, for example, a camera or a mobile phone to pass on the message from the Divine to people – as happens in the case of the Pentecostal Church – she adopted other means, often employed by male religious specialists, that authenticated her supernatural power and knowledge and her relationship to spirits. One such means was 'divine writings' – coded messages sent by sprits to Súng. When Súng communicated with a spirit, she noted down its message in secret symbols and then translated its meaning to her clients. The 'divine writings' served to mediate between her and the divine in a way that not only validated her person in the face of criticism from men, but was also visible to her clients.

Women were more understanding towards Súng than men. Some of them took Súng's possession seriously and insisted that she was under the power of the world of the dead (*coi âm*), just like Gia. They believed that the ghosts with whom Súng had established a relationship were coming from Huế because she spoke a Huế accent during possessions. Súng, however, denied that she had any contacts with ghosts from the ancient capital of Vietnam. Instead, she claimed, she had been chosen by the higher world of Buddha and bodhisattvas (*coi thiên*), who were showing their mercy by reducing suffering on Earth. This is similar to Thailand, where Irvine Walter (1984) has observed that some 'modern' spirit mediums claimed a higher status by emphasizing their Buddhist qualities. They maintained that they were possessed by Guan Yin or some other respected figure from the Buddhist pantheon and, at the same time, established links with low-ranking spirits outside the Buddhist realm.

Ahern (1975: 206–207) likewise noted that women in Chinese culture were free to play a predominant role in the cults of 'low-ranking' supernatural spirits. Women could worship or even be possessed by souls of the dead or the 'little low goddesses' who were believed to bring sons or to cure sickly children. The close association of such goddesses with childbirth made them less 'clean' than other spirits. However, in the context of Vietnam, I do not think that we can talk about such a rigid dichotomy. Many authors argue that 'heavy spiritual fate' is a precondition for one's possession (e.g., Trần Thị Ngọc Diệp 1974; Nguyen Thi Hien 2002; Norton 2009; Endres 2011). Súng also believed that her spiritual fate was heavier than other people's, though not as heavy as the fate of those who were possessed by a ghost, as Gia was. In her view, ghosts that were just starting to cure people usually chose to work through a person with a very difficult fate. This helped them accumulate merit and accomplish enlightenment, thereby cultivating their spirits and improving their chances of being promoted to the Buddha's heaven. Such a person could be a woman or a man. When the ghost collects enough merit it moves to the other world. However, to find a suitable person who can facilitate this metamorphosis is not an easy task. As Súng explained, some of these persons should have a sequence of at least seven or eight lives stretching back over a long time. In this way Súng emphasized a crucial difference between her and Gia. Súng claimed that she was selected by the Buddha Mother who, in contrast to ghosts, did not need to improve her *karma*. Being Buddha herself, the Buddha Mother turned to Súng because of her compassion for those who were suffering. Súng's possession, therefore, served a higher purpose than Gia's possession did because it aimed to help humankind by fulfilling the will of the Buddha.

Súng was possessed by the Buddha Mother, who was considered to be the main divinity of the Cao Đài religion (see Hoskins 2015; Ninh 2017). According to Súng – who had only a very loose connection to Cao Đài practices – the Buddha Mother was born from the union of Mother of Earth (*Địa Mẫu*) and Father of the Heavens (*Ông Trời*).[13] She embodied only positive aspects of womanhood (such as motherhood) and granted all wishes that were addressed to her with a 'sincere heart'. Nguyen Thi Hien (2002) explains that in the context of spirit possession cults, a 'sincere heart' means an unwavering faith in spirits and their supernatural power. In Vietnam, a 'sincere heart' is often considered a factor determining a spirit's preference. When Súng's husband told me that his wife had been chosen by the Buddha Mother only because of her heart, he was in fact speaking about her fervent and sincere belief in the Buddha Mother's manifestation and compassion. The 'sincere heart' also formed the basis of Súng's relationship with her clients. She stressed that the medicines she prepared following the instructions of the Buddha Mother could only work when one had strong faith.

Súng considered the Buddha Mother to be 'sweet' (*ngọt ngạo*) and 'compassionate' (*từ bi*); she was also the nearest to the Buddha's heaven. She was responsive to all who acknowledged her without any discrimination. This, however, caused some problems when it came to curing. Some diseases were caused by malicious ghosts, and effective treat-

---

13. The Buddha Mother might be identified with the high-status Chinese goddess Eternal Mother, who is conceived by Chinese people as 'preceding in time of creation, in status, and in authority all the other deities of both Buddhist and Taoist pantheons' (Sangren 1983: 10). Sangren points out that Eternal Mother is a virgin unstained by the pollution of childbirth who lacks earthly incarnation since she precedes all other deities (1983: 14).

ment required that the Buddha Mother be violent. This she ultimately resolved by using the power of other goddesses. Therefore, sometimes the Buddha Mother sent her younger sister, the Divine Mother of the Mountains (*Sơn Thánh Mẫu*), who, in contrast to the Buddha Mother, was violent and fierce (*hung*), had little pity for ghosts, and dealt harshly with them. She mercilessly expelled the evil ghosts causing the sickness from the body and thereby cured the person. Depending on the patient's problems, the Divine Mother of the Mountains occasionally used lower-ranking spirits to cure sick men. If the sick persons were children, then other 'little goddesses' would be called to help.

Transforming crisis into accomplishment

In the previous paragraphs I discussed Súng's interpretation of her possession, her new identity as a spirit medium, and her strategy to authenticate her person. In this section, I develop my analysis further and say a few words about the complex and difficult situation in which Súng found herself before engaging in religious practices. Súng was a married woman in her early forties. Her husband had been a teacher in a primary school, but he gave up his profession when they opened the restaurant. When I conducted my research in 2006 and 2007, their two youngest children, both boys, were still at home, while the eldest child, a daughter, had just entered university. According to Súng – and confirmed by other people in Sa Huỳnh – her restaurant had not turned a profit since they opened the business in 1992. A few years before, she had been forced to sell a piece of her land adjacent to the Sa Huỳnh beach to her neighbour, the rich owner of the successful roadhouse. This neighbour has since constructed a hotel just behind Súng's house. However, Súng still ran up debts and started to suffer from depression.

The situation became even more difficult when the daughter insisted on going to study in Ho Chi Minh City. Súng described her daughter as particularly ambitious and determined, and no one could dissuade her from studying. She went to Ho Chi Minh City with her teacher from grade school, an unmarried thirty-year-old woman who decided to complete her education and earn a master's degree. They rented a small room with a kitchen and lived together. In 2006, Súng's daughter passed an examination and started to study banking. She received three million VND (about €100) from her mother to pay for the first semester, but it was not enough and she asked Súng for more money. Súng had to go into debt again. The situation started to reach a critical point just before the Lunar New Year in 2007, when her daughter asked again for an additional four million VND (€137) to pay for the second semester, rent, and other living expenses. Súng only managed to save up 1.5 million VND (€50), which she sent to her daughter. The girl returned home to celebrate the Lunar New Year with her family and cried that she would have to give up her studies if her parents could not pay for her schooling. Súng felt like she was in a dead-end situation: her debts were growing by the day and she was on the verge of bankruptcy, while her daughter continued demanding money.

A number of authors argue that many spirit mediums, before adopting their new role, encounter difficult social situations and look for a solution to resolve the mental and emotional consequences of the problems they face in the present social, political, and economic situation (Walter 1984; Kendall 1996a, 2009; Kitiarsa 1999; Salemink 2008c, 2010; Endres 2011). In the case of Thailand, Walter (1984) observes that the traditional dominance of Thai women in most forms of small trade is inextricably linked to the commercialization of the spirit possession cult. The recent reinvigoration and intensification of the economy in Vietnam led Taylor (2004: 88) to a similar conclusion. He argued that various petty traders carry out transactions with spirits in the same way they do in everyday life: they negotiate a loan, seek advance contributions, and make a promise to pay off their debts. Such cultivation mirrors their business with clients, creditors and debtors. In turn, Weller (1994, 1998) stresses that traditional values seem to be drained from life whenever market relations begin to dominate social relations. Individuals' growing independence and autonomy deepen anxiety because every individual is in charge of his/her own future. This anxiety is related more to securing a profit in a constantly changing socio-economic context than it is to losing orientation in life. This, inevitably, might create tensions that need to be solved and controlled. Salemink (2008c: 157) observes that in Vietnam, the spiritual security sought via spirit mediums not only compensates for the insecurity related to the volatile market but, above all, creates the 'social capital necessary for investing confidently in new (or old) enterprises, thus enhancing economic security of the traders, their dependants, business partners and clients'.

Súng's financial problems found unexpected relief from the Buddha Mother, who came down from heaven and appeared in Súng's body on New Year's Eve. The goddess calmed her down, saying that she knew about Súng's problems and her worries about her daughter, who studied at the expense of her family's health. She said that the ten years in which Súng and her husband had lived in want had come to an end. Súng was offered *lộc* (Buddha's blessing), which she should share with other people. Overcome by sadness due to the people's suffering, the Buddha Mother had come back to Earth (*Bà ở trên về đây*) and for the next twenty years would use Súng's body to cure those who were sick.

Súng's husband believed that those who were possessed by a ghost (*tà nhập vào*) or a divine spirit (*thần nhập vào*) could not escape their fate. Being caught by the ghost or spirit, one had to serve (*bắt phải làm*) or he or she would become mad. On the other hand, from the moment the person was appropriated by a spirit and became its servant, he or she usually experienced a substantial upturn in business. After the Lunar New Year's incident, Súng's restaurant was inundated for several days with customers who spent enough money to pay for the daughter's semester. On the eighth day of the first lunar month, the girl left Sa Huỳnh to continue her studies in Ho Chi Minh City. Since the appearance of the Buddha Mother on the eve of the Lunar New Year, Súng's business has improved significantly. Travellers stopped and ordered meals at Súng's restaurant almost every day. Súng began to pay off her debts in instalments of 50,000 VND (€1.70), and a small sum of money was still left for day-to-day expenses. She was also able to regularly send her daughter 1.2 million VND (€40) to cover her expenses. Some villagers in Sa Huỳnh took the improvement in Súng's material situation as proof that she really was possessed.

Súng said that the Buddha Mother did not let her charge people for her services. However, she was allowed to accept whatever money the people offered. On one day, when I was waiting with other women for the appearance of the Buddha Mother, one of them asked me how much she should pay to Súng. The people did not expect the spiritual consultation to be free; for them, it was completely natural that they should give at least small change to Súng. As in a typical transaction when two sides exchange items of certain value, Súng's service was rewarded with money. Súng and her husband had never refused such tokens of gratitude and always claimed that the money they earned was spent on buying ingredients and preparing medicaments.

Súng's clientele was predominantly made up of people from a neighbouring commune and Bình Định Province rather than her own co-villagers, who were not sure how to react to her new role. As in Gia's case, fishermen asked for amulets to protect them when fishing; housewives enquired about the fate of their children, health, and prospects of earning money; traders looked for guarantees and luck in business; and sick persons asked for medicine. However, as Súng stated, her most important task was healing. She stopped eating meat and devoted herself to Cao Đài and Buddhist studies. In the evenings she read books, made notes, and practised 'spiritual writing'. The Buddha Mother taught Súng to write signs that originated in the 'other world'. Súng scrawled them with red felt-tip pens on a white sheet of paper and then laid a twisted string of different coloured threads symbolizing the consecutive levels of heaven on the paper and folded it up. Such charms were always prepared individually for each person. Súng's husband became her assistant during the possessions. If someone could not understand Súng, he interpreted her words. Over time Súng trained herself in the preparation of medicaments, her amulets and charms became more colourful, and her handwriting became more professional. The surface of the table she used for preparing amulets gradually grew to be covered with new felt-tip pens and threads in all sorts of colours. Her husband prepared them for every séance, cut paper into pieces for making charms and amulets, gave blessed water to patients and produced medicaments. All charms and amulets had their own expiry date (*hết lộc, hết hàng sử dụng*), and patients who wanted to extend the validity of their powers were advised by Súng and her husband to return for new ones.

In the case of Thailand, Walter (1984) argues that 'modern' spirits are inclined to emphasize that they are not only possessed by Buddhas or bodhisattvas, but that they also help decrease people's sufferings, improve their *karma*, and help them accumulate merit that would allow them to enter Buddha's heaven after death. The possessed persons might even change their diet and become vegetarian. Some spirit mediums even go so far as to claim that they have stopped menstruating and are incapable of having sexual relations with men. When such abstention happens, the marital roles are reversed and the male becomes the subordinate ritual officiant and servant to the spirit of his wife (1984: 320). Soon after the spirit medium resolves the original problem affecting her mental condition, she might become 'an avenue for competition and possible material success as part of the process' (ibid: 322). The spirit medium becomes skilled in using ideology convincingly and establishes herself as a respected authority who might even attract powerful and wealthy clients (ibid: 316).

Salemink (2008b) observes that during spirit possession ritual in Vietnam, gender and sexual boundaries are constructed and transgressed. Women might adopt behaviour that is normally associated with and re-served for men. I am not sure whether Súng really identified with mascu-line roles, but she certainly could not be possessed as a 'real woman' – the Buddha Mother ceased to possess her when she was menstruating. Thus, Súng had to work out her own strategy to validate her person as, above all, a 'real' spirit medium. Similar to what Walter described for Thailand, during Súng's spirit séances, the roles of husband and wife were reversed and Súng adopted the authoritative role of 'master', while her husband was her ritual officiant and servant. Súng considered herself an adept of Buddhist divinity; this role required her to transform her body into a pure vessel (*xác*) that could be 'ridden' by the Buddhist deity, so she also tried to conform to Buddhist prescriptions by becoming vegetarian.

In describing Súng's possession I have sought to demonstrate how, through the everyday encounter with a deity in the privacy of her home, Súng not only solved her own economic problems, but also provided an explanation for the prior failure of her business, which was caused by her heavy spiritual fate. On the verge of a breakdown, she found enough strength and creativity to establish herself not so much as a successful owner of a restaurant, but rather as a respected and knowledgeable spirit medium. In this context, I argue that authentication of ritual identity is a gendered process. Súng's quest for authenticity and authority and her ultimate success became possible by constructing and transgressing symbolic boundaries and incorporating such practices as preparing medicines, perfecting her 'spiritual writing', and devising a convincing ideology of her spirit possession – means previously reserved exclu-sively for men in Sa Huỳnh. Moving beyond ordinary limitations, Súng employed powerful means to transcend her gender role and sexuality and to authenticate and constitute herself as a gifted spirit medium who might even challenge men's control of 'sacred' values, power, authority, and authenticity in the village.

Conclusion

Let me conclude by proposing another way to interpret the vignette at the beginning of this chapter. As I illustrated, the goddess Thiên Y A Na in Sa Huỳnh was a deity of the past, associated with men's religiosity; she had ceased to represent any threat to the local community, especially to women. Thus, the spoiled chicken might be seen as reflecting the dramatic change in the local cosmology: the goddess's decline and her powerless status caused by her travel to the Buddhist heaven. In this sense, the chicken sacrifice becomes the symbolic representation of changes in the power relations between men and women, in which men were losing not only the protection and interest of the goddess, but also their religious dominance.

Women's narratives of Thiên Y A Na's transformation from a fierce spirit to a benevolent one and their notions that the goddess served individual rather than communal needs opened up a new space for an alternative interpretation. Thus, I read the paradoxes and contestations that exist in the ritual domain by looking at women who – located outside of male authority – demonstrated their agency by challenging prevailing ideas and inserting their own interpretations into the framework of dominant local discourses. Relegated to the domestic domain, women turned their zone of ritual exclusion and marginality into a space of creativity and agency. In this space, they sought alternative meanings for themselves other than the domesticity prescribed by the neo-Confucian tradition. Instead of openly resisting men's dominance, they stretched, through various kinds of performance, the boundaries of dominant ideas about what constitutes religious authenticity and authority and created a religious context that involved them as women. In this light, the religious practices appear to be constructed, shaped, and reshaped not only at the intersection of state and village, but also of gendered interpretations and performances. In a nutshell, the 'authentication' of their ritual identity is a *gendered* practice involving power relations as women construct and validate their new ritual identity and transcend the boundaries of the spirit world and their own gender.

Figure 9: Monks, cadres and fishers during the 'Celebration for the Peace of the Paracels and Spratlys', Lý Sơn Island.

Shifting Confrontations in the State–Religion–Society Triadic Relationship

There is a voluminous literature on religion in Vietnam in which religion is pitched against the state or, alternatively, the state is pitched against society. This book deals with this complex, triadic relationship, not by debunking the binary relations that make it up, but by exploring how various protagonists in this book – state officials, religious figures, fishermen, and women – enact, debunk, and re-enact these relations in shifting alliances and changing contexts. In small coastal villages in central Vietnam it is precisely the model of these triadic relations – state–religion–village – that I have sought to capture in terms of hierarchical opposites and self-contradictory dynamics at the intersection of religious and secular frames. I have shown that these binaries are unstable and shifting, but can still be harnessed and manoeuvred by skilled actors in their practical negotiation of power. Based on fine-grained ethnography, this model has allowed me to theorize shifting binaries in ways that go beyond the usual debates over the state–society or state–religion oppositions. In Vietnam, embodied and enacted religious experience seldom leaves the state out, as the state offers the dominant semiotic ideology (see Keane 2007) in which discussions and negotiations are framed – not necessarily a secular frame, but an 'immanent frame' (Taylor 2007) that politicizes religious practices and turns politics into a religious exercise.[1]

---

1. Charles Taylor (2007) uses the term 'immanent frame' to refer to a way of thinking about the material word without any reference to transcendent power.

The centrality of the maritime periphery

The ethnographic material for this book comes from a region in central Vietnam that remains little studied, especially in comparison to the northern Red River Delta or the Mekong Delta in the south, which have been the focus of the vast majority of foreign and Vietnamese scholars. I have challenged that preference and shown that the maritime periphery of the South China Sea is *central* for anthropological analyses of the relationship between state, religion, and society in Vietnam. What Erik Harms (2011b: 4) calls 'peripheral vision as one moment in a mobile field of vision' and Salemink (2018a: 1) terms 'an alternative historical periodization' with reference to the regional centrality of Vietnam's Central Highlands might turn out to be a useful optic through which to reconfigure the binary categories of land and sea. By taking the strategic centrality of the South China Sea in central Vietnam seriously (see Salemink 2018a) and by taking fishing populations and their relations with the surrounding sea and land environments as point of departure, I have demonstrated that Vietnamese society is not exclusively rooted in bounded agrarian village communities (cf. Scott 1976; Popkin 1979) nor predominantly oriented towards the sea. This observation goes to the heart of Keith Taylor's (1998: 951) argument that different modes of being and 'acting Vietnamese' exist through times and terrains. Instead of looking at fishers exclusively through the homogenizing lens of national or regional histories, it is worth remembering that places – regardless of scale – constitute not monolithic but rather heterogeneous entities entangled in complex relations through which they are constructed within and across international, national, and local encounters (Appadurai 1996). A maritime peripheral optic reveals that the understudied fringe of the South China Sea in central Vietnam is important because it is pertinent to understanding the performance of national sovereignty as it is played out through the triangulate relationships that exist among state, religion, and society.

Throughout the book I argue that in the performance of and for the nation, the international disputes over the South China Sea have, paradoxically, drawn peripheral places such as Lý Sơn Island into the centre, turning the old hierarchy between the land and the sea on its head. In this changing aesthetics of the nation, the continental landmass becomes ex-centric and the margins become centred, culminating in the common image of Lý Sơn as the 'navel of the nation' (*rốn bao của cả nước*

Việt Nam)[2] and thus shifting the balance of power in the seemingly immutable binary relationship between mainland and island and between the agrarian and maritime worlds. Following the new patriotic slogan 'The entire Vietnamese nation turns to the sea' (*cả Việt Nam hướng về biển*), many Vietnamese citizens now identify with the island and its territorial vulnerability – alone out there in the middle of the sea, between Vietnam's land mass and the disputed Paracel and Spratly archipelagos – in the belief that fishers are those who bear the brunt of the defence of the nation's sovereignty.

Taking into account Central Vietnam's specific regional histories, its slower rate of socio-economic transformation compared to that of the North and the South, and the geopolitics that plays an increasing role in the region, fishing communities in central Vietnam do not represent an 'exemplary' situation, but rather a peripheral and unsettled one characterized by relations with the state that are not only significantly different from those of other parts of Vietnam, but also vary from place to place within Central Vietnam. The peripheral status of central Vietnam and, thus, of the two fieldsites – Sa Huỳnh and Lý Sơn – refers not just to geographical scale, but to their different levels of (dis)connectedness to state power. When I returned to Sa Huỳnh seven years after my doctoral fieldwork, the Forbidden Hill – access to which had been relatively free since the 1990s – had once again been turned into a military observation post and, therefore, a restricted zone, due to its border status and strategic position. In that sense, Sa Huỳnh and Lý Sơn display the historical, social, and political unevenness of both the region and the place. Each setting stands out in its own right as a 'centrality' marked by the distinctive and unique character of the interactions between state, religion, and society. As my ethnography shows, it is ultimately Lý Sơn Island that, more than mainland Sa Huỳnh, has successfully capitalized on its geographical and historical connection to the South China Sea, taking advantage of the politically imbued image of what it means to be a 'maritime nation' at a time when the sea has become a

---

2. By the time of my fieldwork from May to August 2014, Lý Sơn had become a destination for a new style of patriotic tourism in coastal areas that is increasingly popular among urban Vietnamese, mostly from Hanoi and Ho Chi Minh City. I frequently heard the phrase 'navel of the nation' used in reference to Lý Sơn during my conversations with tourists, including retired high-profile cadres who came expressly to demonstrate their solidarity with fishing communities.

global geopolitical flashpoint regarding disputed sovereignty over the Paracels and Spratlys. Yet this regained centrality of Lý Sơn has become a double-edged sword, simultaneously connecting islanders with the mainland and sidelining and even marginalizing them through the capital investments that flow in and out of the island. The politically and economically harnessed remoteness of the island does not necessarily decrease with connectivity; rather, it takes centre stage as various social actors, including provincial and local officials, 'hold a stake' in particular visions of development (Saxer and Andersson 2019: 145). In this book I have shown how provincial authorities turn Lý Sơn's religious festivals and spaces of worship into axes of cultural-*cum*-economic capital in the newly emerging patriotic tourism industry on the island. This, however, is a topic that deserves a separate study.

The findings presented in this book show that the continuing em-bodied and enacted tensions between villagers, state representatives, and religious authorities are experienced as real binary relations – Việt versus Cham, mainland versus island, fishers versus farmers, male versus female, and ancestor versus ghost – that proliferate, shift, and blur over time. But it would be an oversimplification to try to understand fish-ing communities' entanglement with these different binary relations through the lens of the commonly invoked religious–secular dichotomy. If anything, my ethnography indicates the inadequacy of homogeneous notions of the religious versus the secular, as well as of state versus soci-ety and mainland versus island at the local, national, and global scales. These are not universal categories, but rather binary relations with spe-cific histories and genealogies that are constantly enacted, debunked, and re-enacted in the present and in the specific geographies that add their own weight to these processes. At times, these binaries assume sharper contours and become more visible; at other times the opposing elements collapse into one another and disappear – it all depends on the particular histories, genealogies, and geographies in which the binary relations play out. In this book I have sought to capture these relations, both in their powerful momentum and at their weakest points.

Beyond the religious–secular binary

Much recent scholarship on religion in Asia and the West is framed in terms of the religious–secular binary. Whereas the conceptualization of religion in Europe has emphasized its gradual marginalization within an emergent public space that has increasingly been defined as secular since the Protestant Reformation (Asad 1993, 2003), in Asia, it was presumed that, until relatively recently, religion shaped entire civilizations, moral codes, and social structures, extending into the political sphere of ruling dynasties and competing kingdoms. Existing as overlapping vernacular traditions or in orthodox, scriptural forms that were often non-deistic, religion in non-Islamic Southeast Asia was neither based on a shared belief in a unified doctrine nor on the monotheistic notion of a 'jealous God' demanding exclusive devotion (Salemink 2009a, 2009b; DuBois 2011). In contrast to post-Reformation Christian Europe, religion in imperial-era East Asia – including China and Vietnam – was not controlled by religious authorities that were organized independently of 'secular' authorities. Religion was 'diffused' throughout the different segments of society and controlled by a political leadership that simultaneously represented a cosmic order and acted as mediator between 'this' and the 'other' worlds (Duara 1988: 156).

In that sense, there was not a religious sphere that was clearly distinguishable from a secular sphere. The modern understanding of religion based on 'conceptual dichotomies between the religious domain and this-worldly, secular domains of political and economic practice' (Salemink 2018b: 124; see also DuBois 2009; van der Veer 2013) emerged in Asia only through European imperialism and the formation of nation-states as the main political entities. As Asian colonies morphed into independent nations, vernacular religions became politicized, modernized, and separated from the 'secular' state, which sought to bring them in line with new state orthodoxies. In this period of secularization, the communist-led countries of China, Vietnam, and Laos were more motivated than non-communist ones to reduce and control religions – a point to which I will return later.

The institutional organization of religion and politics in modern nation-states in Asia was not limited to vernacular religious practices, but also included world religions – Buddhism, Hinduism, Christianity, and Islam – which have been fundamental to the development of national citizenship and national identity the world over (Turner 2006). While the separation of religion from the secular relegated religion to the private realm of individual beliefs (Casanova 1994; Asad 2003), the same process also paradoxically allowed religious practices to enter the public space under the guise of national identity, thereby ritually shoring up political power and instrumentalizing religion. In his book *Formations of the Secular*, the anthropologist Talal Asad advanced the following idea about the interdependence of *religion* and the *secular*:

> [A]lthough religion is regarded as alien to the secular, the latter is also seen to have generated religion. Historians of progress relate that in the premodern past secular life created superstitious and oppressive religion, and in the modern present secularism has produced enlightened and tolerant religion. Thus the insistence on a sharp separation between the religious and the secular goes with the paradoxical claim that the latter continually produces the former. (2003: 193)

In contrast to the Weberian model according to which religion and politics became institutionally separated, Asad (2003) argues that neither religion nor the secular are historically stable entities, but are, in a dialectical sense, genealogically and historically fluid and co-constitutive.

In their edited volume *Varieties of Secularism in Asia*, Niels Bubandt and Martijn van Beek (2012: 13) aptly noted that, depending on the 'demographic, religious and cultural make-up' of the nation-state in question, the relationship between 'religions' and the state is not stable; rather, it is constantly redefined and shaped within a given doctrine of secularism. Secularism is essential to defining social and political forms of the 'nation' and to defining citizenship and religious minorities vis-à-vis the imagined 'nation' (Bubandt and van Beek 2012). Such essentialization and reification of national self-representation is often achieved by appropriating the tropes and imaginary of dominant creeds such as Buddhism, Hinduism, Christianity, and Islam, thereby creating new orthodoxies and orthopraxies linked to the nation.

In Vietnam, however, there is no 'dominant religion', even though most of the religious traditions are tied in some way to one or another of the institutionalized religions. As I have suggested, not all of them formulate and impose standardized religious knowledge and practice in the sense of the 'unified authority' that exists in scriptural monotheistic traditions or in the form of an ethno-nationalist ideology. In contrast to notorious cases of ethno-religious purification in, for example, India and Myanmar, it could be argued that Vietnam is a relatively peaceful 'religioscape', to use Turner's (2006: 213) felicitous paraphrase of Arjun Appadurai (1996).

This book highlights the binary oppositions in the religious–secular relations in Vietnam that give rise to various shifting pragmatic positions that cannot be reduced to a single trajectory of authority, power, or resistance in debates about what counts as authentic religion and national culture, and what counts as threats to them. What we are dealing with here is, rather, a transformative aspect within religious–secular binary relations that is not simply assimilative or adaptive. These relations draw on 'concealed' opportunities, political assemblages, cultural repertoires, and a modern discourse of the nation that asserts people's right to religious practices while confirming the legitimacy of the state's semiotic ideology.

Blurring the boundaries between religion and politics

Throughout this book I have shown that in Vietnam the secularizing trend took a new course during the most active years of the Đổi Mới period of economic reform (1986–mid-1990s), when the state relaxed its antisuperstition campaigns and gradually withdrew from a secular–rationalist interpretation of religion as 'unscientific' and 'irrational'. This new course focused on the attempt to transform certain religious forms into the more secular concepts of 'cultural' and 'national heritage', thereby politicizing religious practices. The 'political' within this frame was not necessarily secular, as is clear from numerous rituals adopted by the state in Vietnam – during both the High Socialist and reform eras. The Vietnamese state's commemorative initiative to glorify the historic Paracel and Spratly navy and to preserve all temples and records related to its activities on Lý Sơn Island is a case in point (Chapter 5). Thus, I have shown that the Vietnamese state spared no efforts to connect religion with nationalism when 'foreign' culture became a perceived threat during Vietnam's global integration. Such attempts to validate those religious practices that are in line with state objectives and to condemn those which bear a 'superstitious and heterodox' character could be seen as a *continuation* of the practices of the precolonial monarchy. Among these legacies – dating back to imperial times – is the modern practice of communist-led Vietnam to grant certificates to heroes, divinities, and temples that bear the hallmark of historical and national importance. In neo-Confucian states such as China and Vietnam, the imperial-era governance of and administrative control over religion shielded the interests of the ruling elite, including the emperor, by preventing 'heterodoxy'

– religious beliefs and practices not congruent with the state-approved orthodox version of neo-Confucianism (Do 2003; Taylor 2007: 31–32; Pham Quynh Phuong 2009; DuBois 2009; Brook 2009). These states suppressed and persecuted people who worshipped gods and spirits that were not part of the official registry (Yang 1967). Like the imperial court, today the current communist state of Vietnam seeks to increase its legitimacy through the careful selection and canonization of those historic figures who epitomize moral and patriotic values and fit into the nation-state semiotic ideology.

As I tackled the ways in which state and non-state actors sought to navigate the state and religious semiotic ideologies by continuously making, unmaking, and remaking secular and religious binaries, one of the main questions that drove my research referred precisely to the regulatory character of the state regarding religious practices. In Vietnam, the universal category of religion – *tôn giáo* – only emerged through modern state formation that reconfigured the understanding of vernacular religious practices – now also referred to in terms of modern, Sino-Vietnamese categories such as *tín ngưỡng* (religious beliefs) and *mê tín dị đoan* (heterodox superstition) – and set them up in opposition to science. At the same time, many political categories can trace their pedigrees back to religion. One example is the Buddhist term *giác ngộ* (enlightenment), which was adopted in Vietnamese Marxist discourse as (class/political) consciousness (see Salemink 2018b). Throughout the book I have shown that religious practices are permitted precisely at the intersection of the modern state's definition of religion (*tôn giáo*) and the seemingly more individual notion of belief (*tín ngưỡng*), and allowed to enter the secular public sphere only under the banner of 'culture' or 'national heritage' (Chapter 2). As in other parts of Asia, in Vietnam the communist-led state constructs and controls the space of secularity in such a way that religious discourses and practices cannot challenge the state's legitimacy or moral authority (Salemink 2015).

The politicized and institutionalized religious field in Vietnam cannot be fully understood without recognition of the distinctive polytheistic character of religious practices that often lack the type of orthodoxy and orthopraxy prescribed by scriptural religions in Europe. In contrast to Abrahamic traditions, the cosmologies I encountered in Vietnam's coastal communities are not based on monotheistic religious traditions, nor do they embody absolute norms and moral imperatives. While Confucianism and Buddhism are considered two semiotic religious ideologies in Vietnam, any discussion of moral conduct – as in the case of Lady Roi or Gia – involves reference to political rather than religious norms. For most of the people introduced throughout this book, Confucianism operates as a ritualized-but-secular form of social control, as Confucian ethics determine how a person should properly act within a kin group, within a community, and within society at large, without much explicit reference to gods and deities. Hồ Chí Minh recast the meaning of Confucian virtue by introducing new values into his 'revolutionary ethics' (*đạo đức cách mạng*), such as 'benevolence', 'righteousness', 'knowledge', 'courage', and 'incorruptibility' (Giebel 2004: 182). In addition to traditional morality, which extols virginity and honour, this 'new morality' ideology – which promoted the collective values of patriotism and solidarity against individuality – was tactically mobilized by Anh, the representative of the Phạm Lineage Association, in his attempt to obtain state recognition for his female ancestor and to have her included in the pantheon of Paracel–Spratly heroes. By composing her *lý lịch* (political biography) in a way that emphasized her contribution to national history while backgrounding other aspects that were not congruent with the desired political image, Anh elegantly manipulated religious and political categories.

From the state's perspective, the spirits enshrined in temples have nothing to do with religion, but rather with the question of what should or should not be considered 'national tradition'. Let me return for a moment to the book's opening vignette describing Sa Huỳnh fishers' desire to institutionalize their worship of the wooden statue recovered from the South China Sea as 'historical and cultural heritage' and their ultimate failure to convince the state authorities of the non-superstitious character of their religious practice. This vignette further demonstrates that when such vernacular religious practices transgress the boundaries between public and private, they can appear as matter out of 'proper' secular or religious place, as defined within a particular national context. However, in this book I have tried to transcend the division between religion and the secular by demonstrating that encounters between state and non-state actors are grounded in social life and specific historical and political contexts across global, national, and local scales. An ethnographic approach that connects discrete events, practices, and places has allowed me to demonstrate the continuous proliferation of binary oppositions within the frame of the state–religion–village triadic relationship, as well as how this process varies regionally and locally. It is my hope that the reader has been able to see the proposed model of triadic relations not as static and fixed, but as a *changing* and *changeable* construct. In that sense, the success of the residents of Lý Sơn to enter the public space and secure a 'proper' place for their religious practices on the national level captures the mutability of tactical positions through which various subjectivities are evoked and performed. In turning all temples and records related to the activities of ancestors who were part of historic Paracel–Spratly flotilla into artefacts proving Vietnam's 'cultural' and 'national heritage' in the South China Sea, Lý Sơn fishers redefined their position within binaries of religion and politics, state and society, and mainland and island.

The experience of fishers in Sa Huỳnh also highlights the contingency and unpredictability of the institutionalization of religion and the state's attempt to draw a clear line between acceptable vernacular religious practices and those considered superstitious. If in Lý Sơn the shift in geopolitical imaginaries turned all temples related to the Paracel–Spratly flotilla into 'national heritage', in Sa Huỳnh the actual shift of the location of the Quan Âm statue made the Forbidden Hill a hybrid space of 'folk' beliefs and Buddhism that was re-interpreted by local cadres in terms of traditional 'culture' and by the Buddhist monk in terms of 'superstition'. While fishers did not identify fully with either of these extreme visions, they were careful in their practices not to upset either side. The symbolic potency of the Forbidden Hill was, therefore, produced not only by circulating statues, temples, and ritual practices, but also by the competing power and visions of fishers, state officials, and Buddhist modernizers. It is precisely a changing and changeable binary opposition within this triad that created the ambivalent position of the Forbidden Hill – the hybrid that is neither the exclusive monopoly of the state nor of the people, but rather a matter of shifts in dominant semiotic ideologies.

Navigating authoritative state and religious semiotic ideologies

Before Nha successfully guided his fellows to the Paracels in 1982 (see Chapter 1), he first made a secret pilot trip on his own. Showing me

his logbook, Nha pointed out the list of names he gave to all important landmarks and features he encountered on this virgin trip to the
Paracels. He did not have a nautical map and the administrative map
stolen from the local People's Committee Office gave him only a rough
idea of the geography. Making entries in his logbook and putting marks
on the administrative map, Nha recorded a changing seascape: the rocks
that emerged during ebbs and flows, a coconut tree growing on a small
islet, currents, and passing birds – anything that would allow him to
determine his position and distance from Lý Sơn. In those days, Nha's
boat did not have a navigation system; he was not able to specify latitude
or longitude, nor did he know the speed of his boat. But he had two
valuable pieces of information, namely that the distance from Lý Sơn
to a certain point in the Paracels was 147 nautical miles (ca. 272 km)
and that the length of his boat was 20 metres. He knew that piloting and
manoeuvring involves information about three factors that are essential
for navigation: time, speed, and distance. Standing on the bow of the
boat he counted down seconds to estimate how many nautical miles his
boat was covering in one hour. Once he estimated how many miles his
vessel travelled in 60 minutes, he was able to determine the speed of his
boat and the distance from Lý Sơn to any point in the sea.

Navigating to the Paracels required Nha to steer his boat carefully
on a zigzag course to avoid submerged rocks. Throughout the book, I
have used 'social navigation' (Vigh 2010) as a metaphor to illustrate how
people change their position vis-à-vis the triadic relationship between
state, religion, and society. Like Nha, who took a 'zigzag course' to avoid
hidden rocks, people carefully navigate their ways through the opposing
religion-state or state-society poles to reach a desired destination. The
temporary binaries that emerge can be imagined as analogous to the
mythical Greek monsters Scylla and Charybdis, lying in wait on either
side of the narrow waters and threatening the navigators, who in turn
act this way or that, depending on their position within the sea 'terrain'.
Like these mythical monsters-*cum*-landmarks in the seascape, the semiotic ideologies of state and religious authorities are important and even
necessary reference points for people; however, if ignored or overlooked
on the map of everyday politics, they can pose insurmountable hazards
to the navigator. In that sense 'social navigation' is not limited to chronic
crises created by war, structural poverty, or endemic violence and crime,

as Henrik Vigh (2008, 2012) theorizes, but can equally be deployed in situations where order exists alongside the unpredictability and mutability created by authoritative semiotic ideologies.

There is also the question of politics. It is important to recognize that the art of navigating different binary oppositions requires of actors the ability to give a political dimension to everyday practice while seizing the 'opportunity' (Certeau 1984). For that reason, the binaries are not just mutually interdependent, but also temporally variable, as they materialize and dissolve at various points in time among different groups of actors. This is quite different from Harms's (2011a) argument about the persistence of ideal binary categories in Vietnamese society, despite people's everyday experiences that contradict the existence of such clear-cut spatial and class-inflicted oppositions in real life. Harms shows that people hold onto highly reductionist concepts such as 'urban' versus 'rural' and 'inside' versus 'outside' because these categories allow them to understand the world and to organize their relations within society. However, my ethnography points in a rather different direction, namely that those binaries are never politically neutral, as fishers use them to make claims not just on the state but also on religious authorities and on the hierarchical agrarian society. The poles of these binaries are not fixed *per se*; in practice, fishers construe, construct, enact, and deconstruct these oppositions in multiple ways and with different effects. The various binaries – spatial, political, social – emerge at the same time but with momentary, precarious, and shifting alliances and coalitions between different actors.

In that sense, my argument is closer to Michael Herzfeld's (2016) study of residents of Bangkok's old quarter, who navigate between seemingly self-contradictory positions of authoritarianism and egalitarianism in negotiations with authorities over the fate of their neighbourhood. The ability to adapt authoritative semiotic ideologies in their own interests is particularly important in the case of marginalized fishing communities that for centuries were stateless, constituting a subordinate social category within the settled hierarchical agrarian society of Vietnam (see Subramanian 2009). Exhibiting pragmatic choices and allegiances within the state–religion–village triadic relation, fishers are not easily captured by the simplified state–society or state–religion dyad, as they had to also manoeuvre across and within the spatial and social division of inland and coast that kept them outside of the *làng* system for so long. What characterizes fishers is their use of words, signs, and symbols pertaining to both the state and religious semiotic ideologies. This allows them not only to play powerful state and religious modernizers against one another, but also to navigate the dominant agrarian Vietnamese society to which they have only very recently been admitted as an integral part of 'authentic Vietnamese culture'.

The cases of Sa Huỳnh and Lý Sơn do not just display different dynamics regarding their relation with the state; they also point out nuances regarding the position of such subaltern groups as fishers. The state-initiated process of restructuring the religious domain and abolishing the hierarchical system of the communal house – formerly the religious and political centre of the village – led to the enhancement of the social position of fishers vis-à-vis farmers in both places. In the context of economic liberalization and due to increasing demands for marine products in domestic and international markets, the fishers are getting richer and starting to play a more important role in the village through ritual investment in agriculture-oriented temples. However, the fishers of Lý Sơn, and not those of Sa Huỳnh, have been able to enhance their position not only economically, but also as political actors in the context of the geopolitical tensions between Vietnam and China. In the end, it is the islanders' fishing operations at sea and their bravery that are mediatized on a national and global stage and celebrated by mainland tourists.

The ethnographic examples in these chapters illustrate that, in their desire to enact their local worship and rituals, fishers willingly engage with the sophisticated forms of state and religious discipline. Whereas fishers cannot escape or act as autonomous actors outside the triadic relationship with state and religious authorities, I have shown that they often employ tactical improvisations drawing on selected political and religious repertoires when encountering and countering forms of state and religious discipline. Rather than openly resisting these disciplinary regimes, they resort to what Achille Mbembe (1992) called 'indiscipline', a practice of inverting, subverting, and ridiculing official disciplinary forms while seemingly going along with them. Without using the term 'indiscipline', Michel de Certeau (1984: xv) made an important point about it, namely, that these improvised tactics are 'multiform and fragmentary, relative to situations and details, insinuated into and concealed within devices whose mode of usage they constitute, and thus lacking their own ideologies and institutions', but still conform to certain rules and logics.

This observation leads me to Kathrine Bowie's (2017) historical and ethnographic study on the politics of humour and its role in Thai peasants' popular re-enactments of the classic Buddhist text *Vessantara Jataka*. Bowie shows quite persuasively that social actors in feudal Thailand sometimes intentionally interjected humour into religious performances to criticize the existing political hierarchy of royalty and monastic orders, and yet at the same time to conceal the critique. Bowie's (2017: 206) argument about humour as 'a weapon of the weak' and Certeau's point about the ability of the 'weak' to manipulate events in order to turn them into 'opportunities' are both brought out clearly in my ethnography, which shows that both state and non-state actors within local communities frame religion in terms of 'culture' and, above all, 'national heritage', thereby 'nationalizing' and 'politicizing' religion. This mesh of different disciplining strategies and improvised tactics of indiscipline allows fishers, state officials, and religious modernizers to extract specific cultural practices from a rich repertoire of religious and state semiotic ideologies that give legitimacy to the state's project and simultaneously to the fishers' preferred forms of religious life.

A closer look at fishers' religious expressions reveals that religious and state semiotic ideologies are used not just to legitimize their vernacular religions, but also tacitly to displace the power of the agrarian society, male hierarchy, state officials, and religious modernizers. Like fishers, women constituted a subaltern group that suffered from discrimination in the village religious space but also took advantage of the state's cultural policies, though with varying results in Lý Sơn and Sa Huỳnh. In both places, female villagers do not openly resist men's dominance in the religious landscape of central Vietnam's coastal society but, through various kinds of transgressive performances, create a context that involves them as women. However, in contrast to Lý Sơn, where men continued to define communal house orthodoxy and women were still perceived in terms of the 'uncleanliness' associated with menstruation and female sexuality, women in Sa Huỳnh were able to break the no-female taboo and enter the Thiên Y A Na temple on the Forbidden Hill. Tactically seizing the 'opportunity' of male notions of the spiritual impotence of the goddess, Sa Huỳnh women successfully asserted their own religious vision of the Forbidden Hill. Thus, I have argued that the authentication of women's religious identity – located outside of male authority – is a power-laden gendered practice, as women construct and validate their new ritual identity and symbolically cross the boundaries between 'this world' and the world of imaginative communion with gods and spirits from their own gender position.

Another ethnographic example – that of Gia, a recognized healer in Sa Huỳnh – indicates how indiscipline brings a kind of rationalism that allows seemingly opposing sides to enter into a form of silent collaboration. There were actual confrontations, but also short-lived pragmatic alliances and manipulations of semiotic ideologies that allowed the cadres and religious figures to achieve their contradictory goals within the same ideological frame. Defending a Buddhist statue against the police, Gia blurred the distinction between the religious and political realms – and hence between the opposing poles of a secular–religious binary – in such a way that his actions would not be seen by authorities as superstitious. By insisting that the statue of the Buddhist bodhisattva Quan Âm was worth saving not for its religious potential as an object of worship, but rather for its aesthetic qualities and potential to beautify the landscape, and for that reason rightfully belonged in a secular space, Gia insinuated himself into the logic of the more 'powerful' state authorities. In other words, by articulating his religious desire within the dominant semiotic ideology of the state, Gia managed to subvert the latter in an act of indiscipline. A different ethnographic example is afforded by the Buddhist monk who, promoting a modern vision of religion cleansed of non-Buddhist elements and propagating ascetic forms of self-cultivation, refused to accept the local folk practices as part of his religious duty of ritual care. He sought a radical break from local religious traditions by resorting to the pre-Đổi Mới rhetoric that equated 'superstition' with the 'peasant class'. The monk's attitude reflects the dichotomy between Buddhist orthodoxy and the fishers' presumably heterodox and heteropractic (from an orthodox point of view) beliefs and practices. It also points to a wider issue of competing forms of morality within religious and state semiotic ideologies.

I have focused on the art of navigating the state and religious authorities by fishers in the South China Sea periphery. By attending to the complexity of the ethnography, I offer a form of ethnographic theorizing that foregrounds fishers in a triangular relationship with figures of state and religious authority. These figures sometimes engage in conflicts and sometimes align with each other, depending on the context and on how individual actors articulate different aspects of religious and state semiotic ideologies and enact indiscipline. In *Religion in Contemporary China: Revitalization and Innovation*, Adam Chau (2011: 8) characterizes the relationship between the Chinese Party-state and religion as a 'politics of articulation' in which a 'diverse array of religious ideas and activities … articulate smoothly with the main body politic of the nation-state'. Chau invokes the image of a centipede to depict the nation-state, with its body representing the central state apparatus and its legs signifying the many diverse actors and their often contradictory visions and desires:

> As long as the centipede is moving forward, it probably doesn't care if a few of its legs have minds of their own or are pretending to be moving in synchronicity with the other legs but are in fact moving sideways or even backward. (Chau 2011: 8)

This is a powerful metaphor, but it still presents the state as a monolithic body even as it synchronizes a multitude of visions. If I look more closely at local practices of state and non-state actors, I imagine the state–society–religion interactions as a beehive composed of a well-organized and hierarchical colony of bees that can shift their roles in the hive as they act across various complex relationships. In this sense, rather than acting as a single monolithic body, the state functions like a beehive that consists of a multiplicity of bodies that select different directions and mutualistic relationships within their environment, but never lose sight of the overall hive, which is captured in a dominant semiotic ideology. These different directions and mutualistic relationships become part of visions that are authoritative rather than contradictory. This book has shown that people do productively engage with rather than ignore these ideologies, while still managing to navigate the powerful binaries whenever and wherever they arise.

Moving from the metaphor of the beehive to the wider frame of state–religion–society as a triad of contested categories within the dominant semiotic ideologies of the state and orthodox Buddhism, I argue that religious practices are enacted and co-produced locally by the state through its diverse agents and agencies, by religious reformers through their purifying discipline, and by various categories of villagers who use indiscipline as a local tactic when acting on behalf of their gods. Focusing on local-level confrontations, I have demonstrated that binary opposi- tions of various types of discipline, or discipline versus indiscipline, reli- gious versus secular, or rationalized religious doctrines versus vernacular religions, do exist, but these distinctions are not clear-cut. By exposing the extent of improvisation and tactics of legitimation, I have shown that these binary relations are mutually constitutive, as various categories of social actors compete to gain advantage against the backdrop of the process of purification of religion. State agents, religious authorities, and fishers actively sharpen, interrupt, shift, or blur the binary relations between them but, at the same time, they continuously seek to maximize their tactical positions within and across those binaries by selectively accepting, purifying, and subverting state and religious semiotic ideolo- gies in ways that best serve their specific locale and interests. Still, when the Scylla of the powerful state and the Charybdis of religious authority confront each other in this triadic relationship, local people are the ones who, little by little, subtly and skilfully navigate the waters and influence events in ways that make a real difference.

Bibliography

Official documents

Công Báo [Official Gazette] (1955). Sắc Lệnh số 234-SL ngày 14-6-1955 ban hành chính sách tôn giáo [Decree no. 234-SL of 14-6-1955 on the promulgation religious policy], Chủ tịch nước Việt Nam dân chủ cộng hòa [President of the Democratic Republic of Vietnam], số [no.] 11, 154–155.

———— (1955a). Nghị định số 559 -TTg ngày 14-7-1955 định mức thuế nông nghiệp cho những phần ruộng đất mà nhà thờ, nhà chùa, thánh thất được sử dụng từ sau cải cách ruộng đất [Decree no. 559 - TTg of 14-7-1955 on agricultural tax normalization of land used by churches, Buddhist pagodas, and oratories since the land reform] Thủ Tướng Chính phủ [Prime Minister], số [no.] 12, 172.

———— (1956). Thông tư số 954 - ngày về việc bảo vệ những di tích lịch sư [Circular no. 954 - TTg on the protection of places of historical interest], Chánh văn phòng [Chief of the Secretariat], số [no.] 20, 189.

———— (1960). Thông Tư Số 165/VH/VP ngày 2-2-1960 về việc bảo quản, sử dụng, tu sửa các công trình kiến trúc chưa xếp hạng (đình, chùa, lăng, miếu, cầu, quán, nhà thờ, mồ mả, v.v...) và các động sản phụ thuộc (bia, đồ thờ, đồ trang trí, cây cổ thụ, v.v...) [Circular Letter no. 165/VH/VP of 2-2-1960 on the preservation, use, and repair of architectural constructions that have not been yet classified (communal houses, pagodas, imperial tombs, temples, roadside shrines, palaces, churches, graves, etc.) and personal assets (tombstones, cult objects, decoration objects, century-old trees, etc.)], Bộ Văn Hoá [Ministry of Culture], số [no.]19, 338.

———— (1962). Quyết định số 313-VH/VP ngày 28-4-1962 về việc xếp hạng những di tích, danh thắng toàn miền Bắc [Decision no. 313-VH/VP of 28-4-1962 on the classification of monuments and places of natural beauty in North Vietnam] Bộ Văn hoá [Ministry of Culture], số [no.] 21, 340.

———— (1966). Chỉ thị số 188-TTg/VG ngày 24-10-1966 về việc bảo vệ và phát huy tác dụng của di tích lịch sử trong thời gian chống Mỹ cứu nước

[Directive no.188-TTg/VG of 24-10-1966 on the protection and development of places of historical interest at the time of resistance against the American aggressors for national salvation], Hội Đồng Chính Phủ [Government Council], số [no.] 13, 270.

———— (1973). Chỉ thị số 88-TTg ngày 26-4-1973 về việc chấp hành chính sách đối với việc bảo vệ các chùa thờ Phật và đối với tăng ni [Directive no. 88 -TTg of 26 - 4 -1973 on the implementation of the policy on protection of Buddhist pagodas and clergy], Thủ Tướng Chính phủ [Prime Minister], số [no.] 15, 252-254.

———— (1974). Quyết định số 15-VH/QĐ ngày 13-3-1974 về việc xếp hạng di tích lịch sử và văn hóa đợt III [Decision no. 15-VH/QĐ of 13-3-1974 on the classification of historical and cultural monuments, 3rd stage], Bộ trưởng Bộ Văn hóa [Minister of Culture], số [no.] 4, 51.

———— (1975). Quyết định số 09-VH/QĐ ngày 21-2-1975 việc xếp hạng di tích lịch sử và văn hóa đợt IV [Decision no. 09-VH/QĐ of 21-2-1975 on the classification of historical and cultural monuments, 4th stage], Bộ trưởng Bộ Văn hóa [Minister of Culture], số [no.] 6, 91.

———— (1980). Quyết định số 92-VH/QĐ ngày 10-7-1980 xếp hạng 17 di tích lịch sử và văn hóa [Decision no. 92-VH/QĐ of 10-7-1980 on the classification of 17 historical and cultural monuments], Bộ trưởng Bộ Văn hóa và thông tin [Minister of Culture and Information], số [no.] 12, 230–232.

———— (1982). Quyết định số 147-VH/QĐ ngày 24 -12-1982 xếp hạng 8 di tích lịch sử và văn hóa [Decision no. 147-VH/QĐ of 24-12-1982 on the classification of 8 historical and cultural monuments], Bộ trưởng Bộ Văn hóa [Minister of Culture], số [no.] 25, 532.

———— (1984). Pháp Lệnh ngày 31-3-1984 bảo vệ và sử dụng di tích lịch sử, văn hóa và danh lam, thắng cảnh [State Law of 31-3 -1984 on the protection and use of places of historical and cultural interest and of beautiful landscape], Hội đồng Nhà nước [National Council], số [no.] 8, 154.

———— (2001). Luật Di sản văn hóa, số 28/2001/QH10 ngày 29/6/2001 [State Law on Cultural Heritage, no. 28/2001/QH10 ngày 29/6/2001], Chủ tịch Quốc hội [Chairman of the National Assembly], số [no.] 34, 2231–2243.

———— (2002). Nghị Định của Chính phủ số 92/20002/NĐ-CP ngày 11/11/2002 quy định chi tiết thi hành một số điều của Luật Di sản văn hóa [Decree of the Government no. 92/2002 NĐ-CP of 11/11/2002 on elaboration of the implementation of some clauses of State Law on Cultural Heritage], Chính Phủ [Government], số [no.] 61, 4045-4066.

——— (2002a). Quyết định số 01/2002 QĐ-BVHTT ngày 02/1/2002 về việc ban hành Quy chế công nhận danh hiệu gia đình văn hóa, Lăng văn hóa, Khu phố văn hóa [Decision no.01/2002 QĐ-BVHTT of 02/1/2002 on promulgation regulations on granting a honorouble title of Cultural family, Cultural village and Cultural quarter], Bộ Trưởng Bộ Văn Hóa Thônh Tin [Minister of Culture and Information], số [no.] 20, 1333-1340.

UBND Tỉnh Quảng Ngãi and Sở văn Hoá Thông Tin, *Báo cáo của Sở VHTT Quảng Ngãi về việc xây dựng tôn tạo khu di tích Hoàng Sa - Trường Sa trên huyện đảo Lý Sơn* [Report of the Office of Culture and Information of Quảng Ngãi on reconstructing and embellishment of a Zone of the Paracel - Spratly on Lý Sơn Island]', Quảng Ngãi, 2001.

Unpublished Manuscripts

Đảng Bộ Phổ Thạnh [Phổ Thạnh Party Committee]. (1985). Phổ Thạnh.

Gia Phả - Hộ Võ Văn. [Family annals - Hộ Võ Văn] kept by the Võ Văn lineage, An Vĩnh commune, Lý Sơn District, Quảng Ngãi Province.

Gia Phả - Hộ Phạm Văn. [Family annals - Hộ Phạm Văn] kept by the Phạm Văn lineage, An Vĩnh commune, Lý Sơn District, Quảng Ngãi Province.

Hồ sơ di tích lịch sử - họ Phạm Văn [The dossier of historical sites of the Phạm Văn lineage]. (2005). Tộc họ Phạm Văn. Vĩnh commune, Lý Sơn District, Quảng Ngãi Province.

Hương ước, Đức Phổ [Village convention of Đức Phổ District]. (1937). Hanoi: École Francaise D'Extrême – Orient.

Phan Đình Độ. (n.d.). Tín *ngưỡng* cúng việc lễ của cư dân ở đảo Lý Sơn [Religious beliefs and tradition of the inhabitants of Lý Sơn Island], Chi hội Văn nghệ dân gian Quảng Ngãi.

Tiểu sử chùa Từ Phước. (n.d.). Thạch By, xã Phổ Thạnh, tỉnh Quảng Ngãi [Từ Phước Pagoda's Chronicle. Thạch By, Phổ Thạnh commune, Quảng Ngãi Province].

Published sources cited in Vietnamese
(English translation of titles in brackets)

Bộ Ngoại Giao Uỷ Ban Biên Giới Quốc Gia. (2013), *Tuyển tập các châu bản Triệu Nguyễn về thực thi chủ quyền của Việt Nam trên hải quần đảo Hoàng Sa và Trường Sa* [Collection of Official Documents of the Nguyen Dynasty on the Exercise of Sovereignity of Vietnam over the Paracels and Spratlys Archipelagoes], Nhà Xuất bản Tri thức, Hà Nội.

ĐNTN-LTNV, Đại Nam Thống Nhất Chí – Lục Tỉnh Nam Việt [Gazetteer of Great Vietnam – The Six Southern Province]. (1973 [1882]), Tu Trai Nguyễn Tạo trans. Republished Saigon: Nha Văn Hóa.

Đỗ Quang Hưng. (2004). Phải chăng tôn giáo mâu thuẫn với chủ nghĩa xã hội [Is it Right that Religion is at Variance with Socialism?] *Nghiên cứu Tôn giáo* 5, 10–17.

Đoàn Ngọc Khôi. (2004). *Lý lịch di tích. Đền thờ Âm Linh Tự và mộ Lính Hoàng Sa* [Historical record: Temple of the Dead and graves of the Paracels' soldiers]. Xã An Vĩnh, huyện Lý Sơn, tỉnh Quảng Ngãi, 1–23.

Đồng Khánh Địa Dư Chí [Descriptive Geography of the Emperor Đồng Khánh]. (2003[1885]). Hanoi: EFEO, vol. 3.

Hà Văn Tăng and Trương Thìn. (1999). *Tín ngưỡng - mê tín* [Religious Beliefs-Superstition] Hà Nội: Nhà xuất bản Thanh niên.

Hardy, Andrew. (2008) Núi và biển trong lịch sử kinh tế Chămpa và Việt Nam [Mountains and the sea in the economic history of Champa and Vietnam], in *Văn hóa biển miền Trung và văn hóa biển Tây Nam Bộ* [Maritime culture of the Central region and maritime culture of the Southwest] (pp. 88–102). Hanoi: Nxb Từ điển Bách khoa.

Lê Quý Đôn. (1972 [1776]). *Phủ Biên Tạp Lục* [A Compilation of the Miscellaneous Records When the Southern Border was Pacified], vol.1, Saigon: Phủ Quốc Vụ Khạnh Đặc Trách Văn Hóa.

Ngô Đức Thịnh. (2001). *Tín ngưỡng và văn hóa tín ngưỡng ở Việt Nam* [Beliefs and the Religious Culture in Vietnam]. Hà Nội: Nhà xuất bản Khoa học xã hội.

Ngô Đức Thọ and Nguyễn Văn Nguyên. (2006). *Quốc sử quán triều Nguyễn: Đồng khánh địa du chí, tỉnh Quảng Ngãi* [National History of the Nguyễn Dynasty: Đồng Khánh's Geography of the Country, Quảng Ngãi Province], Quảng Ngãi: Viện nghiên cứu Hán Nôm [Institute of Hán Nôm Language].

Nguyễn Đăng Vũ. (2001). Từ việc xác lập nguồn gốc đội Hoàng Sa nghĩ về việc tôn tạo các di tích liên quan trên đất Quảng Ngãi [On the Establishment of the Origin of Hoang Sa Army: Deliberations on the Preservation of Various Historical Sites Connected with the Quảng Ngãi Area], *Tạp chí văn hóa nghệ thuật*, 11, 31–33.

——— (2002). Lễ khao lề thế lính Hoàng Sa [Customary Ceremony of Replacing a Former Soldier with a New Recruit]', *Tạp Chí Nghiên Cứu Đông Nam Á*, 5, 54–59.

———— (2006). Tục thờ cúng âm hồn dọc biển [Cult of anonymous souls on the coast], *Tap chí cẩm thành* 48 (10): 27–34.

Nguyễn Đoá and Nguyễn Đạt Nhơn. (1939). Địa Dư tỉnh Quảng Ngãi [Geography of Quảng Ngãi Province]. (Huế: Imprimerie Mirador (Vien –De), Quai de la Susse).

Nguyễn Duy Thiệu. (2002). *Cộng đồng ngư dân ở Việt Nam* [Fishers Communities in Vietnam].Hà Nội: Nha xuất Bản khoa học xã hội.

Nguyễn Hữu Thông. (2001). *Tín ngưỡng Thờ Mẫu ở miền Trung Việt Nam* [*Beliefs concerning Mother worship in Central Vietnam*]. Huế: Thuận Hóa.

Nguyễn Q. Thắng. (2008). *Hoàng Sa Trường Sa Lãnh thổ Việt Nam: Nhìn từ Công pháp Quốc tế* [Vietnam's territory of the Paracels and Spratlys: The view from the International Law]. Hà Nội: Nhà Xuất bản Tri thức.

Nguyễn Quang Ngọc and Vũ Văn Quân. (1998). 'Tư liệu về nguồn gốc, chức năng và hoạt động của đội Hoàng Sa' [Documents on the Origin, Tasks and Activities of the Paracel Team], *Tạp Chí Khoa học Đại Học Quốc gia Hà Nội* XIV no.3.

Nguyễn Thị Kim Bình. 'Đời sống làng xã tỉnh Quảng Ngãi qua các bản hương ước' [Village Life of Quảng Ngãi Province through the 'Convention'], http://www.archives.gov.vn/cong_bo_gioi_thien_tl/mlnews.2006= 9-18.75735954401, access on 18 September 2006.

Nguyễn Văn Mạnh. (1999). *Văn hóa làng và làng văn hóa ở Quảng Ngãi* [Village culture and cultural village in Quảng Ngãi]. Huế: Nhà Xuất Bản Thọan hóa.

Tạ Chí Đài Trường. (2005). *Thần, Người, và Đất Việt* [Deities, People and the Land of Việt]. Hà Nội: Nhà xuất bản Văn Hoá Thông Tin.

Toàn Ánh. (2005 [1968]). *Nếp Cũ - Làng Xóm Việt Nam* [Old customs – Vietnamese Village]. HCHM: Nhà Xuất Bản Trẻ.

Trần Thị Ngọc Diệp. (1974). Ngưỡng đồng bóng [Beliefs of Spirit Possession]. *Khảo Cổ Tập San (Bulletin de L'institute de Recherches Archeologiques Transactions of the Archaeological Research Institute, Saigon),* (8): 64–74.

Trương Thìn. (1999). Tôn trọng tín ngưỡng và bài trừ mê tín dị đoan [Respecting Beliefs and Abolishing Superstitions]. In Hà Văn Tăng and Trương Thìn, *Tín ngưỡng - mê tín* [Religious Beliefs-Superstition] (pp. 112–126). Hà Nội: Nhà xuất bản Thanh niên.

Sơn Hồng Đức. (1975). Thử khảo sát về quần đảo Hoàng Sa [An Attempt to Investigate the Paracel Archipelago], *Sử Địa* 29, 1–3.

Published Sources cited in Western languages

Ahern, Emily M. (1975). The Power and Pollution of Chinese Women. In Margaret Wolf and Roxane Witke (eds), *Women in Chinese Society* (pp. 193–214). Stanford, California: Stanford University Press.

Amer, Ramses. (2002). *The Sino-Vietnamese Approach to Managing Boundary Disputes.* Durham: International Boundaries Research Unit.

Anagnost, Ann S. (1985). *Hegemony and the Improvisation of Resistance: Political Culture and Popular Practice in Contemporary China.* Ann Arbor: University of Michigan.

——— (1987). Politics and Magic in Contemporary China. *Modern China*, 13 (1): 41–61.

——— (1994). The Politics of Ritual Displacement. In Charles F. Keyes, Laurel Kendall and Helen Hardacre (eds), *Asian Visions of Authority: Religion and the Modern States of East and Southeast Asia* (pp. 221–254). Honolulu: University of Hawai'i Press.

——— (1997). *National Past-times: Narrative, Representation, and Power in Modern China.* Durham: Duke University Press.

Anderson, Benedict R. (1991). *Imagined Communities: Reflections on the Origin and Spread of Nationalism.* London and New York: Verso.

Antony, Robert J. (2014). 'Righteous Yang': Pirate, Rebel, and Hero on the Sino-Vietnamese Water Frontier, 1644–1684. *Cross-Currents: East Asian History and Culture Review*, 3 (2): 319–348.

Appadurai, Arjun. (1996). *Modernity at Large: Cultural Dimensions of Globalization.* Minneapolis: University of Minnesota Press.

Ardener, Edwin. (2012). 'Remote areas': Some theoretical considerations. *Hau: Journal of Ethnographic Theory*, 2(1): 519–33.

Asad, Talal. (1993). *Genealogies of Religion: Discipline and Reasons of Power in Christianity and Islam.* Baltimore: The Johns Hopkins University Press.

——— (2001). Reading a Modern Classic: W.C. Smith's 'The Meaning and End of Religion.' In Hent de Vries and Samuel Weber, *Religion and Media* (pp. 131–147). Stanford, California: Stanford University Press.

——— (2003). *Formations of the Secular: Christianity, Islam, Modernity.* Stanford, California: Stanford University Press.

Ashiwa, Yoshiko and David L. Wank. (2009). *Making Religion, Making the State: The Politics of Religion in Modern China* (pp. 1–21). Stanford University Press: Stanford, California.

Avieli, Nir. (2012). *Rice Talks: Food and Community in a Vietnamese Town.* Bloomington, Indiana: Indiana Univeristy Press.

Bélanger, Danièle. (2004). Single and Childless Women of Vietnam: Contesting and Negotiating Female Identity? In Lisa Drummond and Helle Rydstrøm (eds), *Gender Practices in Contemporary Vietnam* (pp. 96–116). Singapore: Singapore University Press.

Bohannan, Laura. (1952). A Genealogical Charter. *Africa: Journal of the International African Institute,* 22 (4): 301–315.

Boudarel, Georges. (1991). L'insertion du pouvoir central dans les cultes villageois au Vietnam: Esquisse des problèmes à partir des écrits de Ngô Tat Tô. In Alan Forest, Yoshiaki Ishizawa and Leon Vandermeersch, *Cultes populaires et societétés asiatiques: Appareils cultuels et appareils de pouvoir* (pp. 87–144). Paris : Centre National de la Recherche Scientifique, l'Université Paris, l'Institute of Asian Cultures, l'Université Sophia (Tôkyô).

Bowie, Katerine A. (2017). *Of Beggars and Buddhas: The Politics of Humor in the Vessantara Jataka in Thailand.* Wisconsin and London: The University of Wisconsin Press.

Brandtstädter, Susanne. (2003). The Moral Economy of Kinship and Property in Southern China. In Christopher M. Hann (ed.), *The Postsocialist Agrarian Questions: Property Relations and the Rural Condition* (pp. 419–420). Münster: LIT.

Brook, Timothy. (2009). The Politics of Religion: Late-Imperial Origins of the Regulatory State. In Yoshiko Ashiwa and Dawid L. Wank (eds), *Making Religion, Making the State: The Politics of Religion in Modern China,* (pp. 22–43). Stanford: Stanford University Press.

Bubandt, Niels and Beek, Martijn van (2012). *Varieties of Secularism in Asia: Anthropological Exploration of religion, politics and the spiritual.* London and New York: Routledge Taylor and Francis Group

Cadière, Leopold. (1955–1957). *Croyances et Pratiques Religieuses des Vietnamiens* (Vol. 1–3). Saigon: École Française D'Extrême-Orient.

Casanova, José. (1994). *Public Religions in the Modern World.* Chicago: University of Chicago Press.

Certeau, de Michael. (1984). *The Practice of Everyday Life.* Berkeley: University of California Press.

Chapman, John. (2007). The 2005 Pilgrimage and Return to Vietnam of Exiled Zen Master Thích Nhất Hạnh. In Philip Taylor (ed.) *Modernity and*

Re-Enchantment: Religion in Post-Revolutionary Vietnam (pp. 297–341). Singapore: ISEAS.

Chao, Emily. (1999). The Maoist Shaman and the Madman: Ritual Bricolage, Failed Ritual, and Failed Ritual Theory. *Cultural Anthropology,* 14 (4): 505–534.

Chau, Adam Yuet. (2006). *Miraculous Response: Doing Popular Religion in Contemporary China.* Stanford, California: Stanford University Press.

Ciorciari, John D. and Chen Weiss, Jessica. (2016). Nasionalist Protests, Government Responses, and the Risk of Excalation in Interstate Disputes. *Security Studies,* 25 (3): 546–583.

Chou, Cynthia. (2003). *Indonesian Sea Nomads: Money, Magic, And Fear of the Orang Suku Laut.* London and New York: RoutledgeCurzon.

——— (2010). *The Orang Suku Laut of Riau, Indonesia: The Inalienable Gift of Territory.* London and New York: RoutledgeCurzon.

Coleman, Elisabeth B. and White Kevin. (2006). In Coleman, E. B. & White, K. (eds), *Negotiating the Sacred: Blasphemy and Sacrilege in a Multicultural Society,* (pp. 1–13). Canberra: ANU E Press.

Connerton, Paul. (1999). *How Societies Remember.* Cambridge: Cambridge University Press.

Day, Tony. (2002). *Fluid Iron.* Honolulu: University of Hawai'i Press.

Đặng Nhiêm Vạn. (1998). *Ethnological and Religious Problems in Vietnam,* Hanoi: Social Sciences Publishing House.

Didier, Bertrand. (1996). The Thay: Masters in Hue, Vietnam. *Asian Folklore Studies,* 55 (2): 271–286.

DiGregorio, Michael. (2001). Iron Works: Excavating Alternative Futures in a Northern Vietnamese Craft Village. Unpublished PhD thesis. Los Angeles: University of California.

——— (2007). Things Held in Common: Memory, Space and the Re-constitution of Community Life. *Journal of Southeast Asian Studies,* 38 (3): 441–465.

DiGregorio, Michael, and Oscar Salemink. (2007). Living with the Dead: The Politics of Ritual and Remembrance in Contemporary Vietnam. *Journal of Southeast Asian Studies,* 38 (3): 443–440.

——— (2003). *Vietnamese Supernaturalism: Views from the Southern Region.* London and New York: RoutledgeCurzon.

Do, Thien. (1997). Popular Religion in Contemporary Southern Vietnam: A Personal Approach. *Sojourn,* 12 (1): 64–91.

Douglas, Mary. (2001). *Purity and Danger: An Analysis of the Concept of Pollution and Taboo.* London and New York: Routledge. First published in 1966.

Dror, Olga. (2002a). *Opusculus de Sectis apud Sinenses et Tunkinenses. A small Treatise on the Sects among the Chinese and Tonkinese: A Study of Religion in China and North Vietnam in the Eighteenth Century.* Ithaca, NY: Cornell University.

———(2002b). Đoàn Thị Điểm>s <Story of the Vân Cát Goddess> as a Story of Emancipation. *Journal of Southeast Asian Studies,* 33 (1): 66–67.

——— (2007). *Cult, Culture, and Authority: Princess Lieu Hanh in Vietnamese History.* Honolulu: Univeristy of Hawai'i Press.

Drummond, Lisa. (2004). The Modern 'Vietnamese Woman': Socialization and Women's Magazines. In Lisa Drummond and Helle Rydstrøm (eds), *Gender Practices in Contemporary Vietnam* (pp. 158–178). Singapore: Singapore University Press.

Duara, Prasenjit. (1988). *Culture, Power, and the State: Rural North China 1900–1942.* Stanford California: Stanford University Press.

——— (1991). Knowledge and Power in the Discourse of Modernity: The Campaigns Against Popular Religion in Early Twentieth-Century China. *Journal of Asian Studies,* 50 (1): 67–83.

——— (1995). *Rescuing History from the Nation: Questioning Narratives of Modern China.* Chicago: University of Chicago Press.

DuBois, Thomas D. (2009). *Casting Faiths: Imperialism and the Transformation of Religion in East and Southeast Asia.* London: Palgrave Macmillan.

——— (2011). *Religion and The Making of Modern East Asia.* Cambridge: Cambridge University Press.

Durand, Maurice. (1959). *Technique et pantheon des mediums Viêtnamiens (đồng) [Technique and Pantheon of Vietnamese Mediums].* Paris: EFEO.

Durkheim, Emile. (1995 [1915]). *The Elementary Form of Religious Life.* New York: Free Press.

Elias, Norbert, and John Scotson. (1994). *The Established and the Outsiders: A Sociological Enquiry into Community Problems.* London: Sage Publication.

Endres, Kirsten W. (2000). *Ritual, Fest und Politik in Nordvietnam: Zwischen Ideologie und Tradition.* Münster: LIT Verlag.

—— (2001). Local Dynamics of Renegotiating Ritual Space in Northern Vietnam: The Case of the Dinh. *Sojourn*, 16 (1): 70–71.

—— (2002). Beautiful Customs, Worthy Traditions: Changing State Discourse on the Role of Vietnamese Culture. *Internationales Asienforum*, 33 (3–4): 303–322.

—— (2007). Spirited Modernities: Mediumship and Ritual Performativity in Late Socialist Vietnam. In Philip Taylor (ed.), *Modernity and Re-Enchantment: Religion in Post-Revolutionary Vietnam* (pp. 194–220). Singapore: ISEAS.

—— (2008). Engaging the Spirits of the Dead: Soul-Calling Rituals and the Performative Construction of Efficacy. *Journal of the Royal Anthropological Institute* (14): 755–773.

—— (2011). *Performing the Divine: Mediums, Markets and Modernity in Urban Vietnam.* Copenhagen: NIAS Press.

Erndl, Kathleen. (1993). *Victory to the Mother: The Hindu Goddess of Northwest India in Myth, Ritual and Symbol.* New York: Oxford University Press.

Evans, Grant. (1998). *The Politics of Ritual and Remembrance: Laos since 1975.* Honolulu: University of Hawai'i Press.

—— (2002). Between the Global and the Local There Are Regions, Culture Areas, and National States: A Review Article. *Journal of Southeast Asian Studies*, 33 (1): 147–162.

Fabian, Johannes. (1985). Religious Pluralism: An Ethnographic Approach. In Wim van Binsbergen and Matthew Schoffeleers, *Theoretical Exploration in African Religion* (pp. 138–163). London and Boston: Routledge and Kegan Paul.

Fall, Bernard. (2005 [1961]). *Street Without Joy: The French Debacle in Indochina.* Stackpole Books: Mechanicsburg.

Firth, Raymond. (1964). *Malay Fishermen: Their Peasant Economy.* London: Routledge and Kegan Paul.

FitzGerald, Frances. (1972). *Fire in the Lake: The Vietnamese and the Americans in Vietnam.* Boston: Atlantic-Little, Brown and Company.

Fjelstad, Karen and Nguyen Thi Hien. (2006) *Possessed by the Spirits: Mediumship in Contemporary Vietnamese Communities.* Ithaca, NY: Cornell University Press.

Foucault, Michael. (1975). *Discipline and Punish: The Birth of the Prison.* New York: Random House.

Foucault, Michael. (1991). Governmentality. In Graham Burchell, Colin Gordon, and Peter Miller (eds), *The Foucault Effect: Studies in Governmentality*, (pp. 84–104). Chicago: University of Chicago Press.

Geertz, Clifford. (1973). *The Interpretation of Culture: Selected Essays*. New York: Basic Books.

———— (1979). *Central Problems in Social Theory: Action, Structure, and Contradiction in Social Analysis*. London: Macmillan Press.

Giebel, Christoph, (2004). *Imagined Ancestries of Vietnamese Communism: Ton Duc Thang and the Politics of History and Memory*. Seattle: University of Washington Press.

Goody, Jack. (1961). Religion and Ritual: The Definion Problem. *British Journal of Sociology*, 12 (2): 142–64.

Gourou, Pierre. (1936). *Les paysans du delta Tonkinois*. Paris: Editions d'Art. et d' Histoire.

————(1940). *L'utilisation du Sol en Indochine francaise*. Paris: Centre D'Études de Politique Étrangère.

Grafe, Regina, and Oscar Gelderblom. (2010). The Rise and Fall of the Merchant Guilds: Re-thinking the Comparative Study of Commercial Institutions in Premodern Europe. *Journal of Interdisciplinary History*, 40 (4): 477–511.

Granet, Marcel. (1975 [1925]). *The Religion of Chinese People*. Trans. M. Freedman. Oxford: Clarendon Press.

Grossheim, Martin. (1996). Village Laws (*hương ước*) as a Source for Vietnamese Studies. In Philippe Le Failler et Jean Marie Mancini (eds), *Việt-Nam Sources et Approches* (pp. 103–123). Aix-en-Provence: Pub. de l'Université de Provence.

Gupta, Akhil, and James Ferguson. (1992). Beyond 'Culture': Space, Identity, and the Politics of Difference. *Cultural Anthropology*, 7 (1): 6–23.

Hall, Kenneth R. (2011). *A History of Early Southeast Asia: Maritime Trade and Societal Development, 100–1500*. Lanham, New York, and Toronto: Rowman and Littlefield.

Hann, Christopher M. (2006). Introduction: Faith, Power, and Civility after Socialism. In Christopher M. Hann et al., *The Postsocialist Religious Question: Faith and Power in Central Asia and East-Central Europe* (pp. 1–26). Münster: LIT Verlag.

Hardy, Andrew. (2005) A View from Linh Thái Mountain: Historical Peregrinations into Chăm Culture' in Nguyễn Văn Kự, Ngô Văn Doanh & Andrew Hardy (eds), *Pérégrinations culturelles au Champa* (pp. 49–63). Hanoi: EFEO- Nxb Thế giới.

——— (2009). Eaglewood and the Economic History of Champa and Central Vietnam. In Andrew Hardy, Mauro Cucarzi and Patrizia Zolese (eds), *Champa and the Archeology of Mỹ Sơn (Vietnam)* (pp. 107–126). Singapore: NUS Press.

Hardy, Andrew and Nguyễn Tiến Đông, (2019). The Peoples of Champa: Evidence for a New Hypothesis from the Landscape History of Quảng Ngãi. In Arlo Griffiths, Andrew Hardy and Geoff Wade (eds), *Champa: Territories and Networks of a Southeast Asian Kingdom* (pp. 121–143). Paris: EFEO.

Harms, Erik. (2011a). *Saigon's Edge: On the Margins of Ho Chi Minh City*. Minneapolis and London: University of Minnesota Press.

——— (2011b). The Critical Difference: Making Peripherial Vision Central in Vietnamese Studies. *Journal of Vietnamese Studies*, 6 (2): 1–15.

——— (2012). Beauty as Control on the New Saigon: Eviction, New Urban Zones, and Atomized Dissent in a Southeast Asian City. *American Ethnologist* (39): 735–50.

Hayton, Bill. (2014). *The South China Sea: The Struggle for Power in Asia*. New Haven and London: Yale Univeristy Press.

——— (2019). The Modern Origins of China's South China Sea Claims: Maps, Misunderstandings, and the Maritime Geobody. *Modern China*, 45(2): 127–170.

Hefner, Robert. (1997). 'Introduction.' In R. W. Hefner and P. Horvatich (eds), *Islam in an Era of Nation-states: Politics and Religious Renewal in Muslim Southeast Asia* (pp. 3–42). Honolulu: University of Hawai'i Press.

Herzfeld, Michael. (2016). *Siege of the Spirits: Community and Polity in Bangkok*. Chicago and London: The University of Chicago Press.

Hickey, Gerald. C. (1964). *Village in Vietnam*. New Haven and London: Yale University Press.

Hillman, Ben. (2004). The Rise of the Community in Rural China: Village Politics, Cultural Identity and Religious Revival in a Hui Hamlet. *The China Journal*, (51): 53–73.

Ho, Engseng. (2006). *Graves of Tarim: Geneaology and Mobility across the Indian Ocean*. Berkeley, Los Angeles, and London: University of California Press.

Ho Tai, Hue Tam. (1995). Monumental Ambiguity: The State Commemoration of Ho Chi Minh. In K. W. Taylor and J. K. Whitmore (eds), *Essays into Vietnamese Past* (p. 273). Ithaca: Cornell University.

———— (2001). Introduction: Situating Memory. In Hue Tam Ho Tai (ed.). *The Country of Memory: Remaking the Past in Late Socialist Vietnam* (pp. 1–20). Berkeley: University of California Press.

Ho Tai, Hue Tam, and Lê Hồng Lý. (2008). The Revenge of the Object: Villagers and Ethnographers in Đồng Kỵ Village. *Asian Ethnology,* 67 (2): 323–343.

Hoang Ba Tinh. (2006). *Floating People: Potentials and Challenges.* Hanoi: Vietnam National University Publishing House.

Hoang, Van Chung. (2017). *New Religions and State's Response to Religious Diversification in Contemporary Vietnam: Tensions from the Reinvention of the Sacred.* Springer Int. Publishing AG.

Hoeppe, Götz. (2007). *Conversation on the Beach: Fishermen's Knowledge, Metaphor and Environmental Change in South India.* New York: Berghahn Books.

Hoskins, Janet A. (2015). *The Divine Eye and the Diaspora: Vietnamese Syncretism Becomes Transpacific Caodaism.* Honolulu: University of Hawai'i Press.

Jamieson, Neil L. (1985). The Traditional Vietnamese Village. *Inter Culture,* 18 (1): 2–40.

———— (1993). *Understanding Vietnam.* Berkeley, Los Angeles and London: University of California Press.

Kammerer, Cornelia A., and Nicola Tannenbaum. (2003). Introduction. In Nicola Tannenbaum and Cornelia A. Kammerer (eds), *Founders' Cults in Southeast Asia: Ancestors, Polity, and Identity* (pp. 1–14). New Haven: Yale University, Southeast Asia Studies.

Keane, Webb. (2003). Semiotics and the Social Analysis of Material Things. *Language and Communication,* 23: 409–425.

———— (2007). *Christian Moderns: Freedom and Fetish in the Mission Encounter.* Berkeley: University of California Press.

———— (2008). The Evidence of the Senses and the Materiality of Religion. *Journal of Royal Anthropological Institute,* S110–S127.

Kehl-Bodrogi, Krisztina. (2006). Islam Contested: Nation, Religion and Tradition in Post-Soviet Turkmenistan. In Christopher M. Hann et al., *The*

Postsocialist Religious Question: Faith and Power in Central Asia and East-Central Europe (pp. 125–146). Münster: LIT Verlag.

Kendall, Laurel. (1985). *Shamans, Housewives and Other Restless Spirits: Women in Korean Ritual Life.* Honolulu: University of Hawai'i Press.

——— (1996a). Korean Shamans and the Spirits of Capitalism. *American Anthropologist,* 98 (3): 512–527.

——— (1996b). The Cultural Politics of 'Superstition' in the Korean Shaman World: Modernity Constructs Its Other. In Linda H. Connor and Geoffrey Samuel, *Healing Powers and Modernity: Traditional Medicine, Shamanism and Science in Asian Societies* (pp. 25–41). Westport, CT.: Greenwood Publishing.

——— (2009). *Shamans, Nostalgias, and the IMF: South Korean Popular Religion in Motion.* Honolulu: University of Hawai'i Press.

Kerkvliet, Benedict J. Tria (2005). *The Power of Everyday Politics: How Vietnamese Peasants Transformed National Policy.* Ithaca and London: Cornell University Press.

Kertzer, David. (1988). *Ritual, Politics and Power.* New Haven: Yale University Press.

Keyes, Charles F. (1984). Mother or Mistress but Never a Monk: Buddhist Notions of Female Gender in Rural Thailand. *American Ethnologist,* 11 (2): 223–241).

——— (2002). National Heroine or Local Spirit? The Struggle over Memory in the Case of Thao Suranari of Nakhon Ratchasima. In Tanabe Shigeharu and Charles F. Keyes (eds), *Cultural Crisis and Social Memory: Modernity and Identity in Thailand and Laos* (pp. 113–135). London: RoutledgeCurzon.

Keyes, Charles F., Laurel Kendall, and Helen Hardacre (eds). (1994a). *Asian Visions of Authority: Religion and the Modern States of East and Southeast Asia.* Honolulu: University of Hawai'i Press.

——— (1994b). Introduction: Contested Visions of Community in East and Southeast Asia. In Charles F. Keyes, Laurel Kendall and Helen Hardacre (eds), *Asian Visions of Authority: Religion and the Modern States of East and Southeast Asia,* (pp. 1–18). Honolulu: University of Hawai'i Press.

Khuat, Thu Hong. (2004). Sexual Harassment in Vietnam: A New Term for an Old Phenomenon. In Lisa Drummond and Helle Rydstrøm (eds), *Gender Practices in Contemporary Vietnam,* (pp. 117–136). Singapore: Singapore University Press.

Kipnis, Andrew. (2001). The Flourishing of Religion in Post-Mao China and the Anthropological Category of Religion. *The Australian Journal of Anthropology*, 12 (1): 32–46.

Kirsch, Thomas A. (1973). *Feasting and Social Oscillation: A Working Paper on Religion and Society in Upland Southeast Asia*. Ithaca: Cornel University. Southeast Asian Program.

—— (1985). Text and Context: Buddhist Sex Roles/Culture of Gender Revisited. *American Ethnologist* 12 (2): 302–320.

Kirsch, Thomas G. (2004). Restaging the Will to Believe: Religious Pluralism, Anti-Syncretism and the Problem of Belief. *American Anthropologist*, 106 (4): 699–709.

Kitiarsa, Pattana. (1999). You May Not Believe, But Never Offend the Spirits: Spirit-medium Cult Discourses and the Postmodernization of Thai Religion. Unpublished PhD thesis. Seattle: University of Washington.

Kleinen, John (1999a). *Facing the Future, Reviewing the Past: A Study of Social Change in a Northern Vietnamese Village*. Singapore: ISEAS.

—— (1999b). Is there a 'Village Vietnam'? In Bernhard Dahm and Vincent J.H. Houben (eds), *Vietnamese Villages in Transition: Background and Consequences of Reform Policies in Rural Vietnam* (pp. 1–41). Passau: Passau University.

Kleinen, John, and Manon Osseweijer. (2010). *Pirates, Ports and Coasts in Asia: Historical and Contemporary Perspectives*. Singapore: Institute of Southeast Asian Studies; Leiden, Netherlands: International Institute for Asian Studies.

Kumar, Ratheesh. (2016). Temporality as Value: Ethnography and the Question of Time. *Journal of Human Values*, 22 (1): 46–56.

Kwon, Heonik. (2006). *After the Massacre: Commemoration and Consolation in Ha My and My Lai*. Berkeley, Los Angeles and London: University of California Press.

—— (2009). *Ghost of War in Vietnam*. Cambridge: Cambridge University Press.

Latour, Bruno. (1993). *We Have Never Been Modern*. Cambridge, MA: Harvard University Press.

Leach, Edmund R. (1954). *Political System of Highland Burma: A Study of Kachin Social Structure*. Boston: Beacon Press.

Leshkowich, Ann Marie. (2014). *Essential Trade: Vietnamese Women in a Changing Marketplace*. Honolulu: University of Hawai'i Press.

Lewis, I. M. (1966). Spirit Possession and Deprivation Cults. *Man (NS)*, 1 (3): 307–329.

—— (2003). *Ecstatic Religion: A Study of Shamanism and Spirit Possession.* London and New York: Routledge.

Lhamo, Yeshe Choekyi. (2003). The Fangs of Reproduction: An Analysis of Taiwanese Menstrual Pollution in the Context of Buddhist Philosophy and Practice. *History and Anthropology,* 14 (12): 157–178.

Li, Tana. (1998). *Nguyễn Cochinchina: Southern Vietnam in the Seventeen and Eighteenth Centuries.* Ithaca, NY: Cornell University Press.

—— (2006). A View From the Sea: Perspectives on the Northern and Central Vietnamese Coast. *Journal of Southeast Asian Studies,* 37 (1): 83–102.

Luong, Van Hy. (1988). Discursive Practices and Power Structure: Person-Referring Forms and Sociopolitical Struggles in Colonial Vietnam. *American Ethnologist,* 15 (2): 139–253.

—— (1992). *Revolution in the Village: Tradition and Transformation in North Vietnam, 1925–1988.* Honolulu: University of Hawai'i Press.

—— (1998). Vietnamese Kinship: Structural Principles and the Socialist Transformation in Twentieth-Century Vietnam. *Journal of Asian Studies,* 48 (4): 741–756.

—— (2003). Gender Relations: Ideologies, Kinship Practices, and Political Economy. In Hy Van Luong (ed.), *Postwar Vietnam: Dynamics of a Transforming Society* (pp. 201–224). Singapore: ISEAS.

—— (2009). Rural Migration to Hồ Chí Minh City: A Tale of Two Regions. In Hy Van Luong (ed.), *Urbanization, Migration, and Poverty in a Vietnamese Metropolis: Hồ Chí Minh City in Comparative Perspectives* (pp. 77–102). Singapore: NUS.

Mahmood, Saba. (2005). *Politics of Piety.* Princeton, NJ: Princeton University Press.

Malarney, Shaun K. (2001). 'The Fatherland Remembers Your Sacrifice': Commemorating War Dead in North Vietnam. In Hue Tam Ho Tai (ed.), *The Country of Memory: Remaking the Past in Late Socialist Vietnam* (pp. 46–76). Berkeley: University of California Press.

—— (2002). *Culture, Ritual and Revolution in Vietnam.* London: Routledge Curzon.

——— (2003). Return to the Past? The Dynamics of Contemporary Religious and Ritual Transformation. In Hy Van Luong (ed.), *Postwar Vietnam: Dynamics of a Transforming Society* (pp. 225–256). Singapore: ISEAS.

——— (2007). Festivals and the Dynamics of the Exceptional Dead in Northern Vietnam. *Journal of Southeast Asian Studies*, 38 (8): 515–540.

Malinowski, Bronislaw. (1961 [1922]). *Argonauts of the Western Pacific: An Account of Native Enterprise and Adventure in the Archipelagoes of Melanesian New Guinea*. New York: Dutton.

Mandair, Arvind-Pal S. (2009). *Religion and the Specter of the West: Sikhism, India, Postcoloniality, and the Politics of Translation*. New York: Columbia University Press.

Marcus, George E. (1995). Ethnography in/of the World System: The Emergence of Multi-Sited Ethnography. *Annual Review of Anthropology* (24): 95–117.

——— (1998). *Ethnography Through Thick and Thin*. Princeton, NJ: Princeton University Press.

Marr, David G. (1981). *Vietnamese Tradition on Trial, 1920–1945*. Berkeley, Los Angeles and London: University of California Press.

Mbembe, Achille. (1992). The Banality of Power and the Aesthetics of Vulgarity in the Postcolony. *Public Culture*, 4 (2):1–30.

MacLean, Kenneth. (2014). From Land to Waters: Fisxing Fluid Frontiers and the Politics of Lines in the South China/Eastern Sea. In James A. Anderson and John K. Whitmore (eds), *China's Encounters on the South and Southwest* (pp. 370–394). Laiden, Boston: Brill.

——— (2016). Unbuilt Anxieties: Infrastructure Projects, Transnational Conflict in the South China /East Sea and Vietnamese Statehood. *TRaNS: Trans-Regional and -National Studies of Southeast Asia*, Available on CJO DOI: https://doi.org/10.1017/trn.2016.3

McAlister, John T., and Paul Mus. (1970). *The Vietnamese and Their Revolution*. New York: Harper and Row.

McElwee, Pamela. D. (2016). *Forests Are Gold: Trees, People, and Environmental Rule in Vietnam*. Seattle and London: University of Washington Press.

Meyer, Birgit. (2006). Religious Revelation, Secrecy and the Limits of Visual Representation. *Anthropological Theory*, 6 (4): 431–453.

Morris, Rosalind C. (2000). *In the Place of Origins: Modernity and Its Mediums in Northern Thailand*. Durham, NC: Duke University Press.

Murray, Dian H. (1987). *Pirates of the South China Sea 1790–1810*. Stanford, CA: Stanford University Press.

Mus, Paul. (1948). *The Role of the Village in Vietnamese Politics*. Pacific Affairs XXII (9): 265–272.

———(1952). *Viêt-Nam, Sociologie d'une Guerre*. Paris: Edittions du Seuil.

Navaro-Yashin, Yael. (2007). Make-believe papers, legal forms and the counterfeit: Affective interactions between documents and people in Britain and Cyprus, *Anthropological Theory*, 7 (1): 79–98.

Ner, Marcel. (1940). Chronique de l'année 1940 – Indochine Française, Annam-ethnologie, *Bulletin de l'Éçole Française d'Extrême-Orient*, 40 (2): 475–477.

Ngo Thi Ngan Binh. (2004). The Confucian Four Feminine Virtues (tu duc): The Old Versus the New – Ke thua Versus phat huy. In Lisa Drummond and Helle Rydstrøm (eds), *Gender Practices in Contemporary Vietnam* (pp. 47–73). Singapore: Singapore University Press.

Ngô, Tâm T. T. (2016). *The New Way: Protestantism and the Hmong in Vietnam*. Seattle and London: University of Washington Press.

Nguyen The Anh. (1995). The Vietnamization of the Cham Deity Po Nagar. In Keith W. Taylor and John K. Whitmore (eds), *Essays into Vietnamese Pasts* (pp. 42–50). Ithaca, NY: Southeast Asia Program Publications, Cornell University.

Nguyen Thi Hien. (2002). The Religion of the Four Palaces: Mediumship and Therapy in Viet Culture. Ph.D. dissertation. Bloomington: Indiana University.

Nguyễn Tuấn Anh. (2010). Kinship as Social Capital: Economic, Social and Cultural Dimensions of Changing Kinship Relationship in a Northern Vietnamese Village. Unpublished PhD. Thesis. Amsterdam: Vrije Universiteit.

Nguyễn Văn Huyên. (1995 [1945]). *The Ancient Civilization of Vietnam*. Hanoi: The Gioi Publishers.

Nguyên Van Ky. (2002). Rethinking the Status of Women in Folklore and Oral History. In Gisele Bousquet and Pierre Brocheux (eds), *Việt Nam Exposé: French Scholarship on Twentieth-Century Vietnamese Society* (pp. 87–107). Ann Arbor: University of Michigan Press.

Nguyen-vo, Thu Huong. (2008). *The Ironies of Freedom: Sex, Culture, and Neoliberal Governance in Vietnam*. Seattle and London: University of Washington Press.

Ninh, Thien-Huong. (2017). Race, Gender and Religion in Vietnamese Diaspora: The New Chosen People. *Cham*, Switzerland: Palgrave Macmillan.

Ninh, Kim N. B. (2002). *A World Transformed: The Politics of Culture in Revolutionary Vietnam, 1945–1965.* Ann Arbor: University of Michigan Press.

Norton, Barley. (2009). *Songs for the Spirits: Music and Mediums in Modern Vietnam.* Urbana: University of Illinois Press.

Nye, Malory. (2000). Religion is Religioning: Anthropology and the Cultural Study of Religion. *Scottish Journal of Religious,* 20 (2): 193–234.

Ortner, Sherry B. (1995). Resistance and the Problem of Ethnographic Refusal. *Comparative Studies in Society and History,* 37 (1): 173–193.

——— (2001). Specifying Agency: The Comaroffs and their Critics. *Interventions,* 3 (1): 76–84.

——— (2006). *Anthropology and Social Theory: Culture, Power and the Acting Subject.* Durham and London: Duke University Press.

Ota, Atsushi. (2010). Pirates or Entrepreneurs? Migration and Trade of Sea People in Southwest Kalimantan c.1770–1820. *Indonesia,* 90: 67–96.

Pearson, Michael N. (1985). Littoral Society: The Case for the Coast. *The Great Circle: Journal of the Australian Association for Maritime History,* 7 (1): 1–8.

——— (2003). *The Indian Ocean.* London and New York: Routledge.

——— (2006). Littoral Society: The Concept and the Problems. *Journal of World History,* 17 (4): 353–373.

Pedersen, Morton A. (2011). *Not Quite Shaman: Spirit Worlds and Political Lives in Northern Mongolia.* Ithaca, NY: Cornell University Press.

Pelley, Patricia M. (2002). *Postcolonial Vietnam: New Histories of the National Past.* Durham: Duke University Press.

Pham, Charlotte Minh Ha. (2013). The Vietnamese Coastline: A Maritime Cultural Landscape. In Satish Chandra and Himanshu Prabha Ray (eds), *The Sea, Identity and History: From the Bay of Bengal to the South China Sea* (pp. 94–137). Delhi: Society for Indian Ocean Studies.

Pham Charlotte, Lucy Blue and Colin Palmer. (2010). The Traditional Boat of Vietnam, An Overview. *International Journal of Nautical Archaeology,* 39 (2): 258–277.

Pham Quynh Phuong. (2009). *Hero and Deity: Tran Hung Dao and the Resurgence of Popular Religion in Vietnam.* Chiang Mai: Mekong Press.

Phan Huy Lê. (2006). Research on the Vietnamese Village: Assessment and Perspectives (pp. 25–41). In Tran Nhung Tuyet and Anthony J. S. Reid (eds), *Việt Nam: Borderless Histories*. Madison: The University of Wisconsin Press.

Phinney, Harriet M. (2005). Asking for a Child: The Refashioning of Reproductive Space in Post-War Northern Vietnam. *The Asia Pacific Journal of Anthropology*, 6 (3): 215–230.

Reid, Anthony. (1999). *Charting the Shape of Early Modern Southeast Asia*. Chiang Mai: Silkworm Books.

Rydstrøm, Helle, and Lisa Drummond. (2004). Introduction. In Lisa Drummond and Helle Rydstrøm (eds), *Gender Practices in Contemporary Vietnam* (pp. 158–178). Singapore: Singapore University Press.

Salemink, Oscar. (2007). The Emperor's New Clothes: Re-fashioning Ritual in the Huế Festival. *Journal of Southeast Asian Studies*, 38 (3): 559–582.

———— (2008a). Trading Goods, Prestige and Power: A Revisionist History of Lowlander–Highlander Relations in Vietnam. In Peter Boomgaard, Dick Kooiman and Henk Schulte Nordholt (eds), *Linking Destinies: Trade, Towns and Kin in Asian History* (pp. 51–69). Leiden: KITLV Press.

———— (2008b). Embodying the Nation: Mediumship, Ritual and the National Imagination. *Journal of Vietnamese Studies*, 3 (3): 261–290.

———— (2008c). Spirits of Consumption and the Capitalist Ethic in Vietnam. In Pattana Kitiarsa (ed.), *Religious Commodifications in Asia: Marketing Gods* (pp. 147–168). London and New York: Routledge.

———— (2009a). Afterword: Questioning Faiths? Casting Doubt. In Thomas D. DuBois, *Casting Faiths: Imperialism and the Transformation of Religion in East and Southeast Asia*, (pp. 257–263). London: Palgrave Macmillan.

———— (2009b). Secularization, Sacralization and Bricolage: Syncretizing Categories of 'Religion' and 'Superstition' in Post-Secular Vietnam. Paper presented at workshop on Religion, Identity and Conflict, consortium of African and Asian Studies Inaugural International Conference. Leiden University, 26–28 August.

———— (2010). Ritual Efficacy, Spiritual Security and Human Security: Spirit Mediumship in Contemporary Vietnam. In Ellen Bal, Thomas Hylland Eriksen and Oscar Salemink (eds), *A World of Insecurity: Anthropological Perspectives on Human Security* (pp. 262–289). London/Ann Arbor: Pluto Press.

———— (2013). Appropriating Culture: The Politics of Intangible Cultural Heritage in Vietnam. In Hue-Tam Ho Tai and Mark Sidel (eds), *Property and Power: State, Society and Market in Vietnam*. New York and London: Routledge.

———— (2015). Spirit worship and possession in Vietnam and beyond. In B. S. Turner and O. Salemink (eds), *Routledge Handbook of Religions in Asia*, (pp. 231–45). London and New York: Routledge.

———— (2016a). Scholarship, Expertise, and Regional Politics of Heritage. In O. Salemink (ed.) *Scholarship and Engagement in Mainland Southeast Asia*. Bangkok: Silkworm Books.

———— (2016b). Described, Inscribed, Written Off: Heritagisation as (Dis) connection. In P. Taylor (ed.) *Connected and Disconnected in Vietnam: Remaking Social Relationships in a Post-socialist Nation*, (311–345). Canberra: Australian National University Press.

———— (2018a). The Regional Centrality of Vietnam's Central Highlands. In *Oxford Research Encyclopedia of Asian History*, Oxford University Press.

———— (2018b). Southeast Asia is Theoretical Laboratory for the World. *SUVANNABHUMI* 10 (2): 121–142.

Sangren, Stephen P. (1983). Gender in Chinese Religious Symbols: Kuan Tin, Ma Tsu, and the 'Eternal Mother'. *Signs*, 9 (1): 4–25.

———— (1987). *History and Magical Power in a Chinese Community*. Stanford, California: Stanford University Press.

Saxer, Martin and Andersson, Ruben. 2019. The Return of Remoteness: Insecurity, Isolation and Connectivity in the New World Disorder. *Social Anthropology* 27 (2): 140–155.

Schwenkel, Christina. (2009). *The American War in Contemporary Vietnam: Transnational Remembrance and Representation*. Bloomington and Indianapolis: Indiana Univerisity Press.

Scott, James C. (1976). *The Moral Economy of the Peasant: Rebellion and Subsistence in Southeast Asia*. New Haven: Yale University Press.

———— (1990). *Domination and the Art of Resistance: Hidden Transcripts*. New Haven, CT: Yale University Press.

———— (1998). *Seeing Like a State: How Certain Schemes to Improve the Human Condition Have Failed*. New Haven: Yale University Press.

Serjant, Robert B. (1995). *Farmers and Fishermen in Arabia: Studies in Customary Law and Practice*. Aldershot, Hampshire, Great Britain and Brookfield, Vermont: Variorum.

Sheng-Ti Gau, M. 2012. The U-shaped Line and a Categorization of the Ocean Disputes in the South China Sea. *Ocean Development and International Law* 43, 1:57–69.

Sidnell, Jack, and Merav Shohet. (2013). The Problem of Peers in Vietnamese Interaction. *Journal of the Royal Anthropological Institute*, 19 (3): 618–638.

Siu, Helen F. (1989). Recycling Rituals: Politics and Popular Culture in Contemporary Rural China. In Perry Link, Richard Madsen and Paul G. Pickowicz, *Unofficial China: Popular Culture and Thought in the People's Republic* (pp. 121–137). Boulder, San Francisco and London: Westview Press.

Solheim, Wilhelm. G. (1988–1989). A Brief History of the Dongson Concept. *Asian Perspective*, 48 (1): 23–30.

Soucy, Alexander D. (2007). Nationalism, Globalism and the Re-establishment of the Trúc Lâm Thiền Buddhist Sect in Northern Vietnam. In Philip Taylor (ed.), *Modernity and Re-Enchantment: Religion in Post-Revolutionary Vietnam* (pp. 342–370). Singapore: ISEAS.

———— (2012). *The Buddha Side: Gender, Power, and Buddhist Practice in Vietnam*. Honolulu: University of Hawai'i Press.

Southworth, William. (2004). The Coastal States of Champa. In Jan Glover and Peter Bellwood (eds), *In Southeast Asia from Prehistory to History* (pp. 209–233). London and New York: RoutledgeCurtzon.

Stanner, William E. H. (1967). Reflection on Durkheim and Aboriginal Religion. In M. Freedman (ed.) *Social Organization: Essays Presented to Raymond Firth*. (pp. 217–240) London: Cass

Subramanian, Ajantha. (2009). *Shorelines: Space and Rights in South India*. Stanford, California: Stanford University Press.

Sutton, Donald S. and Kang Xiaofei. (2009). Recasting Religion and Ethnicity: Tourism and Socialism in Northern Sichuan, 1992–2005. In Thomas D. DuBois (ed.), *Casting Faiths: Imperialism and the Transformation of Religion in East and Southeast Asia* (pp. 190–214). London: Palgrave Macmillan.

Szonyi, Michael. (2008). *Cold War Island: Qumoy on the Front Line*, Cambridge University Press, Cambridge.

Tagliacozzo, Eric. (2009). Navigating Communities: Race, Place, and Travel in the History of Maritime Southeast Asia. *Asian Ethnicity*, 10 (2): 97–120.

———— 2011. A Sino-Southeast Asian Circuit: Ethnohistories of the Marine goods Trade. In E. Tagliacozzo and Wen-Chin Chang (eds), *Chinese*

Circulations: Capital, Commodities and Networks in Southeast Asia, (pp. 432–454). Durham, NC: Duke University Press.

Taylor, Charles. (2007). *A Secular Age.* Cambridge, MA. and London: the Belknap Press of Harvard University Press.

Taylor, Keith W. (1983). *The Birth of Vietnam.* Berkeley: University of California Press.

———— (1998). Surface Orientation in Vietnam: Beyond Histories of Nation and Region. *Journal of Asian Studies,* 57 (4): 949–978.

Taylor, Keith W., and John K. Whitmore (eds). (1995). *Essays into Vietnamese Pasts.* Ithaca, NY: Southeast Asia Program Publications, Cornell University.

Taylor, Philip. (2001). *Fragments of the Present: Searching for Modernity in Vietnam's South.* Honolulu: University of Hawai'i Press.

———— (2003). The Goddess, the Ethnologist, the Folklorist and the Cadres: Situating Exegesis of Vietnam's Folk Religion in Time and Place. *The Australian Journal of Anthropology,* 14 (3): 383–401.

———— (2004). *Goddess on the Rise: Pilgrimage and Popular Religion in Vietnam.* Honolulu: University of Hawai'i Press.

———— (2007). Modernity and Re-Enchantment in Post-Revolutionary Vietnam. In Philip Taylor (ed.), *Modernity and Re-Enchantment: Religion in Post-Revolutionary Vietnam* (pp. 1–56). Singapore: ISEAS.

Thayer, Carlyle A. (2010). The United States and Chinese Assertiveness in the South China Sea. *Security Challenges,* 6 (2): 69–84.

Tonan, Ajia Kenkyu. (2008). Village versus State: The Evolution of State-Local Relations in Vietnam until 1945. In Philip Papin (ed.), *Parcours d'un historien du Việt Nam: Recueil des articles écrits par Nguyễn Thế Anh* (pp. 747–766). Paris: Les Indes savantes.

Tran, Nhung Tuyet, and Anthony J. S. Reid, eds (2006). *Việt Nam Borderless Histories.* Madison: University of Wisconsin Press.

Trần Quốc Vượng. (1992). Popular Culture and High Culture in Vietnamese History. *An Interdisciplinary Journal of Southeast Asian Studies,* 7 (2): 5–38.

Trouillot, Michel Rolph. (1995). *Silencing the Past: Power and the Production of History.* Boston: Beacon Press.

Truong Huyen Chi. (2001). *Changing Processes of Social Reproduction in the Northern Vietnam Countryside: An Ethnographic Study of Đồng Vàng Village (Red River Delta).* Ph.D. dissertation. Toronto: University of Toronto.

———— (2004). Winter Crop and Spring Festival: The Contestations of Local Government in a Red River Delta Commune. In Benedict J. Tria Kerkvliet and David G. Marr, *Beyond Hanoi: Local Government in Vietnam* (pp. 110–136). Singapore: Institute of Southeast Asian Studies.

Tsing, Lowenhaupt Anna. (1993). *In the Realm of the Diamond Queen: Marginality in an Out-of-the-Way Place*. Princeton: Princeton University Press.

———— (1999). Becoming a Tribal Elder, and Other Green Development Fantasies. In Tania Li (ed.), *Transforming the Indonesian Uplands: Marginality, Power and Production* (pp. 159–200). Singapore: Harwood Academic Publishers.

Turner, Bryan. S. (2006). Religion and Politics: Nationalism, Globalisation and Empire. *Asian Journal of Social Science*, 34 (2): 209–224.

Turner, Bryan. S. and Salemink, Oscar. (2015). Introduction: Constructing Religion and Religions in Asia. In Bryan S. Turner and Oscar Salemink (eds), *Routledge Handbook of Religions in Asia* (pp. 1–14). London and New York: Routledge.

Van der Port, Mattijs. (2005). Circling around the Really Real: Spirit Possession Ceremonies and the Search for Authenticity in Bahian Candomblé. *Ethos*, 33 (2): 149–179.

———— (2011). (Not) Made by the Human Hand: Media Consciousness and Immediacy in the Cultural Production of the Real. *Social Anthropology*, 19 (1): 74–89.

Van der Veer, Peter. (2013). *The Modern Spirit of Asia: The Spiritual and the Secular in China and India*. Princeton, NJ: Princeton University Press.

Van der Veer, Peter and Hartmut Lehmann. (1999). *Nation and Religion: Perspectives on Europe and Asia*. Princeton, NJ: Princeton University Press.

Van der Veer, Peter and Stephen Feuchtwang. (2009). The Comparative Sociology of India and China. *Social Anthropology*, 17 (1): 90–108.

Vickery, Michael. (2009). A Short History of Champa. In Andrew Hardy, Mauro Cucarzi and Patrizia Zolese (eds), *Champa and the Archeology of Mỹ Sơn (Vietnam)* (pp .45–60). Singapore: NUS Press.

Vigh, Henrik. (2008). Crisis and Chronicity: Anthropological Perspectives on Continuous Conflict and Decline. *Ethnos*, 73 (1): 5–24.

———— (2010). Youth Mobilisation as Social Navigation. Reflection on the concept of dubriagem. *Cadernos de Estudos Africanos* (18–19): 140–164.

Vo, Nghia M. (2012). *Legends of Vietnam: An Analysis and Retteling of 88 Tales.* Jefferson, North Carolina: McFarland and Company, Inc., Publishers.

Walter, Irvine. (1984). Decline of Village Spirit Cults and Growth of Urban Spirit Mediumship: The Persistence of Spirit Beliefs, the Position of Women and Modernization, *Mankind,* 14 (4): 315–324.

Wang, Wensheng. (2014). *White Lotus Rebels and South China Pirates: Crisis and Reforms in the Qing Empire.* Cambridge and Massachusetts: Harvard University Press.

Warren, James F. (1981). *The Sulu Zone, 1768–1898.* Singapore: Singapore University Press.

Watson, James. L. (1985). Standardizing the Gods: The Promotion of Tien Hou (Empress of Heaven) Along the South China Coast 960–1960. In Nathan David Johnson, Andrew Nathan, and Evelyn Rawski (eds), *Popular Culture in Late Imperial China* (pp. 292–324). Berkeley and Los Angeles: University of California Press.

Weber, Max. (1951). *The Religion of China: Confucianism and Taoism.* Glencoe, IL: The Free Press.

———— (1966). *The Sociology of Religion.* London: Methuen.

Weller, Robert P. (1994). Capitalism, Community, and the Rise of Amoral Cults in Taiwan. In Charles F. Keyes, Laurel Kendall and Helen Hardacre (eds) *Asian Visions of Authority: Religion and the Modern States of East and Southeast Asia* (pp. 141–165). Honolulu: University of Hawai'i Press.

———— (1998). Divided Market Cultures in China: Gender, Enterprise, and Religion. In Robert W. Hefner (ed.), *Market Cultures: Society and Morality in the New Asian Capitalism* (pp. 78-103). Boulder, CO: Westview Press.

Werner, Jayne S. (2009). *Gender, Household and State in Post-Revolutionary Vietnam.* London and New York: Routledge.

Wheeler, Charles. (2001). Cross-Cultural Trade and Trans-Regional Networks in the Port of Hoi An: Maritime Vietnam in the Early Modern Era (China). Ph.D. dissertation. New Haven, Connecticut: Yale University.

———— (2006). Re-thinking the Sea in Vietnamese History: Littoral Society in the Integration of Thuận-Quảng, Seventeenth-Eighteenth Centuries. *Journal of Southeast Asian Studies,* 37 (1): 123–153.

———— (2015). Placing the 'Chinese Pirates' of the Gulf of Tonking at the End of the Eighteenth Century. In Eric Tagliacozzo, Helen F Siu, and Peter C.

Perdue (eds), *Asia Inside Out: Connected Places* (pp. 30–63). Cambridge and London: Harvard University Press.

White, John. (1824). *A Voyage to Cochin China*. London: Longman, Hurst, Rees, Orme, Brown, and Green.

Whitmore, John K. (2006). The Rise of the Coast: Trade, State and Culture in Early Đại Việt. *Journal of Southeast Asian Studies*, 37 (1): 123–153.

Wolf, Arthur P. (1974). *Religion and Ritual in Chinese Society*. Stanford, California: Stanford University Press.

Wolf, Margery. (1975). Women and Suicide in China. In Margery Wolf and Roxane Witke (eds), *Women in Chinese Society* (pp. 111–142), Stanford, California: Stanford University Press.

Wolters, Oliver W. (1988). *Two Essays on Đại-Việt in the Fourteenth Century*. New Haven CT: Council of Southeast Asian Studies, Yale Center for International and Area Studies.

Wong Tze Ken, Danny. (2016). Cham-Viet Relationship in Binh Thuan under Nguyen Rule from the Late Seventeenth Century to Mid-eighteenth Century. In Ooi Ket Gin & Hoang Anh Tuan (eds), *Early Modern Southeast Asia, 1350–1800*, (pp. 210–230). London: Routledge

Xi, He and Faure, David. (2016*). The Fisher Folk of Late Imperial and Modern China: An historical anthropology of boat-and-shed living*. London and New York: Routledge.

Yang, C. K. (1967). *Religion in Chinese Society*. Berkeley: University of California Press.

Young, Glennys. (1997). *Powers and the Sacred in Revolutionary Russia: Religious Activists in the Village*. University Park: Pennsylvania State University Press.

Yü, Chün-fang. (2001). *Kuan-yin: The Chinese Transformation of Avoliketeśvara*. New York: Columbia University Press.

Index

Herzfeld, Michael 17–18, 208
heterodoxy 24, 57, 76, 122–3, 203, 211
heteropraxy 122, 211
Hồ Chí Minh 39
Ho Chi Minh City 4, 12, 39, 45–6, 50, 52, 64–5, 114–15, 115n3, 123, 150, 183, 186, 190, 192, 199, 205
Ho Tai 135
Hòa Hảo (religious sect) 62
Hoàng Sa (Paracel Islands) 3, 44, 44n8, 91, 126–7, 142
Hoàng Sa (Sa Huỳnh) 44, 44n8
Hội An 35–8
houses, ancestral 36, 38, 138
Hrê (ethnic group) 7, 37, 170
Huế 12, 36, 38, 41, 90, 171, 173, 188
Hue Tam Ho Tai 135
Hưng (former guerilla fighter) 55–6
Hương (childless woman) 41, 182–4
husband: faithfulness to 148, 150, 183; family of 167, 171, 182; finding 46, 179, 182–3; infertility of 183; loss of 178–9, 182
Hy Van Luong 45, 116, 140
hybridization 149
hybrids 22, 115

ice making 40–1
identity 32, 91, 139–40, 150, 155; collective 140, 156; female 185; national 52, 64, 69, 72, 74, 201–2; women's religious 190, 211
ideologies 60, 63, 71, 157, 210, 212; see also semiotic ideologies
ideology: ethno-nationalist 202; 'of fatalism and predestination' 77; male-dominated religious 166; neo-Confucian 158, 168; 'new morality' 205; official state 15, 18, 60, 63, 71, 157; of spirit possession 194
imaginaries: geopolitical 206; territorial 7, 85, 95, 105
imperial-era governance 71, 90, 146, 203–4
imperial tombs (*lăng tẩm*) 66–7

imperialism, European 201
incantations 76, 171
incense 63, 109, 146–7, 162, 165, 177, 182
India 202
indiscipline 17, 19–20, 23, 27, 55, 71, 107, 113–14, 114n2, 166, 209–13; tactics of 112, 114, 157, 213; see also discipline; purification; semiotic ideologies
Indochina 42
Indochina wars 3, 13, 38–9, 49, 60, 67, 108, 128, 149–50, 155, 175; First 38, 49; Second 13, 38–9, 49, 60, 67, 108, 128, 149–50, 155, 175; see also Vietnam War
Indonesia 8n13, 17, 36, 119
infertility 183–4
inheritance rights 168
Inner Dune Palace (*dinh Cồn Trong*) 82, 85
Inner Region (*Đàng Trong*) 44n8
intellectuals 61, 74, 133, 137, 152
interethnic marriages 31–2; descendants of 32
International Monetary Fund 14
Internet 143
Islam 14, 75, 119, 201–2
ivory 35, 90

Japan 46, 64
jar burials 29n1
Jinmen Island 131, 149
journalists 11, 139, 144, 152
Judaism 14

Kachin society 104
Kalimantan 34
Kang, Xiaofei 75
karaoke gatherings 182
karma 189, 193
Keane, Webb 17, 19, 19n7, 19, 114
Kendall, Laurel 61, 73–4
Kertzer, David 134